THE WORLD UNDER PRESSURE

THE WORLD UNDER PRESSURE

How China and India are Influencing the Global Economy and Environment

Carl J. Dahlman

STANFORD ECONOMICS AND FINANCE
AN IMPRINT OF STANFORD UNIVERSITY PRESS
STANFORD, CALIFORNIA

FOUNDATION® BOOKS

Delhi • Bengaluru • Mumbai • Kolkata • Chennai • Hyderabad
Pune • Thiruvananthapuram

Published by
Cambridge University Press India Pvt. Ltd.
under the imprint of Foundation Books
Cambridge House, 4381/4 Ansari Road, Daryaganj, **New Delhi** 110 002

Cambridge University Press India Pvt. Ltd.
C-22, C-Block, Brigade M.M., K.R. Road, Jayanagar, **Bengaluru** 560 070
Plot No. 80, Service Industries, Shirvane, Sector-1, Nerul, **Navi Mumbai** 400 706
10 Raja Subodh Mullick Square, 2nd Floor, **Kolkata** 700 013
21/1 (New No. 49), 1st Floor, Model School Road, Thousand Lights, **Chennai** 600 006
House No. 3-5-874/6/4, (Near Apollo Hospital), Hyderguda, **Hyderabad** 500 029
Agarwal Pride, 'A' Wing, 1308 Kasba Peth, Near Surya Hospital, **Pune** 411 011
T.C. 25/ 2731 Lukes Lane, Ambujavilasam Road, **Thiruvananthapuram** 695 001

This edition has been published by Cambridge University Press India Pvt. Ltd. by arrangement with Stanford University Press.

First South Asia Edition 2013

ISBN 978-93-82264-64-4

Published by Manas Saikia for Cambridge University Press India Pvt. Ltd. and printed at Sanat Printers, Kundli, Haryana

This book is dedicated to Maria, Ana, Andre, Daniel, Alexandra, and Felisa.

Contents

List of Figures

List of Tables

Preface

I HAVE HAD THE PRIVILEGE of working on China and India for over 30 years, first as an economist at the World Bank for more than 25 years and then as a professor at Georgetown's School of Foreign Service for the last 6 years. During this period, I have visited each country more than 30 times and followed how they have transformed themselves from the most populous poor developing countries to major powers which are changing the global system. Their transformation has been spectacular. As will be developed in the book, the different speeds of their transformation and how far they have progressed are the result of their development strategies and the capabilities of their governments and populations.

In China, it has been largely because of a very shrewd government strategy that has managed an incredible shift from a state-controlled economy to a largely market-driven economy that is the most globally integrated large economy in the world in its participation in world trade. It is the more classic export-led development strategy based on exploiting its comparative advantage based on low labor cost. As a result, it has become a strong manufacturing center for the world.

In India, it has been largely because of a very dynamic private sector that has managed to become internationally competitive, initially in spite of government policy, although in the last 20 years government policy has become progressively more supportive. Its rapid growth is more recent and is due to a large extent to how its private sector has been able to exploit the potential of the information revolution—more specifically, the ability to provide services at a distance. As a result, it has become a global center for information-enabled services.

There is much that can be learned about development strategy from the experience of these two countries. Initially, I set out to write about this. However, with the advent of the 2008–2009 global economic crisis, I realized that the most interesting story was how important these two countries had become and how they were changing the world. As I focused on their relationship with the global system, I found that it was critical to understand more about the nature of that system and its evolution. This led me to look into how economic power shifted and the relationship between countries changed as that power shifted. This reinforced my appreciation of the important role of technological innovation and technological catch-up in economic development. It also led me to focus on the role of tertiary education and knowledge as elements critical to swift economic growth.

Studying the evolution of the global economic system also made me aware of the strong geopolitical elements of the relationships between major countries and the many ways they manifested themselves from trade to finance to technology to security and to global governance. It also helped me see that environmental sustainability was a new element which we have recognized as a binding constraint only more recently.

Combining the study of past power shifts with the new binding constraint of the world's ability to cope with increased carbon emissions that are the by-product of economic development and the very swift development of China and India, I became concerned about the economic stability and environmental sustainability of the global system. The result is this book.

It puts the rapid growth of China and India in the context of our very complex and increasingly interdependent world. It also does some simple extrapolations on their expected future growth. The conclusion, based on the review of historical experience of power shifts, the new binding constraint of the environment, and the gaps in the existing global governance system, is that the current system is unsustainable. We are heading toward major frictions. Managing these tensions is going to be a very big challenge that will take a lot of political leadership among the great powers and more willingness to adjust domestic interests for better longer-term global welfare. This will not be easy, but it must be done. I hope that this book will help to create a greater awareness of what is at stake and an understanding of why some of these issues need to be tackled now.

Acknowledgments

THIS BOOK HAS BEEN six years in the making, and I have many institutions and individuals to thank for making it possible. First, I would like to thank Georgetown University and the Luce Foundation for the generous support I have received over the last six years. Georgetown University offered me a teaching position at the School of Foreign Service funded in part with a grant from the Luce Foundation. Being on the Georgetown faculty has given me the time and perspective to write this book, which would have been impossible to do otherwise. I thank Robert Galluci, former dean of the School of Foreign Service, and Carol Lancaster, current dean, for their great support and encouragement on writing the book. I particularly want to acknowledge the value of a one-semester faculty fellowship leave in the fall of 2008, supported by my department's director, Elizabeth Stephens. During this leave, I was able to work out the structure and do most of the writing of a first draft of this book.

I have benefited greatly from interaction with other faculty members as well as with the students in my classes. Over the last six years, I have taught a course on China and India as emerging global powers, which has allowed me to explore many different dimensions of their history, economic strategy, and impact on the world. The interaction with students in presenting material to them as well as learning from their questions and their work has been extremely valuable. I have also had some excellent student research assistants who have made very valuable contributions. This has included numerous students who helped and were supported through Georgetown's GUROP program as well as students contracted with research funds made available through Georgetown University and the Luce Foundation grant. Among them, I want to particularly thank Sean Liu, Amber Rivera, Zack Wilson, Raja Karthikeya, and Andrew Martinelli. I also thank President John DeGioa for the opportunity to participate in Georgetown's China Initiative, including many workshops with senior officials from the Chinese Central Party School at Georgetown and in Beijing, Chengdu, and Xian. Here I would particularly like to thank Jeff Gibson, who was an invaluable guide on our visits to China. Finally, at Georgetown, I want to thank Carole Sargent for her valuable support and advice on publishing for the academic world. At Georgetown, I also want to thank David Gibbs for some excellent copyediting.

I have also broadened my perspective and learned very much from my faculty colleagues at the School of Foreign Service. I have been particularly fortunate in benefiting from their wide range of expertise and the insights they have offered from fields ranging from history, environment, politics, government, technology, and security studies. Many of them have generously commented on various drafts of this book. Their perspectives have greatly complemented my own background in economics. I would especially like to acknowledge helpful comments from Timothy Beach, Robert Cumby, David Edelstein, Charles King, Robin King, Robert Leiber, Joanna Lewis, Dennis McNamara, Kathy McNamara, John McNeill, Theodore Moran, Michael Nelson, Paula Newman, Robert Shambaugh, Robert Sutter, Scott Taylor, and especially Charles Weiss for our many long discussions and his excellent comments.

I also want to acknowledge the very valuable perspective I acquired on development and the global economic system from my more than 25 years working as an economist at the World Bank. I had the benefit of working on all the major developing countries and particularly on China and India. In the course of my work with the World Bank, I traveled to China and India more than 30 times, traveled extensively within both countries, and discussed issues with senior policy makers, academics, business people, and persons at all levels of society. I specifically want to thank Ramesh Mashelkar and Shuilin Wang for the many insights I acquired in extensive discussions with them over the course of many years. Among various other books, I coauthored two each on China and India with colleagues from the World Bank. These books were extensively discussed with policy makers, business people, and academics in the countries. I want to thank them for their very valuable comments and insights. I also thank several former colleagues at the World Bank who commented on drafts of this manuscript. I particularly want to thank Jean-Eric Aubert, Danny Leipziger, Vinod Goel, and Yevgeny Kuznetsov.

I also want to thank various close friends, including Pieter Bottelier, Thomas Greiner Jr., Ashoka Mody, and Peter Scherer, for their excellent comments and encouragement.

Finally, I especially want to thank Margo Beth Crouppen, acquisitions editor at Stanford University Press, for her patience in waiting for me to complete this manuscript, as well as her excellent advice and editing in completing this manuscript. I also want to thank the two outside reviewers brought in by Margo to comment on my original manuscript. Their very thorough and detailed comments forced me to sharpen and streamline my analysis and contributed to raising the quality of the work.

Needless to say, the opinions in this book are my own, and any faults or mistakes should be attributed to me, not to any of the persons named above.

List of Abbreviations

BRICs	Brazil, Russia, India, and China
CIC	China Investment Corporation
CIS	Commonwealth of Independent States
DAC	Development Assistance Committee
EC	European Community
EU	European Union
FDI	Foreign Direct Investment
G-7	Group of Seven
G-20	Group of Twenty
GATT	General Agreement on Tariffs and Trade
GDP	Gross Domestic Product
GNI	Gross National Income
IBRD	International Bank for Reconstruction and Development
ICT	Information and Communications Technology
IEA	International Energy Agency
IMF	International Monetary Fund
IPCC	Intergovernmental Panel on Climate Change
IPE	International Political Economy
IPR	Intellectual Property Rights
IT	Information Technology
MNC	Multinational Company
NATO	North Atlantic Treaty Organization

NIAEs	Newly Industrialized Asian Economies
NPT	Nuclear Non-Proliferation Treaty
OECD	Organisation for Economic Co-operation and Development
OPEC	Organization of Petroleum Exporting Countries
PPP	Purchasing Power Parity
RCA	Revealed Comparative Advantage
R&D	Research and Development
SDRs	Special Drawing Rights (name of shares of member countries in the IMF)
SITC	Standard Industrial Trade Classification
SWF	Sovereign Wealth Funds
TFP	Total Factor Productivity
TNCs	Transnational Corporations
TOE	Tons of Oil Equivalent
UN	United Nations
UNCTAD	United Nations Conference on Trade and Development
WDI	World Development Indicators
WEF	World Economic Forum
WEO	World Economic Outlook
WEO	World Energy Outlook
WIPO	World Intellectual Property Organization
WTO	World Trade Organization
USTR	United States Trade Representative

THE WORLD UNDER PRESSURE

CHAPTER 1

Rising Powers

THE ECONOMIC RISE OF CHINA AND INDIA since the 1980s is unprecedented in its speed and breadth. These giant countries, which today represent nearly 40 percent of world population, have increased their share of global economic output from 4 percent in 1980 to 18 percent in 2010 in terms of purchasing power parity (an economist's adjustment for what money can buy).[1] Over the same period, their share of global trade has increased from 1 percent to 12 percent. Their rapid entry onto the global stage is creating frictions in trade, finance, foreign investment, intellectual property rights, and competition for natural resources—not to mention concerns about climate change, global governance, security, and balance of power. The world needs to accommodate the rise of these two countries; that much is clear. But this will require difficult adjustments by all major powers, including these two swiftly rising countries themselves. The question is whether the world can accommodate these ascending giants without the aforementioned tensions escalating into major economic and power collisions.

Why This Book? The Rise of These Two Powers Is Stressing the Global System

There are many books on the growth of one or both of these countries.[2] However, none have taken as broad a view of their rise as this book seeks to do, while developing the implications of such a swift upsurge for the global system. Another unique aspect of this book is its historical perspective combined with an appreciation for a new binding global constraint—the limited capacity of the environment to absorb increased CO_2 emissions that are a by-product of economic development because of our reliance on fossil fuels.

Taking a historical view, the speedy development of other countries is not encouraging. Fast-paced changes in economic and political power have typically led to strong hostilities that have tended to spiral into power struggles translated into trade, resource, and ideological wars as well as military conflict. Historically, the world has not faced the environmental constraints that we do. We need to limit the absolute amount of CO_2 emissions to avoid climate change, and this brings a new binding constraint to the swift ascent of China, India, and the world.

The focus of this book is not on the military or security threats from the growth of these two countries but on *the implications of their growth for the global economic system* and *their impact on the environment and geopolitics*. It does not delve into the military and security issues except as a by-product of the two countries' increasing economic size and impact on the environment.

Although the book covers both China and India, the challenges that they pose are qualitatively and substantively different. The biggest and most immediate challenge is posed by China. Its population is nearly a sixth larger, its economy almost three times the size, and its merchandise exports nearly eight times those of India. China uses three times as much energy and emits four times as much CO_2 as India. At current rates of growth in purchasing power parity terms, China will have as big an economy as the United States by 2016. In nominal terms, it is likely to be as big as that of the United States by 2020, once adjustment is made for a gradual appreciation of its exchange rate. It will take India more than four times as long to match the size of the U.S. economy. Furthermore, as an authoritarian, one-party state and hybrid socialist/market economy, China has a different political and economic model from the West, Japan, or India, and its expansion creates an additional concern in terms of geopolitics and ideology.

India is included in our analysis because, if it continues to grow at its recent rate, in about 10 years it will be putting pressure on the global system in the same ways China does today. In 40 years, India may also surpass the United States in economic size, and that will further complicate the dynamics of global power. In addition, there is a risk of collision between China and India over water, possibly other resources, and perhaps economics and ideology. Therefore, focusing on China is not enough. Our story is about two powers that will each shift the global balance on a number of fronts during time frames that overlap and extend over the next half century.

Economically, the world faces competitive pressure from China's increasing exports. Although China's competitive export growth provides consumers with the benefit of low prices for manufactured products, this expansion is displacing workers and companies in developing and developed countries alike. Between 1980 and 2010, China's share of the world's merchandise exports increased from less than 1 percent to 10 percent. No country has had such a massive entry into the global economy in as short a time. In the context of high unemployment and low growth in developed countries, there are growing complaints about currency manipulation and protectionist sentiment against China.

India is pressuring developed economies not with merchandise but with information-enabled service exports. This raises concerns about the off-shoring of knowledge-intensive jobs from developed countries to India. There are also concerns that both countries are growing faster by copying and pirating technology from the rest of the world. Their expanding innovation capability, based on an increase in the number of scientists and engineers and money allocated to research and development, is also influencing their competitive strength, although China is much further along than India. Both countries are becoming important homes to, as well as sources of, direct foreign investment. One question in the world's marketplace is whether they are attracting foreign investment that may have gone elsewhere. Since they are buying natural resources and high-technology companies abroad, another key question is one of security in terms of access to resources, as well as strategically important technology residing in more developed nations.

Environmentally, these two countries' enormous resource needs are a sore subject, as both are resource poor on a per capita basis. Their large demand translates into windfalls for commodity exporters but rising prices for other commodity importers. World competition is particularly strong for energy resources and, between China and India, for water. However, the more significant collision with the environment is not over resources; the main sticking point is CO_2 emissions. If business continues as usual, the CO_2 emissions of China, the United States, and India will be greater by 2035 than the whole world's emissions in 1990.[3] The Kyoto targets are to cut total global emissions below the 1990 level if the irreversible levels of CO_2 for disastrous global warming are to be avoided.

The friction over CO_2 emission stems from the fact that today's rich countries developed without paying for the CO_2 they created. China and India do not want to commit to quantitative limits because the additional costs of reducing CO_2 emissions would slow their growth. They argue that it is unfair to make them pay for a problem created by developed economies whose per capita incomes are 16 to 40 times higher than theirs. Since China, the United States, and India have not formally committed to reducing their emissions, there has not been much progress on a global agreement to deal with the problem.

Some countries, like the United States, are considering legislation that would put a border tax on the carbon content of products from countries like China and India, which are not considered to be doing enough to reduce CO_2 emissions. If such legislation were adopted, there would be an increased risk that trade tensions would escalate to the point where there could be a breakdown of the global trading system into regional blocs.

Structure of the Book: Review the Past to Get Insights into the Present and the Future

Now that we have looked at the chessboard of the world from a bird's-eye view, we will traverse the potential conflicts that we face at the ground level in the hopes of understanding our landscape better and beginning to chart a viable course. The structure of this book is as follows. Chapter 2 focuses on what we can learn from the history of global power shifts. It includes a review of some theories of power shifts, noting additional complexities introduced by the binding global environmental constraints of our day, greater global interdependence in trade and finance, the globalizing activities of multinational companies, and the power of the Internet. It also traces previous changes in the global economic, trade, financial, and underlying technological systems.

Chapter 3 addresses why China and India have been growing faster than the rest of the world for the last 30 years. It considers some similarities and differences in their histories and economic policies to explain their growth rates, the sources of their strengths, and their impact on the world. A large part of their growth is because of how they have leveraged technology that was obtained formally or informally from the rest of the world. In many respects, both countries, but particularly China, are out to regain their former status and prestige and to avenge the humiliation they were forced to endure in the nineteenth century when they were exploited by Western powers.

Chapter 4 explores their growth prospects over the next 20 years. What are the main challenges? How successful are they likely to be in addressing these daunting challenges? Although predicting the future is hazardous and there are always unforeseen events, this chapter concludes that China and India are likely to grow much faster than the rest of the world for the next two decades unless there is a strong protectionist reaction or some major unforeseen disruption. They will also increase their competitiveness because they are strengthening their innovative capability by investing in higher education and research and development (R&D).

Chapter 5 homes in on the economic frictions that China's and India's rapid growth raises for the world. It discusses the positive and negative impacts on other countries through their trade. This includes an analysis of the symbiotic relationship of the financial imbalances between the United States and China that have resulted from China's large trade surpluses and the U.S. deficits, the controversial issue of exchange rates, and the complex issue of the U.S. dollar as the reserve currency. It also analyzes the frictions resulting from the bigger role of both countries as hosts to direct foreign investment as well as in buying up natural resource and high-technology companies in other countries. It analyzes the competitiveness problem created as companies in these two countries copy and steal technology from foreign companies. Finally, it also notes the shifting geopolitical balance between countries with democratic and market-oriented regimes and those captivated by the attractiveness of the authoritarian Chinese model of government and state market relationships.

Chapter 6 explores environmental frictions resulting from the two countries' swift growth. It focuses on their relative resource scarcity, their energy needs, and CO_2 emissions in particular. It also explains that the world is deadlocked over CO_2 emissions because the problem is a zero-sum game. Unless this deadlock can be broken, there is a risk that there will be negative fallout from climate change. The chapter argues that the most straightforward way to break this deadlock is through a major push for more sustainable energy technologies, but that is not happening because not enough resources are allocated to energy R&D. Finally, it points out that the pressures on the environment from the quick development of China and India are a precursor to the pressures that will come as the rest of the world develops. Thus, it is necessary to find more environmentally sustainable development strategies and start helping developing countries implement them rather than copying the energy- and resource-intensive strategies of the developed economies.

Chapter 7 summarizes the shifts in power that are taking place and the friction they are generating. It argues that the existing international system is not able to deal with these tensions. It was designed after World War II for a different configuration of power, is not able to handle new stresses within the traditional areas, and is even less able with the new binding environmental constraint. There is a risk that these frictions could lead to more serious confrontations, including trade wars, ideological wars, and even conventional wars. Here the short-term pressure is coming from the rise of China, which is on track to become the largest economy within a decade in virtually all dimensions of power except military.

The problem with China's rapid rise is that it has been free riding on the global system—enjoying the benefits of the system while not paying the costs and not following some of the rules. The main problem is its trade strategy, where it has been manipulating its currency to strengthen its cost advantage. Free riding also extends to copying and stealing technology from the rest of the world. In addition, China is using access to its large and dynamic domestic market to get foreign companies to divulge their technology. It then helps its firms use the technology to their competitive advantage, including even exporting the products to other countries. China is also free riding by not doing enough to maintain other aspects of the international system—for example, controlling nuclear proliferation.

The rise of China, accelerated by free riding on the global system, is a major challenge for the United States, which was the main architect of the current system and its strongest power. On the environment, this is further complicated because, like China (and India), the United States is also free riding on the environment by not paying for CO_2 emissions. Chapter 7 uses the insights from Chapter 2 to argue that together with the European Union and Japan, the United States needs to engage China to work out a new set of rules and mechanisms that can address the key imbalances and threats and also help create more sustainable development strategies for countries that are being left behind by the more competitive and demanding global economic system.

Because there is much uncertainty about how the world will evolve, Chapter 8 develops three alternative scenarios to help think through the challenges. It argues that the current unsustainable and uncooperative global system could lead to economic tensions between a stronger China and its area of influence and the United States and other similar-minded countries, as well as the negative consequences of climate change due to a lack of shared commitment to curb global CO_2 emissions. An alternative scenario is similar on the economic side but foresees the challenge of global climate change being temporarily solved by some unilateral geo-engineering move by a capable power such as China or India. The most desirable scenario—that of global cooperation to maintain an economically integrated and environmentally sustainable global system—is imaginable but difficult to attain. The chapter also considers the scenario of the impact of a major economic collapse in China. The negative consequences of that scenario make clear that China already is central to the global economic system and reinforce the desirability of working out cooperative solutions.

Accommodation on both the economic and environmental fronts will require changes in the behavior of all parties. While the solutions are relatively straightforward in principle, the political economy of implementing them is difficult because it involves significant costs and changes in behavior of the major powers. The difficulties are also related to the time frames of different political systems and the mind-sets and perceptions of people and nation-states.

The main point I hope to drive home is that our current global system—in terms of trade, finance, technology, environment, and global governance—is not sustainable as it is currently established. At a minimum, the systems will need to accommodate the environmental constraints of climate change, taking into the account the needs of developing countries. In addition, it will be necessary to adjust the economic and political relationships of the main world powers to reflect new power realities among them as well as each nation's relationship with the rest of the world. How smoothly this adjustment is made and how it will affect overall global welfare will depend on the extent to which there is a better understanding of the interdependence of the issues, the stakes of the players, and the benefits of maintaining a cooperative global system.

CHAPTER 2

Insights from History of Power Shifts and Growing Interdependence

THE ARRIVAL OF NEW ENTRANTS on the global economic stage is never an easy or smooth process. The historical record over the last 200 years shows that there are strong frictions between established and rising powers. These involve competition over territory, competition for regional or global dominance, and competition for natural resources (gold and silver in earlier mercantilist times and energy more recently). An important change has been that competition over territories has been replaced largely by competition through trade and finance. There is also ideological competition over governance and economic systems (such as during the Cold War) as well as conflict over human rights and humanitarian concerns.[1] More recent is the realization of environmental constraints in terms of the amount of CO_2 that can be emitted without causing a rise in global temperatures that could have very negative effects on global growth and welfare. Also new is the much greater degree of global competition and interdependence, which raises the need for greater coordination to address global interactions and problems, posing challenges to the architecture of the global system and the actions of the key players. It also raises concerns about the likelihood of trade wars, resource wars, cold wars (over the ideology of state versus market and authoritarian versus democratic regimes), and conventional wars.

The first section of this chapter reviews several theories of international political economy that provide some perspective on power shifts and global stability. The review takes note of four trends that have a strong bearing on the analysis of the impact of the ascent of China and

India in the current global context. The second section of the chapter lays out a framework for thinking about the global system. It emphasizes the complex interdependence among seven areas: economic growth of countries, international trade, international finance, technology, environment, security, and global governance. The third section briefly examines changing economic and geopolitical power over the last 200 years using the framework. Its purpose is to provide a historical context of power shifts and pressures that will be analyzed in the rest of the book. The final section concludes that the history of power shifts is not reassuring. Although the past is not a predictor of the future, it can provide insights. These will be useful for the analysis in the last two chapters of the book.

Conflicting Theories Provide Relevant Perspectives

Three contrasting theories about international relations provide some relevant insights to the examination of the development of new powers. The two main traditions, realist and liberal, both focus on the state as the principal actor.[2] The realist theory focuses on power.[3] Its main proposition is that states pursue power to increase their security.

Liberals also focus on the state as the key actor, but in contrast to the realists' Darwinian, power-centered view, they allow for a more benign world and focus more on growth. The liberal theories have their roots in the mid-eighteenth-century Enlightenment, when some thinkers believed that reason could be employed to make the world a better place. They argue that prosperous, interdependent, democratic states are unlikely to fight each other and that international institutions enable states to avoid war and concentrate instead on building cooperative relationships.[4]

In contrast to the realists, who focus primarily on power as the main objective, the state as the main actor, and the military as the main instrument, neoliberal theorists in international political economy accept that there are important nonstate actors, that economic well-being is another important objective (particularly when military threat is perceived to be in abeyance), and that institutions and agreements are the main instruments.[5] They developed the theory of complex interdependence that will be one of the central thrusts of this book, with some updating and expansion. The insights from this neoliberal theory will be contrasted with the realist theory in the analysis of the global system in Chapter 7.

There is also a different theory, or approach, that has been termed constructivism. It points out that a society's ideas, culture, and concepts of morality also affect the behavior of states and that these can also evolve.[6]

Theories are shaped by the historical contexts in which they are created. Changing events force theories to adapt to new realities and concerns. Thus, for example, hegemonic stability theory was developed in the period after World War II, when the United States was hegemonic and largely developed the rules of the Bretton Woods system (see below).[7] The hypothesis was that there had to be a hegemonic power to ensure stability in what would otherwise be anarchy among state relationships. The theory of hegemonic decline was developed in the 1970s and 1980s, when there were signs that the United States was losing its immediate post–World War II preeminence because of the rapid recovery of Western Europe, the growing military strength of the USSR, and the swift rise of Japan.[8]

A realist theory of power that is relevant to analyze the rise and decline of nations was developed by Robert Gilpin in his classic work *War and Change in World Politics* (1981). Gilpin argues that countries rise to power on economic strength, which is based on resources and technology. Countries expand their power and territory until the costs of expansion offset the benefits. They also seek to control the international system, which is based on the regular interactions among states according to some form of control or governance.[9] The governance of the system depends on the distribution of power among the actors, the hierarchy of prestige (reputation based on economic and military power), and "a set of rights and rules that govern or at least influence the relations among states."[10] The most powerful country generally sets up these institutions.

Gilpin argues that countries that develop power tend to overextend themselves and that their citizens become accustomed to their position of prestige and start working less. On the other hand, because of what he calls the law of uneven development (or what has been called the advantage of backwardness[11]), less developed countries can catch up quickly by assimilating the technology of the leaders. Their swift expansion eventually makes them a challenger to the established power, which then has two options: to increase resources or reduce costs. The first option is preferable but difficult. Citizens of the hegemonic state are less willing to work hard to stay ahead. They react negatively to the government's attempts to increase taxes to invest in greater technological strength and military leadership.

There are four variants to reducing costs. One is to retrench to more defensible positions.[12] This may be feasible and will help the hegemon conserve its strength and preserve its dominant role for more time. A second is to form alliances with other powers that can help contain the rise of the new power. However, there is a risk that the allies will switch allegiance to the rising power. A third variant is to appease the developing power by giving it a greater role in setting the rules of the global system. However, if power continues to shift in favor of the new entrant, it may want to set its own rules. The fourth is a preemptive strike against the rising power before it becomes strong enough to take on the incumbent.[13] Gilpin also makes an important distinction between changes *within* the global system and changes *to* the global system. The former are less disruptive, as the new power basically just demands more influence in the way the system is run. The latter are more disruptive, as it means changing the entire global system, and it tends to be the result of wars over hegemony.[14] So far, the rise of China and India appears to be an example of changes within the existing system rather than changes to the system.

Gilpin wrote this framework in 1981 in the context of what appeared to be the hegemonic decline of the United States in the face of rising Soviet military power and Japanese economic power. However, even during this period of intense Cold War rivalry, he did not believe there was a risk of hegemonic war. The USSR was not out to change the global system, just to expand its control over some other countries and maintain its empire. As it turns out, the threat of the USSR and the economic threat from Japan disappeared when both of these potential challenges faced their own internal crises. More recently, some have argued that the rapid ascent of China, and to a lesser extent India, is a modern version of the same pattern of power shift. Edward Friedman, for example, argued that the rise of China carries risks similar to those resulting from the rise of Germany prior to World War I. He warned that the United States and China needed to cooperate much more to avoid tensions that could lead to war.[15]

Whether the realist, neoliberal, or constructivist approach most accurately reflects reality matters for policy makers trying to affect or anticipate future outcomes. We will come back to these different interpretations of the rise of China and India in Chapter 7 after we have explored some of the challenges their development raises for the global system. Theories also need to take more explicit account of the greater speed, depth, and complexity of global interdependence as well as the importance of environment and technology.

Keohane and others contributed to international political economy (IPE) theory by emphasizing that the state is no longer the sole international actor. He and other neoliberals pointed out that there was a proliferation of new nonstate actors, including issue-oriented nongovernmental organizations, political movements, and human rights and environmental activists. With the development of the Internet and better communications technology such as video and social networking systems, these actors are able to get their message out globally to pressure governments and corporations at very little cost. A good example is the WikiLeaks release of hundreds of thousands of secret U.S. State Department cables in 2010, which revealed details of how the government carried out international relations with various countries. Cyberattacks carried out by lone hackers, independent groups, or organized crime groups also use this new information and telecommunications technology to disable critical infrastructure or even steal valuable military, industrial, and personal information.

The framework developed in this book stresses the need to recognize the complex interdependence noted by Keohane and others. Four trends need to be taken into account. The first three are more a matter of the greater relevance of what were earlier just emerging trends; the fourth is the new concern about the environment.

First, global interdependence has increased significantly since the original development of the theory. A good example is the increase in integration through trade. Since the early 1990s, the share of trade in world economic activity has increased by half, from 35 to 45 percent (depending on whether services are included in addition to merchandise) to 55 to 65 percent.[16] This dramatic expansion of trade has been the result of liberalization of trade regimes as well as of technological advance. In regard to the latter, two developments have been particularly important. One is a rapid reduction in transportation costs as more efficient means of transportation have been developed, including the development of containerization. The second is the revolution in information and communications technology, which has made possible the integration and coordination of vast supply chains of production and distribution networks all around the world. Advances in information technology have also made it possible to trade labor services across countries even without the physical movement of labor, as any service that can be digitized can be traded over the Internet.[17] The critical role of participation in the global economy, including the facilitation of trade in goods and services made possible by advances in information technology, in explaining the swift ascent of China and India will be developed in Chapter 3.

A second element that has increased global interdependence is greater global integration through international finance. Although IPE theorists have noted the importance of trade and finance and have focused on the political economy of these flows, the theory has not fully taken into account the increasing internationalization and interdependence of financial flows and how large financial transactions have become relative to global GDP. Between 2000 and 2008, the value of financial transactions relative to global GDP has almost quadrupled from 342 percent to 1,229 percent.[18] This explosive growth of the financial sector to more than 12 times real global GDP explains in large part the financial collapse of 2008–2009, which shook the whole world not only through the financial flows but also through its negative impact on jobs and production. The smaller impact of this crisis on China and India will be developed in Chapter 4, as will China's role in contributing to global financial imbalances and the strong financial and trade interdependence between China and the United States.

Third, another agent that has become as important as the state is the multinational corporation (MNC). This was noted in Raymond Vernon's 1972 book *Sovereignty at Bay*, which had a direct influence on the thinking of Keohane and Nye. While the discussions of the strength of MNCs as a countervailing power to that of states have somewhat faded from more recent writings of IPE, their power, if anything, has increased. Intrafirm trade among MNCs with their subsidiaries is estimated to account for two-thirds of world trade.[19] In addition, MNCs are the main creators and disseminators of technology. The thousand largest companies account for more than 50 percent of total world R&D.[20] The value added of their production in their home countries and their subsidiaries accounts for 27 percent of global value added.[21] That is an underestimate of their influence on global economic activity because it does not include their indirect impact through backward linkages to suppliers and forward linkages to marketers, distributors, and services. As will be developed in Chapters 3 and 5, MNCs have played an important role in helping India's, and even more so China's, technological catch-up and in integrating them into global supply and distribution systems.

Fourth, as will be developed later in this chapter and expanded in Chapter 6, theory also needs to explicitly take global environmental constraints into account. These are not just from the input availability side but also from the capacity of the environment to deal with the side effects of industrialization in terms of pollution and global warming. It is also necessary to take a global rather than just a state-centric perspective to understand and deal with the increasingly complex interdependence of international relations in light of environmental sustainability constraints that affect the entire planet.

Greater globalization, greater financial interdependence, the expanded role of MNCs, and environmental constraints will figure prominently in this book. The newly prominent role of terrorism, cyberhackers, and NGOs will be touched upon only briefly, although they are important new elements that require greater attention in international affairs.

This Book Uses a Broad Framework to Analyze and Track Power Shifts

This book proposes a new framework for analyzing the global system. Because of the increased importance of flows of resources, knowledge, and people across borders, it necessary to have a broad framework integrating economic, political, and environmental elements. International trade, finance, and technology flows are important contributors to growth as well as indicators of increasing economic strength. Greater economic strength leads to more military capability and greater geopolitical power. In addition, it leads to demands for a louder voice in the international governance architecture. For large countries, economic growth also puts pressure on global environmental resources, including the capacity of the environment to absorb carbon dioxide. These changes in relative power and impact lead to increasing frictions in the international system, which need to be managed carefully lest they turn into more serious problems of global stability and sustainability. The framework therefore includes looking at seven elements: economic size, international trade, international finance, technology, environment, security, and global governance.

Table 2.1 summarizes key events across these seven areas since 1800, with emphasis on critical mileposts for China and India. They have been laid out in parallel in chronological order to help track the interrelationships among the different areas and changing economic power. The relevance of each of the areas will be discussed first. The following section discusses the rise and decline of some of the key countries.

TABLE 2.1 Key events in main areas of framework since 1800

	1800–1850	1850–1900	1900–1920	1920–1940	1940–1960
Economic/Political					
Builds on technology but also requires appropriate economic/political regime to provide stability and incentives to improve economic performance	China peaks at 33.1% of world GDP (all GDP in table measured in PPP) India goes down to 16% After 1820, the UK and USSR overtake France at 5.5% each Germany 3.8% U.S. 1.8%	1870: UK peaks at 9.1% world GDP France peaks at 6.6% Rapid rise of U.S., Germany, and Russia U.S. surpasses UK by 1880, reaches 15% by 1900 China, India lose share rapidly Japan rises after 1870s	UK in decline, falls to 6.5% 1913: Germany peaks at 8.8% Russia also surpasses UK at 8.6% China, India surpassed by U.S., USSR, Germany, and UK Japan continues to rise	Russia surpasses Germany Japan continues to rise	1947: India gains independence 1949: Establishment of People's Republic of China China and India bottom out at 4.2–4.5% of world GDP; both become very inward oriented and autarkic 1950: U.S. peaks at 27.3 % world GDP Russia peaks at 9.6% 1945–1959: Europe rebuilt
Trade					
Rules set by the most powerful to maintain advantage; evolution from mercantilism to limited free trade and more detailed bilateral agreements	UK suppressed India trade 1812–1814 war: U.S. vs. UK over trade 1821: UK formally adopts gold exchange standard 1839–1842: UK vs. China in First Opium War	1856–1860: UK Second Opium War with China 1880s: European tariffs 1890: McKinley tariffs	1898–1901: China Boxer Rebellion against foreign trade and influence, suppressed by Eight-Nation Alliance of major powers (includes U.S.)	1930: Smoot-Hawley Act—global trade wars: trade falls by 1/2 to 2/3 and prolongs Great Depression Gold standard abandoned by UK, other European countries	IMF system based on new gold standard/fixed exchange to dollar

(*Continued*)

TABLE 2.1 *(Continued)*

	1800–1850	1850–1900	1900–1920	1920–1940	1940–1960
International Finance Key to growth and international trade	1825–1826: Global financial crisis starts in UK with sovereign defaults of Latin American countries over stock and commodity bubbles	Major UK capital flows to U.S. and Latin America 1873–1896: UK Great Depression because of overinvestment and increased productivity 1893: U.S. panic because of overbuilding of railroads	1907: Global financial crisis starts with Panic of 1907 in U.S. after collapse of developing country commodity prices 1913: U.S. establishes Federal Reserve Bank, helps make U.S. dollar a reserve currency	1929–1939: Great Depression U.S. Federal Reserve's inability to increase credit deepens and prolongs U.S. depression because of adherence to gold exchange standard	Marshall Plan: $13 billion in grants to help rebuild Europe Large offshore currency markets develop and put pressure on world currencies, including U.S. dollar
Technology Technological breakthroughs underlie the rise of economies, but fast-follower strategies allow some countries to catch up	1829: Start of age of steam and railways UK leads, spreads to Europe and U.S.	1875: Start of age of steel, electricity, and heavy engineering U.S. and Germany lead, overtake UK	1908: Start of age of automobile and mass production U.S. leads, spreads to Europe	Use of steel, petroleum, engines, chemical industry to develop war equipment: artillery, ships, tanks, bombs	1940–1950s: Green revolution in Mexico 1945: Start of nuclear age 1945: U.S. 1949: USSR 1952: UK 1957: USSR Sputnik success shocks U.S. 1960: France

Security					
Concerned with gaining and maintaining power and warding off threats	1803–1815: Napoleonic Wars as France tries to take over Europe	1870: Franco–Prussian War confirms rise of Germany over France	1904–1905: Russo–Japanese War confirms rise of Japan 1914–1917: WWI started by Austro–Hungary and Germany, involves most of Europe and U.S.	1931–1945: Sino–Japanese War for Manchuria over raw materials 1939–1945: WWII started by Germany, involves most of world	Cold War (1945–1991): U.S. bloc vs. USSR bloc 1947: First Indo–Pakistan War (over Kashmir) 1949: NATO established against USSR 1950–1953: Korean War, China supports North Korea 1955: Warsaw Pact among USSR allies to counter NATO
Global Governance					
The strongest set the rules for the global system, following a war or crisis	1815: Treaty of Paris at end of Napoleonic War 1815: Congress of Vienna sets Europe's boundaries for 100 years	1883: Paris Convention for Protection of Industrial Property	1917: Versailles Treaty whereby Germany accepts responsibility, loss of territory, and high war reparations 1919: League of Nations created to avoid war	1939: Collapse of League of Nations because of lack of support by U.S. and German and Japanese violations	1944: Bretton Woods Conference creates: 1945: IMF to stabilize trade and finance 1945: World Bank to reconstruct Europe 1945: GATT to reduce obstacles to trade (India founding member of GATT) 1945: United Nations established as successor to League of Nations

(*Continued*)

TABLE 2.1 *(Continued)*

	1800–1850	1850–1900	1900–1920	1920–1940	1940–1960
Environment Only recognized as constraint after 1971	Spread of coal-based industrialization	First wave of environmentalism; upturn in CO_2 due to coal and deforestation in the West			Global population growth reaches nearly 2% per annum; emergence of oil as major fuel; nuclear power
	1960–1980	**1980–1990**	**1990–2000**		**2000–2010**
Economic/Political Builds on technology but also requires appropriate economic/political regime to provide stability and incentives to improve economic performance	1960: Sino–Soviet split 1960–1989: rapid rise of Japan, peaks at 7.7% world GDP in 1973 1967: Creation of European Community from European Iron and Steel Community, European Economic Community, and European Atomic Energy Community 1970: U.S. falls to 22% world GDP 1972: Nixon recognizes China	1978– : China starts rapid rise after market reforms and opening to trade and foreign direct investment 1970s–1980s: Global concern with Japan's rapid economic rise June 4, 1989: China Tiananmen Square November 9, 1989: Fall of Berlin Wall	1991: Breakup of USSR 1991: Japanese financial crisis stops country's rise 1991: Indian financial/currency crisis leads to economic liberalization, opening to world, and faster growth 1993: European Union established on foundation of European Community		2005: U.S.–China strategic dialogues begin 2008 world GDP: U.S. 20%, China 13%, Japan 6%, India 5% 2008: U.S. and world experience worst economic crisis since Great Depression China and India less affected, maintain positive growth, but at lower levels

Trade				
Rules set by the most powerful to maintain advantage; evolution from mercantilism to limited free trade and more detailed bilateral agreements	August 1971: U.S. drops gold exchange standard December 1971: Major countries revalue vs. U.S. March 1973: World moves to flexible exchange rates	1985: Plaza Accord to depreciate U.S. dollar vs. Japanese yen 1986–1994: Uruguay Round of tariff reductions 1987: Louvre Accord to stop U.S. dollar slide against Japanese yen	1994: Services added to GATT 1994: North American Free Trade Agreement created 1995: World Trade Organization set up as successor to GATT 1999: Start of euro currency	2001: China joins the WTO 2001: Doha Rounds begin 2008: Doha Rounds break down: disagreements between developing and developed countries 2008: China and others question U.S. dollar as reserve currency 2009: China becomes world's largest merchandise exporter
International Finance				
Key to growth and to trade	1973–1974: World stock market crash leads to 1975 global recession; recovery takes 10–20 years Rapid growth of international finance; petrodollars lent to developing countries	1980: Global financial crisis following 1979 rise in oil prices, then collapse of commodity prices 1981: Latin American debt crisis 1987: Black Tuesday crash 1989: Recovery	1990–1993: Global financial crisis and recession from real estate and stock market speculation 1997: Asian financial crisis 1998: Russian financial crisis	2001–2002: Dot-com bust 2008: China becomes largest U.S. financier 2008–2009: U.S. financial crisis leads to global financial crisis

(*Continued*)

TABLE 2.1 *(Continued)*

	1960–1980	1980–1990	1990–2000	2000–2010
Technology				
Technological breakthroughs underlie rise of country, but fast-follower strategies allow some countries to catch up	1960s: Green revolution spreads to India and Philippines 1960: China has its own green revolution 1964: China nuclear 1971: Start of age of information and communications; technology in U.S. spreads to Europe and Asia 1974: India nuclear 1979: Israel nuclear	1983: Nanotechnology 1989: Launch of World Wide Web from ARPANET of the 1970s	1990: Human Genome Project 1994: Intellectual property rights (IPRs) added to GATT 1998: Pakistan becomes nuclear	2005: North Korea becomes nuclear 2005: China sends men to space 2006: China becomes largest industrial design and trademark patentee 2008: China invests in green technology Strong focus on energy efficiency and green technology Start of age of green technology?

Security				
Concerned with gaining and maintaining power and warding off threats	1962: Cuban missile crisis 1962: China–India Border War 1963–1975: Vietnam War (China supports North Vietnam) 1965: Second Indo–Pakistan War (over Kashmir) 1968: Nuclear nonproliferation treaty (NPT) 1971: Third Indo–Pakistan War (creation of Bangladesh) 1971: China enters Security Council 1972: Strategic Arms Limitation Treaty (SALT I)	1979–1987: USSR–Afghan War 1980–1988: Iraq–Iran Oil War 1983: Strategic defense initiative (Star Wars) announced by Reagan, heats up arms race again. 1987: Intermediate Range Nuclear Forces Treaty between U.S. and USSR to reduce nuclear warheads	1990: Iraq invades Kuwait for oil 1991: First U.S. Gulf War against Iraq over its invasion of Kuwait 1999: Fourth Indo–Pakistan War (over Kashmir)	9/11/2001: Terrorist attacks in New York and Washington 2001: Shanghai Cooperation Treaty includes China, Russia, others, not U.S. 2001– : U.S.–Afghanistan War 2003– : Iraq War (Second Gulf War) 2005: China shoots down own satellite. 2005: Concern about North Korea nuclear expansion (China key in six-party talks) 2006: Concern about Iran making nuclear weapon with Pakistani help 2008: U.S.–India Nuclear Accord to counterbalance China

(*Continued*)

TABLE 2.1 (*Continued*)

	1960–1980	1980–1990	1990–2000	2000–2010
Global Governance Strongest set the rules for the global system, following a war or crisis	1964: G-77 in U.N. 1971: China enters U.N. 1975: G-6/G-7	1989: Washington Consensus	1997: G-7 becomes G-8 with Russia's entry	2008: G-20 created in aftermath of 2008 global financial crisis 2008: Beijing Consensus?
Environment Only recognized as constraint after 1971	1972: Limits to Growth Report raises concern about environmental constraints to growth 1973: Oil Crisis I 1979: Oil Crisis II	1987: Montreal Protocol on chlorofluorocarbons and ozone depletion	1992: Rio Earth Summit United Nations Framework Convention on Climate Change 1997: Kyoto Protocol on CO_2 reductions	2007: IPPC Global Warming Report 2008: China becomes largest CO_2 emitter 2008: Oil price shock, food shortages, and commodity price shock 2009: Copenhagen meeting disappoints

SOURCE: Created by author.

Economic Size and Geopolitical Power

As will be developed in the explanation of the growth of China and India in the next chapter, countries grow not only from the accumulation of capital and labor but also from effective government, an economic regime that allocates resources to their most productive use, and improved technology. Effective government includes political stability and good macropolicies such as low inflation, low interest rates, and appropriate foreign exchange rates.

An effective economic system has mechanisms to allocate resources efficiently to improve economic performance, including through interaction with the rest of the world. Improved technology can either be acquired from abroad or developed domestically. Countries that are behind the world-technological frontier can boost their growth by acquiring technology from others. Countries already at the frontier need to continually develop new technology to improve their productivity. Countries that grow fast and become large economically have geopolitical tensions with established powers over resources, markets, ideology, and the governance of the global system.

Shifting economic power to China and India is challenging the global system because of their large economic size and resource use. The rise of China is creating additional frictions because of its authoritarian government and greater government control of the economy. These tensions can lead to trade wars, cold wars, or conventional wars. See Table 2.1 for the interdependence between the ascent of different countries and wars. The rise of Germany in the late nineteenth and early twentieth centuries led to World War I and World War II. The ascent of Japan in the late nineteenth century and the first part of the twentieth century partly led to a quest for resources and to its involvement in World War II. The rise of the USSR after the Communist takeover in 1917, the growth in its military capability after World War II, and its growing geopolitical power led to the Cold War with the United States and its allies from 1945 to 1991. This led to a great diversion of world resources toward military rather than economic uses.

International Trade

Historically, economic power leads to greater military power. Military power was used to expand economic and political power through territorial conquest. To a large extent, trade became a substitute for direct military conquest.[22] Dominant countries pushed mercantilism and imperialism onto colonies. Mercantilism is an economic viewpoint that holds that the wealth of a country is based on increasing its gold and silver assets, that trade is a zero-sum game, and that countries increase their wealth by exporting more than they import and getting gold and silver for the surplus. Mercantilist trade policy encouraged the imports of raw materials and protection and exports of domestically manufactured products. It was developed and widely used from the sixteenth to the nineteenth centuries in the United Kingdom and Europe and is linked to the drive of European countries to expand their territories through colonial conquest. More recently, trade and finance have been used instead of territorial conquest to control weaker countries. The United Kingdom switched to free trade once it had a dominant economic position thanks to the leadership it acquired as the birthplace of the Industrial Revolution.

The period between the two world wars was characterized by trade wars (see the second row in Table 2.1). These started with the Smoot-Hawley tariffs unilaterally imposed by the United States against Canadian imports. Given the negative experience of these trade wars, the major powers, led by the United States, sought to avoid a repeat of them after World War II. They created the General Agreement on Tariffs and Trade in 1947 to reduce tariffs on international trade. The GATT initially focused only on reducing tariffs on commodities. In negotiations of the Uruguay Round (1984–1994), it extended agreements into new areas, including intellectual property, services, capital, and agriculture.[23] Many aspects of this expansion, in particular the agreements on services and intellectual property rights, have been criticized by developing countries.

The World Trade Organization (WTO) was officially established on January 1, 1995, and superseded the GATT. Relevant from the perspective of this book, it approved China's joining the WTO.[24] It also set out an ambitious plan to make globalization more inclusive and to help the world's poor by slashing barriers and subsidies in farming and strengthening assistance to the poor. The so-called Doha Trade Rounds started in 2001 and were supposed to be completed by 2005, but the negotiations have turned out to be contentious. Even though the negotiations were extended, agreement has not been reached. Talks broke down in July 2008 because of disagreements between China and India on one side and the United States and the European Union on the other over agricultural subsidies in developed countries and safeguards for poor farmers in developing countries.[25,26] This will be taken up again in Chapter 8.

Free trade ideology has been internalized by China and to a lesser extent by India. China has prospered by adopting free trade. In a sense, it has turned the tables on the developed countries by being so successful in exports.[27] One of the main reasons for its success has been using direct foreign investment from developed economies to catch up technologically and gain access to global markets through their distribution networks. China's rapid expansion of trade is putting very strong economic restructuring pressure on the rest of the world. This will be developed in Chapters 3 through 5.

International Finance

Growing economic power is also reflected in international finance.[28] Developed countries generally have excess capital, which they invest in poorer developing countries, where they expect to reap higher returns in the case of portfolio investment or bonds or higher profits through direct investment in natural resources (minerals, land) or in the production of goods and services.

The nineteenth century saw very large international capital movements. As the economically dominant and more mature economy, the capital-rich United Kingdom was the source of most of these flows—first to the United States and the empire and then to Latin America and other parts of the world. These were very important to finance the development of new industries in new territories. A large share of them went to finance new infrastructure such as the railroads and electricity networks. The United States became the main source of finance after World War II. But it went from a net capital exporter in the postwar years to a net capital importer owing to the costs of the Vietnam War and the first Gulf War. Because of the growth of its large economy, it also attracted a lot of foreign direct investment.

The global financial system is extremely complex. Historically, it tends to go through cycles of boom and bust that generally affect not only the savers and investors but also the economies of which they are a part. International financial crises also affect the standing and relative power of countries (see the third row in Table 2.1). History is full of examples of international financial crises resulting from real estate and asset bubbles and external price shocks related to sharp increases or decreases of commodity prices.[29]

The 1929 stock market crash followed a major financial bubble involving investment in the automobile industry and the related industries of petroleum, steel, glass, cement, and road construction, as well as electricity and telephone grids and electric motors and appliances that transformed the workplace and the home. There are many explanations for the crash, including overinvestment, the pending Smoot-Hawley tariffs, the attempt of the United Kingdom to refloat the pound to the gold standard, rising income inequality, and insufficient money supply expansion by the Federal Reserve.[30]

The 2008–2009 financial and economic crisis is the deepest downturn the global economy has seen since the Great Depression. There are important parallels but also significant differences between the two crises. Both started in the United States and spread to international markets on account of financial interdependence. In both cases, rapid credit expansion and financial innovation led to high levels of debt, which created vulnerabilities to negative shock. In the 1920s, the financial innovation was the rapid diffusion of installment credit provided by retailers and other nonbank institutions as part of the rapid expansion of consumer-goods sales. In addition, new marketing techniques for stocks and purchases of stock through margin loans led to an overextension of credit and highly leveraged loans.[31] The financial innovation preceding the 2008–2009 crisis was the development and rapid spread of mortgage-backed securities and the rapid development of credit default swaps.

An important difference is that, in the 1929 crisis, there was a contraction of liquidity, which contributed to the recession. In the 2008–2009 crisis, the U.S. Federal Reserve and the central banks of other countries significantly expanded the money supply.[32] In addition, the United States and many other countries have adopted strong fiscal expansionary packages that are helping speed the recovery.[33]

As will be seen in Chapter 4, China and India were not as negatively affected by the 2008–2009 great contraction.[34] China's strength in merchandise exports has led to the accumulation of large foreign exchange reserves. This has resulted in the anomaly that a developing country with per capita income one-sixteenth that of the United States has become a major capital exporter. China uses its large foreign exchange reserves to buy U.S. Treasury bills and other assets. This also helps keep its currency, the renminbi, from appreciating, which helps maintain the competitiveness of its exports. The United States has become China's largest market. It has become the world's largest net borrower, and China has become the largest net lender. This has led to a complex symbiotic relationship between the United States and China, which will be explored in more detail in Chapters 5 and 7.

Technology

Innovation has been critical for the increase in global population as well as in per capita income and welfare.[35] For the first 1,400 years of the past two millennia, the global population grew very slowly. Between 1400 and 1800, both global population and per capita income began to increase simultaneously.[36] This shift was due to the convergence of many factors, in particular the development of ingenious ways to harness wind and water power to augment human and animal energy, and advances in agricultural techniques in irrigation, improved seeds, and multiple cropping. In addition, advances in shipbuilding and navigation technology, including the astrolabe and the compass, led to increased trade and exchange, which expanded markets and specialization.[37]

Both population and per capita incomes rose faster from the 1800s onward. This rapid per capita growth was in large part based on harnessing different forms of energy to increase productivity. A useful perspective on the relationship between innovation and economic growth and institutional structures over the last 250 years has been outlined by Carlota Perez (2002), who developed the concept of technological revolution. This is defined as a powerful and highly visible cluster of new and dynamic technologies, products, and industries capable of bringing about an upheaval in the whole fabric of the economy and of propelling a long-term upsurge of development. It involves strongly interrelated constellations of technical innovations, generally including an important all-pervasive, low-cost input, often a source of energy, sometimes a crucial material, plus significant new products and processes and a new infrastructure.[38]

Perez lists five such revolutions to which I have added another, the nuclear age, before the information revolution, because of its far-reaching significance for the security issue as well as its renewed relevance because of the low CO_2 emissions of nuclear energy. In the context of issues that will be discussed in Chapter 6, it is relevant to note that, with the exception of the information revolution, all of these revolutions are directly related to energy (see the fourth row in Table 2.1 to follow the technoeconomic revolutions). It can also be argued that the information age is related to energy in the sense that it is essentially a technology that allows the very precise management of electricity.[39] It will be argued in Chapter 6 that what the world needs now to ensure global sustainability is a major energy/environment revolution.

The first Industrial Revolution (1770–1840),[40] which started in England, involved the mechanization of cotton spinning and weaving through the use of waterpower and the expansion of canals, roads, and waterways to deal with increased commerce. Many of these innovations in the use of waterpower, canals, roads, and agriculture were developed earlier in China and India and used for agricultural production. In England, waterpower was applied for the first time to industrial production.

The second Industrial Revolution (1830–1890) was the age of steam and railways. The newly developed steam engine powered not only the cotton industry but also railroads and steamships. Simultaneous with demographic changes and enhanced production technology, railroads and steamships supported scale economies and provided new opportunities for specialization and exchange. This revolution also led to the development of railroad lines, ports and depots, telegraph lines along railroad right of ways, universal postal services, and city gas.

The third technological revolution (1875–1930) was based on steel, electricity, and heavy engineering developed in Germany and the United States. In the early nineteenth century, this broad social and economic transformation set the course toward the advanced standard of living that is the hallmark of developed countries today. The development and spread of electricity were particularly important. Almost overnight, power could be distributed in discrete units, including into the home for powering numerous labor-saving devices. This technological change gradually released women into the paid work force and increased output. Another impact on labor augmentation during this period was that gas and then electric lighting increased the length of the workday.

The fourth technological revolution (1910–1970) was based on the development of the internal combustion engine in the United States and Germany combined with rapid dissemination through low-cost mass production. The development of the gasoline and diesel engine untethered power from grids and led to more flexible land transportation. The expansion of the telegraph and then the telephone reduced distances by making it possible to communicate and coordinate activities across space, enlarging markets and furthering opportunities for specialization and exchange.

The nuclear age (1945–present) can arguably be considered another technological revolution. It has included not only nuclear weapons but also rapid development of intercontinental ballistic missiles and satellite technology. It has also included the development of nuclear energy, which is an important though controversial noncarbon-based alternative energy source. In addition, it has included the use of radiation and nuclear material in health not only for the treatment of cancer but also for X-rays and other medical and food applications.

The current technological revolution (1970–present) is based on the development of the transistor and semiconductor in the United States. The development and application of the semiconductor to information processing and communications spawned the current information technology (IT) revolution. It should be viewed as one more epochal innovation wave that is transforming the organization of economic and social activity. Economic development strategy today needs to take into account the evolving productive and developmental logic of information technology. This has been done in China with the production of information technology hardware and the use of IT to organize and coordinate global supply and distribution chains. It has been done in India with the export of information technology–enabled services.

With recent advances in science and technology, we may be at the cusp of another significant technological revolution. With advances in materials science, nanotechnology, and biotechnology, we are beginning to create new materials and to develop new life forms.[41] These technologies potentially have far-reaching implications across a wide range of industries and economic activities. It is still too early to know the full nature of their specific implications and impact.

While technological advances are very important for countries at the technological frontier, particularly if they want to maintain their lead, they are not essential for speedy economic development. Other countries can catch up rapidly by acquiring and making effective use of existing technologies.[42] In fact, the rise of many powers has been based on swift technological catch-up rather than the initiation of major technological revolutions. The basic technologies of the industrial revolutions spread rapidly beyond the United Kingdom. Germany and the United States, with their ample coal reserves, were particularly well placed to take up the new technologies and use the steam engine for industrial power. The United States was also able to take advantage of the transportation cost reductions permitted by railroads to rapidly develop manufacturing and trade throughout the country.

TABLE 2.2 Technological leadership and technological catch-up underpinnings of the rise of countries

UK rapid rise 1790s–1870[a]	Major innovator of first and second Industrial Revolutions
UK relative stagnation 1870–1950	Rest of Europe and U.S. caught up rapidly economically, but UK maintained global naval superiority until 1922
Prussia/Germany rapid rise until 1870	Rapid catch-up with UK coal-based steam engine technologies
Prussia/Germany 1875–1913[a]	Major innovator in steel, petroleum, electricity, heavy engineering, chemicals
German rapid rise in 1930s	Steel, chemicals, modern warfare equipment
Russia in second half of 1700s –1800s	Catherine the Great's rapid catch-up (1762–1796), similar to Peter the Great's rapid catch-up with the West in late 1690s–early 1720s; made Russia a great European power
Russia 1900–1945	Much imitation of the West, but also development of considerable scientific and technological capability, oriented primarily toward the military; forced industrialization 1929–1953 under Stalin
Russia post-WWII	Fast follower in nuclear capability, leader in space technology (Sputnik and missile launchers); however, 1991 breakup shows importance of the economic regime because it did not have an efficient system to shift its highly developed human resources and scientific and technological capability from military to commercial activities
Japan 1870s–WWI and WWII	Fast follower from Meiji restoration with massive imports of technology and knowledge from West and investments in technical and engineering education
Japan post-WWII–1970	*Continued* massive importation of Western technology facilitated by playing a key logistical supporting role in Vietnam War plus heavy investments in engineering education
Japan 1970–present	Reverse engineering and optimization of production processes and product design, with large increases in R&D as percentage of GDP, mostly applied rather than basic; innovator of superior production management systems
U.S. 1800–1875	Rapid catch-up with UK and Europe, copying reverse engineering, hiring foreign talent
U.S. 1870s–1930s[a]	Major innovator in steel, petroleum, heavy engineering, mass production, telegraphy, and investments in research sometimes using German scientists and engineers
U.S. during WWII[a]	Major innovator in nuclear technology: atomic and hydrogen bombs and nuclear energy; atomic bomb ended WWII with Japan and clearly reinforced U.S. hegemony in early post-WWII period
U.S. 1945–1970s	Massive investments in higher education (facilitated by GI bill), and in basic and applied R&D given success of Manhattan Project, expansion of U.S. multinational corporations (MNCs)
U.S. 1975–present[a]	Major innovator in information and communications technologies (ICT) and the Internet revolution, basic research, health, bioengineering, and nanotechnology; *continued* rapid expansion and globalization of MNCs
China since 1978	Rapid catch-up, now complementing with domestic innovation; very high investments in higher education; more higher education students than the U.S. by 2005 and more higher educated population by 2007 (see Chapters 3 and 4)
India since 1991	Rapid catch-up, facilitated by English language and core of engineering graduates that form the nucleus of its rapid rise in software and IT-enabled service (see Chapters 3 and 4)

SOURCE: Created by author.

[a]Leader of major technological revolution.

Table 2.2 summarizes the role of technology leadership versus technology catch-up for the major powers over the last 200 years. China and India have followed in the tradition of lagging powers that catch up through the rapid acquisition of existing technologies. For the discussion to follow in later chapters, the important role of education and highly skilled technical human capital needs to be kept in mind. By investing in tertiary education and R&D, these countries are moving from imitation to innovation.

Environment

As noted by McNeill, the realization that there are environmental constraints on human development is one of the few issues that are truly "new under the sun" in terms of humanity's understanding of its destiny.[43] Unfortunately, the global system has not yet internalized this new binding constraint. Environmental concerns did not enter explicitly into the global debate until the 1970s,[44] although the negative effects of the human impact on the environment were evident much earlier (see the bottom row of Table 2.1). The first alert as to the environmental constraints to growth came with the publication of *Limits to Growth,* written for the Club of Rome in 1972.[45] The main argument was that the world did not have enough resources to support its growing population and increasing level of natural resource use. As it turned out, technology came to the rescue and reduced the environmental constraints. The authors had assumed that demand for environmental resources grew exponentially whereas resource supply grew only incrementally. What they missed was that price increases stimulated saving and innovation to find, develop, and use more resources efficiently. The importance of prices for reflecting opportunity costs and stimulating the search for substitutes and better extraction and processing technologies is a lesson worth remembering when considering how to deal with carbon emissions (see Chapter 6).

The year after the publication of *Limits to Growth,* another event served as a harbinger of environmental constraints to growth: the oil crisis of 1973. The immediate trigger for the oil crisis was the geopolitical action of the Arab oil-producing states striking back at the countries supporting Israel in the 1973 Arab–Israeli War. This was a direct link between security concerns and a key natural resource. A second such link was that petroleum countries had been seeing the price of oil falling because of the rapid depreciation of the dollar. In real terms, the price of a barrel of oil dropped from 1960 until 1971.[46]

There was a second oil crisis in 1979. This time, it was the action of a broader group of countries organized into the Organization of Petroleum Exporting Countries (OPEC). The price rise had a devastating effect on countries that were dependent on oil imports. Particularly hard hit were Japan and oil-importing Latin American countries. Again highlighting the interdependence of the global system, this followed a period when Latin American countries had become highly indebted in hard foreign currencies (mostly dollars) as a result of the internationalization of finance.[47]

There is also a direct interdependence between environment and finance. A study of 137 recessions since 1960 found that the most widespread cause was oil price shocks and that the largest number of recessions were clustered around 1973–1975 and 1979–1981.[48] The oil price shocks also had repercussions on external demand shocks and fiscal and monetary crises. For example, the 1979 oil shock was a key element in the development of the Latin American debt crisis of 1981, as countries that were not able to service their debts when interest rates suddenly rose descended into trade and financial crisis.

In Japan, the second oil crisis redoubled the country's efforts to improve its export competitiveness (to make up for the high cost of oil imports) and to deal with the appreciation of its currency against the U.S. dollar as part of the 1985 Plaza Accord. In the end, this increased productivity made Japan even more of a competitive threat to the United States, and the U.S. trade deficit with Japan was not significantly reduced. The oil crisis was short-lived because President Reagan reduced restrictions on oil production. The spike in oil prices led to increased production and a glut of oil. However, the destabilization of international finance in Latin America led to two decades of macroeconomic instability and very poor growth there, commonly referred to as the lost decades.

One of the first international attempts to deal with the global environmental problem was the Montreal Protocol of 1987. This was a global reaction to the concern that chlorofluorocarbons were leading to serious damage to the stratospheric ozone layer that protects the earth from harmful ultraviolet radiation—most dramatically from a major seasonal decrease in the stratospheric layer over Antarctica and southern Australia. The protocol consisted of a commitment to replace chlorofluorocarbons with less damaging gases. It also involved some technology transfer and funding for the production of alternative refrigerants. The actual cost of reducing the use of chlorofluorocarbons turned out to be much lower than originally estimated.[49]

The first international attempt to control CO_2 emissions was the Kyoto Protocol of 1997, five years after the global Earth Summit in Rio (which, among other things, raised awareness of the link between CO_2 emissions and global warming). However, the Kyoto Protocol did not put any caps on the CO_2 emissions of developing countries, including China and India. It involved a system of charges and trade for CO_2 emissions, the net effect of which was to increase energy prices. The United States did not sign the Kyoto Protocol because of the increased cost that adhering to it would impose on its industries. Many industries also felt that applying the standards would lead to the migration of polluting industries to developing countries such as China and India and therefore put them at a competitive advantage. The Japanese and many European countries did agree to the Kyoto Protocol and have made significant progress in reducing their emissions. However, because the United States did not participate, this overall system has not been effective in reducing global emissions of carbon dioxide.

The next key milestone in awareness about environmental constraints was the release of the Intergovernmental Panel on Climate Change (IPCC) report on climate change in 2007. This group of international experts concluded that there was a direct causal relationship between human activity, particularly CO_2 emissions, and global warming.

There were great expectations for the climate change conference held in Copenhagen in December 2009, but they were not met. All that came out of the conference was a mild statement of intent to deal with the problem of global warming; no binding commitments were made. Chapter 6 will explore the challenges raised by the rapid growth of China and India on demand for raw materials and energy as well as their rapidly increasing CO_2 emissions.

Security and Military Power

In realist theory, security is the main concern of international affairs. Countries will go to war to establish order in an otherwise chaotic world. Problems of security arise from aggression across state boundaries. Causes of war include the desire to gain access to resources or advantageous geographic locations, ideology, religion, or the desire to preempt the rise of other powers. (See the fifth row of Table 2.1 for a chronology of major military conflicts.)

There has been much controversy over the cause of World War I. The most prevalent explanation is that it was a preemptive war through which Germany sought to thwart the threat of the rising power of Russia. The causes of World War II are even more complex, since the interwar years also included the turbulence caused by the Great Depression, which lasted from 1929 until the start of the war. Furthermore, the depression also included a major trade war among most powers. There was also the strong ideological element of Nazism and anti-Semitism.[50]

World War II was followed by the long Cold War (1945–1991) between the United States and its Western allies and the USSR and the countries under its influence. The United States set up the North Atlantic Treaty Organization (NATO) as a mutual defense agreement among Western powers in 1949. In response, the USSR set up the Warsaw Pact in 1955.

The Cold War spilled out into hot proxy wars in Korea (1950–1953) and later Vietnam (1963–1975).[51] In both wars, China supported the side fighting the United States. The Vietnam War in particular was very costly for the United States in terms of war casualties but also in direct and indirect fiscal costs (Table 2.1). Combined with the price rises of the first oil embargo, this drain on resources turned the United States from a net creditor into a net debtor and led to a destabilization of the international financial architecture which had been built on the dollar gold exchange standard. It eventually led to the financial crisis of 1973.

In spite of the proxy wars, the United States, USSR, and other nuclear powers (including China) sought to limit the proliferation of nuclear weapons through the Treaty on the Non-proliferation of Nuclear Weapons (NPT) of 1968. India did not sign this treaty and proceeded to develop nuclear weapons in 1974 and to continue to develop and test them until 1998.[52]

That the two major challengers to U.S. hegemony, Russia on the military side and Japan on the economic side, were both so severely weakened in 1991 created a sense of hubris on the part of the West. In this context, Francis Fukuyama's famous *The End of History and the Last Man* (1992), which argued that the democratic capitalist system was the ultimate goal of history, was widely praised.

That triumphalism proved to be misplaced. The devastating destruction of the U.S. World Trade Center and the bombing of the Pentagon on September 11, 2001, ushered in a major, spectacular new security threat, which has proved difficult to adjust to and deal with. The fact that the U.S. wars in Afghanistan (2001) and Iraq (2003) are still ongoing shows the difficulty of the task. It is not clear that these wars have made the world a safer place; on the contrary, the invasion of Iraq could be argued to have created thousands of new anti-Western terrorists. In geopolitical and moral terms, the United States suffered a tremendous loss of prestige, which will take a long time to recover. The 2008–2009 financial and economic crisis has been another major blow to U.S. prestige and power, serving as a stern reality check.[53] That it originated in the United States—the center of capitalism and the market economy—is particularly significant.

Chapter 7 will explore issues relating to China's and India's internal security, resources, and territorial wars. It will also address concerns about the risks of a possible new Cold War over ideological differences between China's authoritarian hybrid market regime and more market-oriented democracies.

Global Governance

New global governance systems usually result from major hegemonic wars. The end of the Thirty Years' War, with the Treaty of Westphalia in 1648, set the rules that governed interactions among states for the next century.[54] Similarly, the Congress of Vienna at the end of the Napoleonic Wars in 1815 redrew the boundaries of Europe, which lasted roughly until World War I.[55] During the subsequent period, the United Kingdom rose to become a global power and largely set the rules for the international system: free trade, the pound as the major reserve currency, major international capital flows from the United Kingdom to the rest of the world (particularly in the last quarter of the nineteenth century), and continued development and expansion of steam power and railways until technological leadership passed to Germany and the United States in the last part of the nineteenth century.

At the end of World War I, there was an attempt to set up an international governance mechanism to prevent another global war. The Versailles Treaty, signed by the major European powers in 1919, provided for the creation of the League of Nations, which was intended to help arbitrate disputes and avoid future wars.[56] Although the United States was involved in World War I and was one of the four major powers that negotiated the Versailles Treaty, the U.S. Senate refused to ratify the treaty.

The league was unable to stop several aggressions by Italy, Germany, and Japan. Hitler withdrew Germany from the league in 1933 and proceeded to rearm and annex territories. Russia joined in 1934 but was expelled at the end of 1939 because of its invasion of Finland. The league essentially stopped functioning with the onset of World War II but was not formally dissolved until 1946, when it was replaced by the United Nations.[57]

A major development that started even as World War II was still raging was what came to be known as the Bretton Woods system, named after the hotel in New Hampshire where meetings were held by delegates of 44 countries in July 1944. The objective was to avoid the kind of breakdown of the international financial system and worldwide economic depression that had followed the "beggar thy neighbor" policies of the 1930s. The combination of trade protection and currency devaluations to increase the competitiveness of country exports and reduce balance of payments deficits had worsened and prolonged the global economic decline. Trade had become restricted to currency blocs, such as the Sterling Bloc, and had shrunk dramatically as a share of global GDP. The flow of capital and foreign investment was curtailed.

Emerging as the hegemonic world power at the end of World War II, the United States had a strong hand in designing the postwar international system. It was the largest and strongest country, and unlike Europe and Japan, it had not suffered any direct devastation on its soil, aside from the bombing of Pearl Harbor. At the end of World War II, the United States was larger than Western Europe in PPP terms (see Figure 2.1) and accounted for roughly half of world GDP in nominal terms.[58]

The main element of the Bretton Woods system was the obligation of each country to adopt a monetary policy that maintained its currency's exchange rate within a narrowly fixed value in terms of gold. Three key initiatives were undertaken in 1945 to create this new postwar system: the International Monetary Fund (IMF) was established to determine the rules of the international financial system; the International Bank for Reconstruction and Development (IBRD) was established to assist with the reconstruction of Europe; and the General Agreement on Tariffs and Trade (GATT) was established to reduce barriers to trade. The GATT was superseded by the WTO in 1995 (see the sixth row in Table 2.1).

With respect to broader global governance, the basic premise of the League of Nations was incorporated into the United Nations, which

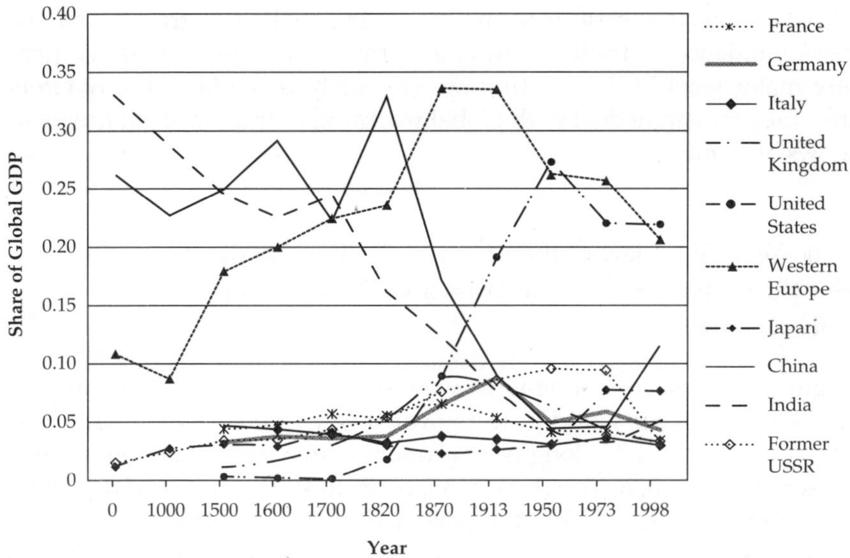

FIGURE 2.1 Changing shares of global GDP: A 2,000-year perspective
SOURCE: Created by author based on data in Maddison (2003).

was founded in 1945 to prevent wars and facilitate cooperation between countries in international law, international security, economic development, social progress, human rights, and the promotion of peace. Virtually all countries of the world are members.[59] There is also a Security Council composed of 15 countries. The major allied powers after World War II (China,[60] France, Russia, the United Kingdom, and the United States) are permanent members, and 10 rotating members are voted in by the General Assembly on a regional basis for two-year terms. The 5 permanent members have veto power on substantive resolutions but not on procedural discussions. This means they cannot bar debate on an issue they do not agree with, but they can block the adoption of a resolution. The workings of the United Nations are slow and somewhat ineffective because of the difficulty of making decisions with so many diverging interests at stake.

These are the main elements of the current global governance system. As will be discussed in Chapter 7, these global institutions are not proving very effective in what is a much-changed world more than 60 years after they were established. Part of the problem is that they do not represent the current alignment of political and economic power.

What's more, the world is facing increasing challenges from global interdependence in trade, finance, and the environment. Finally, there are major gaps in the existing system, such as the lack of any effective mechanism to deal with global warming or international financial flows and imbalances.

2000-Year Overview of the Rise and Decline of Power Shows Frictions Spiral into Wars and Changes of the Global System

Figure 2.1 presents a long-term view of the relative economic importance of the major world powers over the last 2,000 years.[61] Although the accuracy of such a long-term economic time series has been subject to some criticism, its rough outlines serve to show the rise and decline of various countries.[62] For the period prior to 1500, only the data for China, India, Japan, and Russia are tracked.[63] After 1500, data for the United States and the four major Western European countries (United Kingdom, France, Germany, and Italy) are added.

For the first millennium and a half, India and China accounted for roughly one-third and one-quarter of world GDP, respectively.[64] The combined countries of Western Europe did not surpass India until 1740 and China until 1870. What led to the rapid rise of Western Europe and the relative decline of China and India was not that the latter economies collapsed but that Western European countries began to grow more rapidly after the first millennium and a half as a result, among other things, of technological developments and the entrepreneurial drive of their populations. While China and India largely missed the take-off of the first three industrial revolutions, the European countries, the United States, and Japan made rapid strides.

In 1500, Italy was the leading Western European economy thanks largely to its success in trade with eastern Asia. But its economic importance began to decline as other European countries expanded their empires through colonization. At the beginning of the 1800s, the dominant country in Europe was France. Leading an ambitious hegemonic campaign to control large parts of Europe, Napoleon started invading neighboring countries. Other major European powers banded together against France during the Napoleonic Wars (1803–1815) and finally defeated Napoleon at Waterloo.

The country that emerged as the hegemon after the defeat of Napoleon was the United Kingdom. Not only had it played a key role in

Napoleon's defeat, but it was also the leader in the first two industrial revolutions, particularly in the development of coal-based steam power for industrial production (mostly textiles) and the steam railroad, which was also instrumental in exploiting coal deposits as well as for transportation more generally. In 1500, Britain had been the smallest economy among the major Western European countries, with just 1 percent of world GDP. By 1820, it had overtaken France in share of global GDP to become the largest economy in Europe. The United Kingdom would not be larger than China or India economically until the beginning of the twentieth century (Figure 2.1).

A large part of the United Kingdom's success came from its superior naval power. The United Kingdom extended its hegemony and managed its empire through trade and finance. Although the United Kingdom lost most of its American colonies in 1783, it expanded its empire through imperialist colonization and trade to attain a global reach all the way from the Caribbean to Africa, the Middle East, South Asia, and Asia. As the cliché states, at the height of its power, in 1870, the sun never set on the British Empire.

The United Kingdom reached a peak share of 9 percent of global GDP in 1870. By 1880, the United States, then Germany and Russia, had surpassed Great Britain's share. The United States rapidly went on to become the hegemon of the twentieth century, reaching 27 percent of global GDP by 1950 after the destruction of Europe in World War II. (Refer to Table 2.1 and Figure 2.1 to see the interaction between the rise of the United Kingdom and the other countries discussed below.)

In Europe, Prussia took the lead. In 1870, it invaded France and won the Franco–Prussian War (1870–1871). German unification and growth built on the technologies of the early Industrial Revolution, and then Germany took the lead, along with the United States, into steel, electricity, and heavy engineering. In the last 15 years of the nineteenth century, Germany built up its army and navy, although the United Kingdom still remained superior at sea. Germany was particularly concerned with the speed of Russia's development and was ready to go to war to prevent fighting a stronger Russia in the future.[65] It hoped that the United Kingdom and the United States would remain neutral, but it miscalculated. The United Kingdom entered the war, later joined by the United States, and Germany was defeated. During the Great Depression, Germany rebuilt its economy and its military under Hitler. It again launched a war driven by ideology and the desire to conquer territory and gain power. It was again defeated by a coalition of France, the United Kingdom, Russia, and eventually, the United States.

The United States grew rapidly as a fast follower of the technologies of the first two industrial revolutions and then as a major player, along with Germany, in the third (see Table 2.1). U.S. growth was supported by a large internal market that benefited from transportation and communications advances, starting with the railroad. Embracing these technologies brought large cost reductions from extensive economies of scale and scope. The United States was also a land rich in natural resources, including navigable rivers, arable land, timber, and minerals. Yet the true foundation of American economic growth was a fabric of institutions and an economic regime that supported entrepreneurship, experimentation, and risk taking. In fact, the United States may be said to have systematized the process of invention when Thomas Alva Edison created the first industrial research and development laboratory. By 1900, there were more industrial research laboratories in the United States than in Europe.[66]

The other rising world power was Japan, which began to grow more rapidly after the Meiji Restoration of 1868. After the shock of the encounter with Admiral Perry's black ships in Tokyo harbor in 1853 and the realization that the West was much more advanced technologically, Japan embarked on a program of swift catch-up. This included licensing technology, importing capital goods and components from the West, bringing in foreign experts, and sending Japanese abroad to learn about modern technologies.[67] By 1905, Japan had become a major industrial and military power. This was clearly demonstrated when it dealt a devastating defeat to Russia in 1904–1905, a defeat that surprised not only Russia but the other great powers as well. From 1905 to 1945, there was a major state push in Japan to develop heavy industry.

Following the devastation of World War II, Japan rebuilt itself very quickly. It averaged 10 percent growth in the 1960s, 5 percent in the 1970s, and 4 percent in the 1980s. Part of its success lay in its ability to take imported technology apart, redesign it, and put it together again in more efficient ways. Japan also developed very efficient production systems, improving quality and producing products "just in time" to reduce inventories. It reacted rapidly to the 1973 oil shock by developing more energy-efficient production methods and products such as smaller, more energy-efficient cars, which were very successful in the U.S. market. This boosted its international competitiveness, leading to rising trade surpluses and growing foreign exchange reserves. Its projection onto the world scene was dramatic and much noticed. Many books were written on Japan as a superpower, and there was concern around the world that it would be taking over markets,[68] much like the current concern about China's fast expansion of exports.

There Have Been Significant Shifts in Economic Size Even in the Last 30 Years

Table 2.3 traces the changing shares of GDP for the major world economies starting in 1980.[69] Even in this short period, there have been significant changes in the relative size of different economies and regions. Emerging and developing economies have grown faster than developed countries, increasing their share of global GDP from 31 percent in 1980 to 47 percent in 2009.

The developing region that has shown the largest increase is developing Asia.[70] Its share of global GDP more than tripled from 8 percent in 1980 to 23 percent in 2009. By 2005, it had a larger share than the euro countries, and by 2008, it had surpassed the United States.[71] Japan and the Soviet Union, which had been growing rapidly between 1960 and 1980 and were seen as the rising powers after World War II, had a reversal of fortunes. Japan suffered a major financial/economic crisis in 1991 from which it had not fully recovered even before the 2008–2009 crisis. Between 1990 and 2009, Japan lost one-third of its share of global GDP (dropping from 9 percent to 6 percent). The United States lost 4 percentage points, but that was only 20 percent of its share. The Soviet Union fragmented in 1991 into multiple republics, all of which (including Russia) went into major recessions in the early part of the 1990s. By 2000, their share had fallen to 3.6 percent, but it recovered to 4.3 percent by 2009 due to fast development based largely on an expansion of natural resource exports (particularly energy).

The two countries with the most impressive performance are China and India. China's share increased more than sixfold from 2.2 percent of world GDP in 1980 to 12.9 percent in 2009 in PPP terms. By 2010, it surpassed Japan, and by 2010, it reached 65 percent of the size of the United States. India more than doubled its share of global GDP from 2.5 percent in 1980 to 5.2 percent in 2009.

In terms of economic and geopolitical competition, the main players are the United States and China. The European Union is a bigger economic and population bloc than the United States, but it does not have one voice or one military, and it has been more severely affected by the financial and economic downturn and increasing global competition

TABLE 2.3 Share of region/country GDP as a percentage of global GDP in current purchasing power parity prices

	1980	1990	2000	2005	2008	2009
Advanced Economies	**69.10**	**65.49**	**62.89**	**58.69**	**54.75**	**53.39**
Japan	8.66	9.38	7.62	6.83	6.21	5.93
United Kingdom	4.29	3.87	3.59	3.41	3.17	3.03
United States	24.69	23.39	59	22.30	20.54	20.16
Euro Area	N/A	N/A	18.40	16.58	15.53	15.02
Newly Industrialized Asian Economies[a]	1.79	2.78	3.64	3.78	3.79	3.78
Other Advanced Economies (excluding G-7 and Euro Area)	6.01	6.54	7.63	7.57	7.51	7.43
Emerging and Developing Economies	**30.89**	**34.51**	**37.11**	**41.31**	**45.24**	**46.61**
Central and Eastern Europe	3.89	3.25	3.35	3.54	3.60	3.49
Commonwealth of Independent States[b]	N/A	5.49	3.57	4.14	4.54	4.26
Developing Asia	8.02	10.50	15.20	18.39	21.39	23.03
• China	2.19	3.67	7.14	9.47	11.01	12.92
• India	2.55	3.02	3.75	4.30	4.85	5.16
Middle East and North Africa	5.07	4.12	4.19	4.63	4.78	4.92
Latin America and the Caribbean	11.30	8.91	8.81	8.40	8.60	8.51

SOURCE: Created by author using data from IMF *World Economic Outlook* database. Accessed April 11, 2011.

[a] Hong Kong, Singapore, South Korea, and Taiwan.

[b] CIS are former Soviet republics, including Russia.

because its economies are more rigid and still not fully integrated.[72] Japan should also not be forgotten; it is still the world's third largest economy at current market exchange rates (having been surpassed by China in 2010) and has tremendous technological and economic capability. Russia has fallen behind economically, although it is still a significant military power.[73] India is featured in this book because of its population, swiftly growing economic importance, and expanding environmental footprint.

Conclusion: The History of Power Shifts Is Not Reassuring

The historical review of the relationship between rising and established powers and the rule of the international system is not very encouraging. Looking at the last 200 years, all but one of the major global power shifts have resulted in war. The Napoleonic Wars at the beginning of the nineteenth century were a reaction against the territorial expansion of France in Europe. World War I started as a preemptive war by a quickly growing Germany against a developing Russia, which led to a world war to stop German aggression. World War II was a reaction on the part of the United Kingdom, France, and eventually the U.S. alliance to counter Germany's expansion for resources, ideology (Nazism), and power in Europe. Japan's wars in Asia in the first half of the twentieth century were largely due to a quest for natural resources to feed its rapid industrialization. Its participation in World War II was also largely over access to resources (oil in Indonesia, which was protected by the United States and therefore led Japan to bomb the U.S. fleet at Pearl Harbor to preempt the United States' capability to respond).[74] The Cold War divided the world into two opposing ideological camps.

There is one major exception: there was no war when the United States rapidly overtook the United Kingdom in the late 1800s and became the dominant world power in the twentieth century. There are several reasons for this anomaly. First, there was a strong common culture between the United Kingdom and its former colony. Second, until World War II, the United States was considered a regional hegemon by the United Kingdom, which was more concerned with holding on to India and South Africa. Also, the United States was separated from Europe and Asia by two large oceans. Finally, by the time the United Kingdom perceived the United States as a potential global hegemon, it would have been too expensive to take the United States on,[75] not to mention that American dominance after World War II was aided by the devastation of postwar Europe and the United States' large economic size and capacity for innovation.

While the United States remains the world's largest economy and undisputed military power, it has experienced a relative decline in all dimensions of power. Currently, it is particularly weak in terms of its fiscal solvency and its ability to invest in education, research, and physical infrastructure—all critical for maintaining power. Moreover, its political system is hampered by vicious infighting, and its short election cycles have resulted in an orientation toward the short term. The United States has been unable to reduce its global overextension or public expenditures or raise taxes to invest in basic infrastructure for long-term strength. These weaknesses are typical of declining hegemons.

On the other hand, China, the rising power, has a longer-term vision and is investing in all these critical infrastructures. It also has a unique culture and economic and political development model. At the same time, a key nonstate actor that is fundamental for economic and technological power, the U.S. multinational corporation, is losing allegiance to its home country. It is pursuing economic opportunities in the swiftly developing markets of India and, particularly, China, in spite of the latter's authoritarian and less market-oriented regime.

It is important to distinguish between changes in global systems that result from hegemonic wars and changes that result from new powers gaining influence in establishing the rules of the game.[76] The advance of China and India is so far taking place within the existing system, and there is no sign that the two countries intend to change the system itself, at least within the next five to ten years. However, it is clear that changes are taking place in the relative power of China and India versus the United States and the European Union in terms of economic strength, trade, finance, foreign investment, technology, education, military capability, and geopolitical projection. This is part of the rapid catch-up by developing countries with respect to leading countries as they acquire foreign technology and upgrade their domestic innovation capabilities. Within one or two decades, when they have more economic and political power, China and India will want a much greater role in reshaping the global system to meet their interests. The changing relative power and the tensions underlying the systemic challenges from the rise of these two countries, including the role of foreign investment, will be explored throughout this book.

CHAPTER 3

Understanding the Rapid Rise of China and India

CHINA HAS HAD THE HIGHEST rate of growth in the world for the longest time. Between the Communist takeover in 1949 and the mid-1970s, China went through cycles of boom and bust, including a heavy industrialization drive, the disaster of the Great Leap Forward (1958–1960), and a major famine in which an estimated 30 million people died. China's most impressive growth period started with its opening up to the world in the late 1970s under Deng Xiao Ping. China's integration into the world economy started slowly, with the establishment of four export processing zones, but it accelerated, and China eventually joined the World Trade Organization in 2001.

India grew at a yearly average of 2–3 percent from its independence in 1947 until the 1980s. In the 1980s and 1990s, it had average annual rates of growth of 5–6 percent, interrupted by a severe financial crisis in 1991. The crisis forced it to liberalize the economy and put it on a higher growth path. Until recently, India was technologically autarkic—it depended largely on its own technology. It began to grow at near-Chinese rates due in large part to its insertion into international trade through the strength of its high-skilled IT-enabled service export sector. This skilled-service-sector-led growth in a low-income country is something not anticipated by traditional development theory.

What accounts for the very rapid growth of these two economies, and what explains some of the differences in their performance? This chapter provides an overview of the economic rise of China and India to shed some light on where they are coming from and where they may be going, why they have risen so quickly, and what they are trying to achieve.

The first section provides some basic comparative data on China, India, and the United States to put them in perspective. The second section covers some of the similarities in their history, which are helpful to understand what drives them today. The third section examines their growth at an aggregate level through the lens of the economist's basic production function. It shows that their rapid growth and the differences in their rate of growth are partly explained by quick labor force and capital growth. However, the most important source of growth has been technological catch-up.

The next sections go beyond this aggregated analysis to examine some of the similarities and differences in China's and India's development to understand their growth and performance. These include differences in forms of government and development strategies, which in turn lead to differences in industrial structure, performance in growth and welfare, and educational strategies. The two countries have also diverged in how systematically they have tapped global knowledge through trade, foreign direct investment (FDI), technology licensing, foreign education, and copying and reverse engineering. The final section shows that, in spite of their very different starting points and development strategies, the success of both China and India is related to their move toward the market and their insertion into the international economic system. This is likely to increase over time and put greater pressure on the global economic system.

Basic Comparisons

China and India have been growing roughly three times faster than the world average over the past 30 years (Table 3.1). In 2010, China surpassed Japan to become the second largest economy in the world, and India became the tenth largest. In PPP terms, China became the second largest economy in 2001 when it surpassed Japan, and India became the fourth largest in 2006 when it surpassed Germany.

China is distinguished by the very rapid growth of its merchandise exports, from less than 0.8 percent of the world's total in 1980 to 10 percent by 2009, more than seven times that of India.[1] In a sense, China has become the manufacturing workshop of the world. India's strength, on the other hand, has been in the export of services. Its share of global service exports is almost three times that of its merchandise exports, with a strength in information and communications technology (ICT)–enabled services.

TABLE 3.1 Basic economic and social indicators: China, India, U.S., and world

Average Annual Growth of GDP	China	India	U.S.	World Total or Average
1980–1990	9.2	5.7	2.9	3.1
1990–2000	10.4	5.5	3.4	2.9
2000–2008	10.6	7.4	2.0	2.9
2009	9.1	7.6	–2.6	–1.5
2010 (estimate)	10.5	9.7	2.6	4.8
2011 (estimate)	9.6	8.4	2.3	4.2
GNI (2009)				
GNI (nominal billion)	5,028	1,303	14,011	57,861
GNI as Percentage of Global GNI	8.69	2.25	24.21	100.00
GNI per Capita (nominal)	3,650	1,180	46,360	8,727
GNI (million PPP)	9,170	3,758	14,011	71,845
GNI as Percentage of Global GNI (PPP)	12.76	5.23	19.50	100.00
GNI per Capita (PPP)	6,890	3,250	45.640	10,604
Exports (2009)				
Merchandise Exports (millions)	1,201,534	162,613	1,057,054	12,492,190
Merchandise Exports (percentage of world)	9.62	1.30	8.46	100.00
Commercial Service Exports	128,599	90,193	475,979	3,408,648
Service Exports (percentage of world)	3.7	2.65	14.61	100.00
People (2009)				
Population (millions)	1,331	1,155	307	6,775
Population (percentage of world)	19.65	17.05	4.53	100.00
Life Expectancy at Birth (2008)	73	64	78	69
Percentage of People (2005) Below Intl. Poverty Line of:				
$1.25 PPP/day	15.9	41.6	—	25.2
$2.00 PPP/day	36.3	75.6	—	47.0

SOURCE: Created by author based on data from *World Development Indicators* database, except for growth projections which are from IMF, *World Economic Outlook* (October 2010), p. 2.

NOTES: GNI is gross national income. Gross national income is total domestic and foreign value-added claimed by residents of the country. It is the gross domestic product of the country plus net receipts of primary income (such as compensation and property income) to residents from nonresident sources. See World Bank, *WDI* (2010), data notes for Tables 4.1 and 4.2.

Although they are large in population and have been growing very quickly, both are still poor countries. India's per capita income is less than one-fortieth that of the United States in nominal terms and one-fifteenth in PPP terms. China's is one-fifteenth that of the United States in nominal terms and less than one-eighth in PPP terms. The average life expectancy in China exceeds the world average by almost five years (only five years behind the United States), while India's is five years below the world average.

In 1980, India was doing better than China in terms of per capita income. Why have the tables turned over the last 30 years? We will explore that after we look at some of the similarities in their histories.

Some Similarities in Otherwise Very Different Histories

Other than their large populations, five similarities in the history of China and India help to explain their worldview and their development trajectory.[2]

A first similarity is that they are both millennial civilizations responsible for major historical innovations. China developed papermaking, printing, gunpowder, the compass, early seismological detectors, the double-action piston pump, cast iron, the iron plough, the wheelbarrow, the suspension bridge, the parachute, natural gas as fuel, the relief map, the propeller, the crossbow, and the meritocratic civil service.[3] India developed important mathematical concepts (zero, techniques of algebra and algorithms, the square root, the cube root), concepts of the atom, principles of chemistry and medicine, the study of sound and phonetics, principles of mechanical and civil engineering, and metal smelting. In addition, both cultures developed agricultural techniques that could support large urban populations over many centuries.

A second important similarity is that both countries have suffered humiliation from foreign powers. For proud, ancient civilizations, this was traumatic and colored their interactions with the rest of the world, starting with the foundation of their republics in the middle of the twentieth century. India suffered many invasions and takeovers by foreign powers, including most notably the Moguls, who ruled India for several centuries. Britain's East India Company forcibly acquired control of India and ruled much of the country from 1757 to 1858, during which time it extracted its raw materials, spices, and luxury goods and kept Indian workers living at subsistence levels. Eventually, the excesses of the East India Company were so blatant that, following a major rebellion (1857–1858), the British Crown withdrew its monopoly and administered India directly from 1858 until Indian independence in 1947. During this colonial period, Great Britain destroyed what had been a vibrant Indian textile industry, prohibited Indian manufacturers from exporting, and forced India to import British textiles, which were growing rapidly as a result of mechanized production.

China was never fully taken over by foreign powers, but it suffered a loss of control over parts of its cities as a result of mercantilist inroads made by foreign powers interested in Chinese trade. Chief among these was Great Britain. China was not interested in buying British goods, but Britain wanted Chinese silk and spices. Because the Chinese demanded payment in silver, Britain was losing bullion, a serious weakness according to the mercantilist theory of trade that prevailed at the time. To prevent this loss, the British hooked the Chinese on opium and then traded opium—which they obtained from their Indian colony—to pay the Chinese. When the Chinese government objected to this immoral trade and tried to stop it, the Opium Wars were launched.

The First Opium War lasted from 1839 to 1842. Britain won and demanded large reparations from China, including opening four ports to Britain and ceding Hong Kong. The opium trade restarted and led to the Second Opium War, which lasted from 1856 to 1860. Britain again defeated China through its naval and military superiority, and again, China had to pay reparations. As part of the settlement, China was forced to open 10 more port cities, and Britain imposed the most-favored-nation status clause, which meant that China had to extend the trade benefits it was extending to Britain to all the other major powers.[4] Other European powers followed Britain's example of demanding special trading rights. The Japanese invasion of Manchuria in 1931 led to the Second Sino–Japanese War, which lasted from 1937 until the end of World War II.[5] This weakness of the Chinese government was a major loss of face that caused much animosity against the foreign powers. When the Communists took over in 1949, they turned away from the West.

A third key similarity is that both countries were slow to take up the benefits of the first four technological revolutions. This can be seen in the dramatic fall of their share of global GDP from the early 1800s to the middle of the 1900s (see Figure 2.1 in Chapter 2). Both countries fell to their lowest share of global GDP around 1950. The problem wasn't so much internal and external conflict (although there was plenty of that) but that neither country took full advantage of the innovations that characterized the second through the fourth technological revolutions. Perhaps that helps explain both countries' determination to take full advantage of the current ICT and knowledge revolutions.[6]

Another remarkable similarity between these two countries is that they both became modern nation-states within three years of each other. India was founded in 1947 when it obtained independence from the

United Kingdom and has been a democratic nation ever since. China was founded in 1949 when Mao finally pushed Chiang Kai-shek's Nationalist regime off the mainland to the island of Formosa (now Taiwan) and established the People's Republic of China.

A final important similarity is that both countries initially pursued an inward-oriented and autarkic development strategy before gradually opening up and integrating into the rest of the world. Both countries partially turned inward because of their negative experiences with foreign powers mentioned earlier. Both also turned away from the West and toward the USSR. India's first prime minister, Nehru, although an Oxford-educated lawyer, was a Fabian socialist and was attracted by what appeared to be the successful economic model of the USSR, which had become a major industrial power between the world wars and was challenging the United States and the United Kingdom. Mao, a Communist, also turned to assistance from the USSR, the dominant Communist state, with which China shared a long border. As will be seen below, both countries eventually turned away from the inward-oriented Soviet model of strong government intervention to more market-driven and externally oriented systems. Surprisingly, China, the Communist country, started this change earlier than India.

A Macroaccounting for the Differences in Growth

Some explanations for the swift development of China and India and the differences in their growth rates can be gleaned from an economic analysis of the factors of growth. In the standard stylized economic analysis, growth of output is modeled as the result of growth of capital and labor plus some residual, attributed to technological improvement, called total factor productivity (TFP) growth. One of the most comprehensive of such studies, using the same methodology for both countries, has been done by Bosworth and Collins.[7]

Table 3.2 presents results for the decomposition of growth for both countries over the period 1978–2004. It also breaks the analysis into two subperiods, 1978–1993 and 1994–2004.[8] In column three, growth is expressed as output per worker. In columns four to six, it is decomposed in the contribution of physical capital, education, and the residual total factor productivity or technical change.[9]

The bottom rows of Table 3.2 also provide the same decomposition for the high-performing East Asian economies, excluding China, for their period of most rapid growth (1960–1980) as well as for 1980–2003.

TABLE 3.2 Sources of growth: China and India, 1978–2004

				CONTRIBUTION TO OUTPUT PER WORKER		
	Output (1)	Employment (2)	Output per Worker (3)	Physical Capital (4)	Education (5)	Total Factor Productivity (6)
1978–2004						
China	9.3	2.0	7.3	3.2	0.3	3.8
India	5.4	2.0	3.3	1.3	0.4	1.6
1978–1993						
China	8.9	2.5	6.4	2.5	0.4	3.5
India	4.5	2.1	2.4	0.9	0.3	1.1
1994–2004						
China	9.7	1.2	8.5	4.2	0.3	3.9
India	6.5	1.9	4.6	1.8	0.4	2.3
East Asia Excluding China[a]						
1960–1980	7.0	3.0	4.0	2.2	0.5	1.2
1980–2003	6.1	2.4	3.7	2.2	0.5	0.9
1980–1993	7.3	2.7	4.6	2.6	0.6	1.4
1993–2003	4.5	2.0	2.5	1.8	0.5	0.3

SOURCE: Bosworth and Collins (2008), p. 49.

NOTE: Columns 1–3 are average annual growth rates for periods indicated. Columns 4–6 are the percentage points of that growth explained by the contributions of physical capital, education, and total factor productivity.

[a]East Asia in these data includes Indonesia, South Korea, Malaysia, Philippines, Singapore, Taiwan, and Thailand.

These countries serve as a good proxy for the other fastest-growing countries, so a comparison with them gives some insight into the reasons for the high growth rate of China and India.

Three key reasons for the swift development of all these economies stand out. The first is the rapid growth of labor in distinct contrast to its slow growth in advanced countries.[10] The growth of labor in China and India for the period 1978–2004, averaging 2 percent per annum, was the same as that of the East Asian countries in their later period of rapid advance. However, labor growth in the other Asian countries was higher from 1980–2003, particularly at the beginning of that period.

The second reason for the swift development of all these economies it that they have had faster growth of capital than high-income countries.[11] The contribution of capital has been greater in China than in the other high-performing East Asian countries and India, although India has a higher growth rate of capital in the last decade.[12]

The third reason for the swift development of these economics—and in a way, the most significant one for the basic argument of this book—is the contribution of total factor productivity growth.[13] All of these economies have been able to draw upon technology that already existed in advanced economies to play rapid catch-up.[14] The contribution of TFP has been higher in both China and India for the period 1978–2004 than in the East Asian countries. This is partly because China and India started from lower levels of development than the other more advanced East Asian economies.[15]

In comparing the growth of China with that of India, four points stand out. First, as noted, China has been growing faster than India over the entire period. But the difference narrowed from 4.4 percentage points in the first period to just 3.2 percentage points in the second period, and this probably remained true through 2009. Second, while the growth of labor has been the same in both countries for the period 1978–2004, it was higher in the first period. The very sharp drop in labor force growth in China in the second period started before the one-child policy was implemented in 1979. Third, China has used more capital owing to its higher rate of investment,[16] although between 2004 and 2009 the rate of growth of capital in India has increased.[17]

Fourth, China has had much higher TFP growth. The contribution of TFP is higher than the contribution of capital for the entire period for China. As will be argued below, this is because China has had a much more proactive strategy of tapping global knowledge than India. In the second period in China, the contribution of capital is slightly higher than the contribution of TFP, and the difference in the contribution of TFP to growth compared to its contribution in India is slightly less. This is because India began to draw much more on global knowledge during the second period.

Bosworth and Collins also analyze the growth of agriculture, industry, and services (and of labor productivity in each sector) in China and India across the two time periods. In China, output from industry and services grew twice as fast as output from agriculture. In India, industry output also grew roughly twice as fast as that from agriculture, but output from the services sector grew faster than that from industry. In the second period, service output grew almost twice as fast as industry output. Average labor productivity in each sector in China was 70 percent that of India in 1978, but by 2004, it had risen to 110, 130, and 220 percent in agriculture, services, and industry, respectively. Thus, development in China has been driven by faster growth and capital deepening in the industrial sectors as well as by the significant reallocation of labor from low-productivity agriculture to higher-productivity services and industry. In India, it has been driven by faster growth of services, which have the highest labor productivity.[18] However, the reallocation effects of moving labor out of agriculture to industry and services have been lower than in China not only because of lower labor productivity in those sectors but also because there has been less reallocation of labor out of low-productivity agriculture.[19]

In short, China's and India's high rates of development have been due to high growth in labor, capital, and TFP. China's faster growth rate than India's is due to its higher capital growth until recently, and especially to its higher rate of TFP growth, particularly in industry, as well as its faster restructuring out of low-productivity agriculture to higher-productivity industry. The later section on Acquiring Technology from the Rest of the World will look at the extent to which both countries have tapped existing global knowledge as part of their quick catch-up strategies.

The Type and Role of Government

Four key differences between China and India are relevant to understanding their varying rates of growth and future prospects: the type of government and degree of market versus government direction of their economies, their development strategies, their educational strategies, and the extent to which they have drawn on global knowledge.

Authoritarian China Versus Democratic India

China has been an authoritarian one-party state since the Communist takeover in 1949. India has been a democracy since independence from the United Kingdom. A hallmark of China's development since 1978 has been a strong government that has been able to react pragmatically to changing challenges and opportunities. This is aptly summarized in Deng Xiaoping's famous dictum, "Crossing the river by feeling each stone." This pragmatism, combined with the ability of China's authoritarian government to implement new policies quickly, is one of the key reasons China has performed so well. Moreover, although China is an authoritarian government, it has focused on providing economic growth as a way of maintaining legitimacy. This is not a general characteristic of authoritarian governments, as there are many such regimes that control their populations by force and focus on enriching themselves rather than promoting economic growth. What is distinctive about the authoritarian government of China, then, is an implicit social contract: the exchange of political choice for economic growth.

As can be seen from its economic performance and reduction in poverty rates, the government has delivered quite well on this implicit contract (Table 3.1). Since 1978, there has only been one major incident of massive social unrest: the Tiananmen incident in June 1989, when a peaceful prodemocracy movement led by students escalated into violence and threatened to bring down the government.[20]

India has been a democracy since its independence except for a brief interlude in 1977–1978, when Indira Gandhi shut down the Parliament and ruled by decree for 18 months. However, India is a very peculiar type of democracy. Between 1947 and 1977, it was almost a dynasty. Jawaharlal Nehru, the first prime minister, led the country from 1947 until his death in 1964. His daughter, Indira Gandhi, was elected in a sympathy vote in 1965. She led the country until she lost the 1977 election when voters reacted against her autocratic rule. However, she was elected back to power in 1980 and governed until her assassination in 1984. In a repeat of the earlier pattern of a sympathy vote, her son Rajiv Gandhi was elected prime minister in 1984 and governed until a corruption scandal brought him down in 1989. He was assassinated in 1991 while running for reelection.[21] In 2004, in yet another repeat of the pattern, his widow, Sonia Gandhi, an Italian by birth, won. She appointed Manmohan Singh, who had been the successful finance minister during the 1991 crisis, as prime minister.[22]

Since the Congress Party lost control of power in 1989, India has been ruled by weak coalition governments. These coalitions reflect both the strengths and weaknesses of India's democratic tradition. Although very diverse groups can come together in coalition governments, they are coalitions of convenience without strong unity based on common reform agendas. Therefore, these governments generally do not have a mandate to carry out reforms.[23] Even if reforms are passed, they are very hard to implement.

Role and Effectiveness of Government

The government has always played a major role in China's centrally planned economy. However, starting in the late 1970s, the Chinese government began to move slowly toward a market economy. The first phase (1980s–1992) was a period of growing out of the government's central development plan, or "reform without losers." The second phase (1992–the present) was a period of "reform with losers," as state-owned enterprises were downsized or restructured and markets were unified and given more independence.[24] This process accelerated with China's entry into the World Trade Organization. The trade regime was liberalized further, including opening to foreign investment in the service sector. Private property was officially recognized in 2006, and the private sector is now estimated to account for more than 60 percent of economic activity.[25]

Although India has been a democracy since its independence, the early years of the Indian economy were marked by the state playing a very strong role in the economy, including the institution of five-year industrialization plans originally structured on the Soviet model. Government was also strongly against big business. It restricted the growth of large private businesses and reserved a list of several hundred products to very small-scale businesses. Controls on private business began to be lifted in the 1980s. There was further liberalization in the 1990s, which has continued through today.[26] There has been some privatization, but the state still has a strong presence in industry and services.

Both China and India have generally had stabler macropolicies than most developing countries. China has had the stabler macroregime, with low inflation for most of the period since the 1980s. Government plans have been quite clear and stable, and this has facilitated long-range planning by domestic and foreign investors. India has also had a relatively stable macroregime over the last two and a half decades, except for the financial crisis at the beginning of the 1990s. However, its macroenvironment has not been as stable and predictable as China's.[27]

In sum, China and India have differed markedly in their systems of government since their incarnations as modern nation-states. Although coming from different philosophical orientations, the governments of both countries have played a large role in running their economies. However, over time, both moved more toward the market not just internally but also globally (though China much more than India).

Two Contrasting Growth Strategies

China: From Inward-Oriented Command Economy to Labor-Intensive Manufacturing Exporter

Since opening up in 1978, China has followed a more traditional development strategy than India. China started trade liberalization in the late 1980s, about a decade earlier than India. Learning from the success of its Asian neighbors such as Hong Kong, South Korea, Singapore, and Taiwan, it opted for labor-intensive manufactured exports.[28] This started with four export processing zones near Hong Kong and Taiwan. After these proved successful at generating foreign exchange and employment growth, they were expanded to another 19 zones. China eventually committed to joining the WTO, and as part of that process, it committed to significant liberalization of goods and services.

The share of imports and exports in China was 44 percent of GDP by 1990 compared with only 23 percent in India. However, by 2008, the gap had decreased and the share was 66 percent in China and 54 percent in India (Table 3.3). The reduction was largely due to import liberalization in India. Imports as a share of GDP were 20 percent in 1995 and 26 percent by 2007 compared with 9 percent and 25 percent for India, respectively. However, as a result of its more open trade policy, China has been swiftly increasing the technology intensity of its exports. In 1997, the share of high-technology products in its manufactured exports was 22 percent compared with 11 percent in India. In 2008, the share of high-technology products was 29 percent in China compared with only 6

TABLE 3.3 Basic indicators of trade over time: China and India

	China	India
Trade Structure (2008)	*Very heavily manufacturing based*	*Heavily service based (>30% of total)*
Value of Merchandise Exports	$1,428,488	$179,073
Percentage of GDP	33	15
Composition of Merchandise Exports:		
Percentage Manufacturing	93	63
Percentage Primary	7	37
Value of Service Exports	$146,446	$102,562
Percentage of GDP	4	8
ICT Related as Percentage of Service Exports	45	72
High-Tech Exports Percentage of Manufacturing Exports		
1997	22	11
2008	29	6
Imports and Exports as Percentage of GDP		
1980	21	15
1995	44	23
2008	66	54
Merchandise Imports as Percentage of GDP		
1980	N/A	7.5
1995	20	9
2008	26	25
Manufactured Imports as Percentage of Merchandise Imports		
1980	N/A	39
1995	79	54
2008	62	47
Average Tariffs (percentages)		
1990–1992	40.6	83.0
1997	20.9	27.7
2008	3.9	6.1

SOURCE: Created by author from *World Development Indicators*, various years.

percent in India.[29] Part of this difference can be explained by the fact that China imports many of the high-technology components of the electronic products it exports, and many of these exports are made by foreign multinationals exporting from China. However, another part of the explanation is that China has a more highly skilled work force than India and is thus able to produce more sophisticated products. China has also been investing extensively in higher education and in science and technology.

India: From Autarky to Service-Led Growth

Unlike China, which has significantly removed tariff and nontariff barriers to trade, India has until very recently been one of the most closed economies in the world (see Table 3.3). India was forced to liberalize as part of the IMF conditionality for structural adjustment after the 1991 financial crisis. Since then, it has liberalized further,[30] although even by 2008 the average weighted tariffs on manufactured products in India (6.1 percent) were still 50 percent higher than China's (3.9 percent) (Table 3.3).[31]

In China, the rapid development of a large labor-intensive manufacturing export sector led to massive migration of workers from the interior to the coastal provinces; it was one of the largest internal migrations in world history. Exports of manufactured products in China were 50.5 percent of manufactured value added in 1995 and increased to 102.1 percent by 2006. In India, they went from 32.5 percent in 1990 to 69.2 percent in 2006. However, the total volume of manufactured exports from India in 2008 was less than the increase in manufactured exports from China between 2007 and 2008. China's labor-intensive export strategy has transformed the country from an agricultural economy to one with a very large industrial sector (see Table 3.4).

While China's comparative advantage is in the export of manufactured products, India's is in the export of services, especially information technology (IT)–enabled services (74 percent of its service exports compared with 43 percent in China). To a large extent, India was able to get into this business thanks to earlier investments it had made in high-quality engineering education, particularly through the Indian Institutes of Technology (IIT). Indian engineers were already doing some off-shoring work when the Y2K crisis hit at the end of 1999. The demand to help fix the Y2K bug problem in computer and program software was a great boost to Indian ICT exports. Another key factor was the diaspora of Indian engineers and managers to companies in Silicon Valley and elsewhere. They convinced their companies to start sourcing software services and later more general business from India. Many of these services are being performed by Indian engineers working for subsidiaries of U.S. and other foreign companies in India, which have moved there to take advantage of India's lower-cost high-skilled labor. However, the fast upsurge in demand for skilled engineers and other higher-education graduates has led to rising wages because of supply and regulatory constraints.[32]

TABLE 3.4 Contrasting economic structures

	China		India	
Economic Structure (percentage of GDP)	*Heavily* ***industry*** *dominated*		***Services*** *dominated*	
	1980	2009	1980	2009
Agriculture	30	10	38	17
Industry	49	46	26	28
Manufacturing	41	34	18	16
Services	21	44	36	55
Distribution of Labor Force (percentage of total labor)[a]	***Transition*** *out of agriculture*		*Still* ***heavily agricultural***	
	1978	2004	1978	2004
Agriculture	71	47	71	57
Industry	17	23	13	18
Services	12	31	36	25
Structure of Demand	***Investment*** *dominated*		***Consumption*** *dominated*	
	1995	2009	1995	2009
Household consumption	42	35	64	57
Govt. consumption	14	13	11	12
Gross capital formation	42	48	27	35
Exports goods & services	23	27	11	21
Imports goods & services	21	22	12	25
Gross savings	43	54	27	34

SOURCE: Created by author from *World Development Indicators*, various years.

[a]Employment distribution data for India are hard to obtain. These are taken from detailed work for both countries done by Bosworth and Collins (2008).

The portion of India's GDP accounted for by IT and IT-enabled industries (IT/ITES) has risen rapidly from just 1.2 percent in 1998 to 5.2 percent in 2007. Exports have increased from U.S. $1.8 billion to U.S. $40 billion over the same period. Direct employment in these industries has risen from 190,000 to 2,000,000. Although this was only 0.5 percent of India's labor force, it made the sector the largest employer in the organized private sector in the country.[33]

Studies by India's National Association of Software Services (NASSCOM) show that for every job created by IT/ITES industries, three to four additional jobs are created in the rest of the Indian economy. These include direct service providers such as catering, transport, housekeeping, and security, and spending on housing, infrastructure, food, clothing, entertainment, travel, and so on. Thus, the sector is estimated to provide indirect employment for an additional 6.5 million workers.[34]

Very Different Economic Structures as a Result of Contrasting Strategies

Because India did not replicate China's labor-intensive export strategy, it has not undergone the massive structural transformation that has accompanied China's development. (See the share of value added and employment in the economies of the two countries in Table 3.4.) While the share of industry in India's GDP and employment is low for a country at its level of per capita income, China's is higher than would be expected at its level of per capita income. That is because China has become the manufacturing workshop for the world.

One of the obstacles to massive industrialization in India is its restrictive labor legislation, which makes it difficult to fire workers when there are business downturns or when companies need to restructure. Another obstacle is poor infrastructure (see Chapter 4).[35] China has grown faster in part because until recently its investment rate for the past 20 years has been more or less twice that of India. Although much of this investment has been inefficient, high rates of investment allow the embodiment of new technology.

Contrasting Outcomes on Poverty Reduction and Income Inequality

In 1980, the per capita income of India was higher than that of China. However, thanks to China's higher rate of economic growth, its nominal per capita income is now almost three times that of India. Both countries, but especially China, have made impressive gains in reducing poverty. In 2005, the percentage of the population living below the international poverty line of $1.25 PPP a day was 16 percent in China compared with 42 percent in India. The share living below $2 per day jumps to 36 percent for China and 76 percent for India, indicating that a large part of the population is living just barely above the line.[36]

Differences in Educational Strategy Underpin Development Strategies

Bosworth[37] has shown that the average educational attainment of workers in the service sector in India is higher than in industry. It is surprising that a country with low average educational attainment and abundant unskilled and poorly educated labor should develop such a comparative advantage. Thus, there is an education paradox in comparing the export structure of India and China: even though India has a lower general education attainment than China, it has developed a comparative advantage in the high-skilled service sector exports, whereas China has developed a comparative advantage in manufacture service exports. There is a notion that India's rapid service-based growth shows the viability of an alternative development model—namely, it is possible to skip directly from an agricultural to a service-based economy without passing through an industrial stage.

As recently as 1985, China was a poor developing country with low average levels of education, although it already had a literacy rate more than 60 percent higher than India's (see Table 3.5 for the comparative education figures). Over the last quarter century, it has made massive investments in basic education and now has a literacy rate nearly as high as that of developed economies, but India's remains low. Illiteracy is 49 percent among women in India and 25 percent among men.[38] India's basic education system is still very poor, with tens of millions of primary school children out of school.

China also invested in secondary education earlier than India. By 1980, secondary enrollment rates in China were already 50 percent higher than in India. Both countries have increased their secondary enrollment rates since 1985, and China maintains a 16 to 18 percentage point lead over India. China's edge in secondary education has been important in preparing its large labor force for a massive expansion of the industrial sector. It has also helped attract labor-intensive, export-oriented foreign investment.

The high quality of China's educational system is corroborated by the latest round of Organisation for Economic Co-operation and Development global test results of the capabilities of 15-year-olds, in which students from Shanghai placed at the top in all three areas tested: reading, math, and science. Although the students were from Shanghai only, not from all over China, their excellent performance took most observers by surprise.[39] United States students placed average in reading and science but below average in math.[40] India was not included in the tests.

Starting in the late 1990s, China undertook a massive expansion of its tertiary education system to make up for the havoc that was wreaked on it by the Cultural Revolution of 1966 to 1976. In 1980, China had less than half the tertiary enrollment rates of India. By 2009, its enrollment rate had reached 25 percent, while India's had increased only to 13 percent. Because of its large population, China had more students

TABLE 3.5 Education in China and India

	China	India
Literacy Rate (population 15 & older)		
1980	66	41
1995	81	53
2009	94	63
Average Educational Attainment of Adult Population (2005) in Years	7.6	4.7
Gross Primary Enrollment Rate		
1980	113	83
2009	113	117
Secondary Education Enrollment Ratio (percentage)		
1980	46	30
1995	67	49
2009	78	60
Higher Education Enrollment Ratio (percentage)	***Initially very low*** compounded by damage of Cultural Revolution period but has had rapid ramp-up since 1998	***Initially high*** through Indian Institutes of Technology, relatively little expansion and high variance and much low quality
1980	2	5
1995	5	6
2009	25	13
Skilled Labor[a]	***Well-developed*** training market inside and outside firms	***Poorly developed*** training market except for high-tech firms

SOURCE: Created by author from *World Development Indicators*, various years.

[a]Author's assessment based on survey results from World Bank Investment Climate surveys of firms in both countries.

at the tertiary level than the United States in 2006, and 40 percent were in engineering and sciences. However, like India, aside from some key prestige institutions, China's higher educational system has problems of quality. McKinsey, for example, reports that only 10 percent of Chinese and only 25 percent of Indian tertiary graduates are sufficiently prepared to be hired by multinational companies.[41]

Starting in the 1950s, India set up seven Indian Institutes of Technology and later several Indian Institutes of Management, which produced a critical mass of well-educated, English-speaking professionals who have been instrumental in India's emergence in software and

ICT-enabled services. Even so, the overall quality of higher education is poor, with the exception of those institutions mentioned earlier (which produce fewer than 7,000 graduates a year), the Indian Institutes of Science, and some of the regional engineering colleges. The low quality of tertiary education, the regulatory constraints on expanding high-quality institutions, and the limits of private higher education appeared to be a roadblock to India's continued rapid growth in knowledge-intensive services. However, the ICT industry in India has taken initiatives to address this concern, and it appears that the higher-education system is responding, at least with respect to quality IT education. The question is to what extent these reforms can be expanded to the higher-education system more broadly.[42]

The low levels of basic education in India have constrained it from tapping into and assimilating foreign technology. However, in spite of low overall tertiary enrollment rates, India's early investments in quality higher education were critical in positioning it to take advantage of the ICT revolution and the potential of exporting information-enabled services. This illustrates that it is important to distinguish between overall educational attainment and critical mass when looking at large countries.

China had a more literate labor force and was able to quickly expand secondary education, which greatly contributed to the capabilities of the very large number of workers required for its labor-intensive manufactured products export industry. The low cost and high skill levels of its labor force were some key attractions for locating labor-intensive operations to China. On the other hand, the core stock of English-speaking engineering and technical graduates in India and the strong connection of the Indian diaspora to the ICT industry in the United States and Europe were the main attractions in off-shoring IT-enabled services to India. In addition, once India developed a reputation for good-quality higher education services, many foreign firms chose to set up subsidiaries in India to tap into that talent pool, which created a virtuous circle for the swift development of high-skilled services.

China's rapid ramp-up of basic education was part of its strategy to take advantage of global knowledge and turn itself into a knowledge economy. Moreover, unlike India, China has already put in place a massive system to help continuously upgrade the skills of its large labor force.[43] This move toward lifelong learning is a global trend that is more developed in advanced countries.

Sustainability of Service-Led Growth in India

How sustainable is India's rapid growth in information-enabled services exports and in service-based exports more generally? It is clear that India has developed a strong comparative advantage here that could continue to increase, particularly now that the IT sector has adopted standards and is working with higher education institutions and the government to address the issue of graduate quality.

Since so much of the IT-enabled service sector growth has been driven by exports (in particular, to the United States[44]), it has been decoupled from the domestic economy. In the short run, the demand for these export services is likely to be negatively affected by the sharp global economic downturn. There is also the risk of a protectionist backlash in some developed market economies, such as the United States, given the severity of the downturn and continually high unemployment rates. In the medium term, there is a concern that some of the more routine work that was being off-shored could be done by computers and advanced software. In addition, other regions, including China, Central and Eastern Europe, the Middle East, Latin America, and Africa, are moving into this export sector.

However, India's IT firms are also moving up the value chain to more knowledge-intensive activities, including software development and IT integration services, and they are beginning to off-shore some of the more routine work to other countries in the region where wages are lower. There is likely to be increasing globalization of service work, but attracting this work to India and other developing countries is not just a matter of improving tertiary education. As noted in rankings of off-shoring attractiveness such as those used by A. T. Kearney,[45] other important considerations are total compensation costs, work force availability and flexibility, tax and regulatory costs, the country and business environment, infrastructure costs (not just IT services but also electricity, travel, and rental costs), intellectual property, and security. Thus, continuing to attract work to India also requires making progress on the broader investment climate and improving infrastructure, which has been a challenge for developing countries.

The sustainability of rapid service-based growth beyond the IT-enabled service sector depends on the broader growth prospects in India and the world more generally. This is difficult to predict now, given the magnitude of the worldwide economic crisis and the probability that it will lead to significant restructuring of the financial as well as the real sector in the United States and other developed economies. Looking beyond the crisis, though, there certainly is strong potential for continued high productivity increases in the service sector in China and India because these countries are still far behind the technological frontier in many areas, particularly in distribution and retail trade. This continued productivity increase will be spurred by more deregulation and competition.

The concern, however, is that the high-growth, high-productivity sector is not generating much employment relative to the size of the swiftly expanding labor force in India.[46] The challenge will be how to absorb that labor productively into the modern economy. That will require better-educated workers and more manufacturing jobs, along the Chinese model. Based on its track record, the modern service sector alone cannot absorb the rapidly growing labor force. Moving to more labor-intensive and inclusive growth will require addressing broader constraints such as excessively rigid regulation of labor and land markets; further reduction in red tape and in the cost of doing business; and significant improvements in power, transportation infrastructure, and social services.

Manufacturing wages in China have been rising faster than in India. If they continue to rise after the crisis, space will be opened up for greater labor-intensive manufactured exports from India provided that the labor force is better educated and that some of the broader regulatory and infrastructure constraints are addressed.

Acquiring Technology from the Rest of the World

Countries that are still behind the technological frontier in specific industries get higher increases in productivity and improvements in welfare from acquiring already-existing knowledge than by engaging in R&D to push the technological frontier. Creating new knowledge is generally more difficult and riskier and requires much more technological capability. The main means of tapping into global knowledge are trade, foreign direct investment, technology licensing, foreign education and training, and copying and reverse engineering.[47] On all these counts, China has been more aggressive and systematic than India.

The Critical Role of Trade in Technology Catch-Up

Trade is an important means of acquiring global knowledge, as imports of capital goods and components help in the acquisition of embodied technology. Equipment suppliers also provide relevant product and process information. Unlike in India, most merchandise goods imports in China were manufactured products (mostly capital goods and components; Table 3.3). Importing foreign products and services also leads to ideas for copying or reverse engineering similar products or services.

Exporting also forces firms to be aware of what's happening at the global frontier in products, designs, and processes because the exporters have to compete with the best the world has to offer. In addition, foreign buyers often provide product designs as well as production process assistance.[48]

In the 1950s, India followed a very autarkic policy of self-reliance, relying (like China) extensively on massive capital goods imports from the Soviet Union. However, unlike China, India maintained its strongly inward-oriented nationalist policy through the 1980s. During this period, technology policy focused very much on self-reliance. There were also very strong restrictions on foreign direct investment and the licensing of foreign technology.[49] It was only after the trade liberalization of the early 1990s that India began to open up more to foreign technology imports.

Foreign Direct Investment as Key Means to Acquiring Technology and Accessing Foreign Markets

China opened up to foreign investment 1978 in four special economic zones with near free trade status. Through foreign investment, it was able to access world-class technology and inputs, which not only began to modernize the country but also provided needed foreign exchange and employment. The inflows of foreign direct investment into China were several multiples of those into India from the mid-1980s until recently (Figure 3.1). There are at least three reasons for this. First, China opened its regulatory regime to foreign direct investment (FDI) more than 10 years before India, and it did so more broadly. Second, China has many cost advantages over India, even though its labor costs are now generally higher than India's. Transportation is more efficient, service infrastructure is more developed, and red tape for trading physical products is less burdensome. India has one of the most onerous regimes in terms of the cost of doing business, as can be seen from its very low ranking in the International Finance Corporation's (IFC) cost of doing business report for 2010 and 2011. China is ranked 86 and 89, while

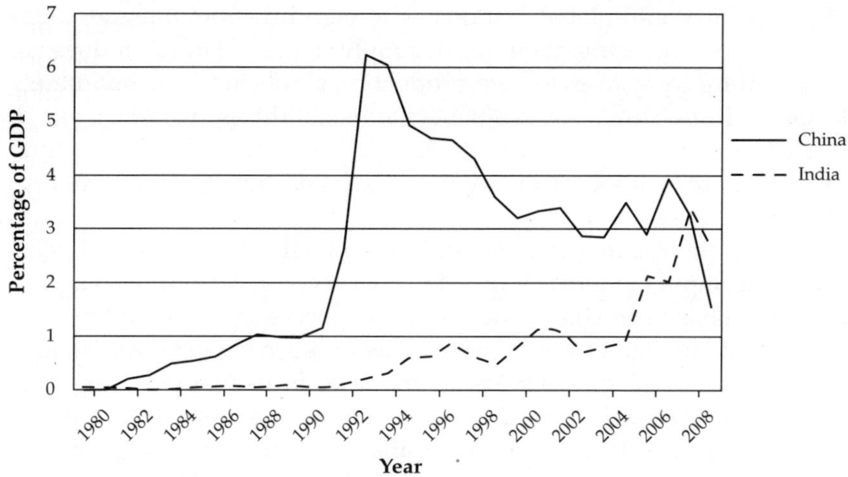

FIGURE 3.1 Foreign direct investment as a share of GDP in China and India, 1980–2008

SOURCE: Created by author based on data from UNCTAD direct foreign investment statistics, available at http://www.unctad.org/Templates/Page.asp?intItemID=1923&lang=1. Accessed November 15, 2010.

India is ranked 132 and 133.[50] Third, China's larger and richer market has been an important pull factor for attracting FDI. As a result, China has been very attractive not just as a production platform for global markets but also for producing for the Chinese market, the world's fastest growing. This strong pull toward manufacturing in China has also permitted the government to encourage strong competition among foreign multinational firms.

Initially, the government forced companies to enter joint ventures with domestic firms and negotiated local and training requirements.[51] This greatly helped the Chinese develop technological and management capability. Once the cost advantage of producing in China became apparent to both the government and multinational companies, the government relaxed the joint-venture requirements to encourage foreign firms to bring their best technologies to China. They did so despite the risk of piracy due to poor intellectual property rights.

The most important contribution of FDI to China has not been capital, since China has had a high savings and investment rate. More important has been access to advanced technology and management through

FDI and entry into global markets as foreign investors integrate their Chinese operations into their global supply chains.[52] The latter does not even require companies to own production plants in China but merely to source from China. An excellent example of this is Wal-Mart, which in 2006 already sourced over U.S. $26 billion from China directly into its retail stores without using intermediaries or even owning local production facilities.

China's success in attracting and making effective use of FDI helps explain its rapid modernization. Many observers have marveled at how fast China has been able to increase its exports and move up the technology ladder. One of the main reasons for such export dynamism is that the bulk of China's exports are made by firms that receive foreign investment. According to Chinese government statistics, enterprises with foreign investment are responsible for over 50 percent of manufactured exports, and that ratio increased from about 50 percent in 2000 to 55 percent by 2006–2008.[53]

Although there is much debate on the exact role of FDI in China's growth, there is no doubt that China would not have developed as fast as it has if it had not made such extensive use of FDI.[54] Foreign direct investment has played a direct role by bringing technology and management to China, providing employment and directly contributing new products and services to China's exports and the domestic economy. Moreover, FDI has indirectly played a role in China's growth by providing products, services, and management and organizational methods that have served as models to be replicated by local enterprises through formal direct links or by copying and pirating.[55] In a way, by effectively using FDI, China has been able to beat the developed countries at the free trade game.

Foreign firms are not as important in India's exports of merchandise goods. From 2003 to 2005, exports of firms with foreign capital in India increased from $3 billion to $5 billion.[56] That represented only about 5 percent of total Indian merchandise exports.

Indian industrial policy protected domestic industry for too long and failed to take advantage of the technology it could get from abroad or the economies of scale and scope of pushing its firms to operate globally. Relatively little FDI went to India before 2005 because of its poor infrastructure and the high transaction costs of operating there. The exception has been in software and ITC-related services, which have not been constrained by regulatory regime or physical infrastructure.

India began to open to FDI in the 1990s and only slowly and selectively. As a result, it got very small inflows. Between 2005 and 2008, India liberalized FDI and trade inflows. In value, they are still smaller than China's, but as a share of GDP, FDI inflows surpassed China's in 2008 (Figure 3.1).

The extent to which China will continue to be successful in attracting FDI remains to be seen. However, as will be developed in Chapter 6, China and India have the tremendous advantage of large and growing markets on their side. In addition, both countries are moving beyond copying and imitating foreign technology, processes, and business organizations to developing their own.

Buying Foreign Technology and Know-How as a Catch-Up Strategy

Both China and India acquire foreign technology through formal technology licensing. Royalty and licensing payments have increased dramatically over the last 20 years. In 2008, China paid more than $10 billion and India slightly over $1.5 billion. Even adjusting for the different sizes of the two economies, China has been licensing more extensively than India. In China, technology-licensing payments as a share of GDP rose from 0.06 percent in 1997 to 0.24 percent in 2008. In India, they rose from 0.04 percent to 0.14 percent over the same period.[57]

Acquiring Knowledge and Capability Through Foreign Education and Training

Sending students abroad for education and training is a very effective way to get nationals, who ideally will return to their home countries, access to foreign knowledge. In 2008, there were nearly 3 million tertiary students studying outside their home country worldwide. The two countries with the most students abroad were China (14.9 percent) and India (5.7 percent). This is not surprising given that they are the world's two largest countries, but it is notable that China's share is much larger than India's, even though their populations are not far apart. A more telling indicator is the number of tertiary students studying abroad as a percentage of total tertiary students studying in the home country. This ratio is roughly 70 percent higher for China compared with India (1.7 percent vs. 1.0 percent).[58] Thus, it is clear that China has been the most active in tapping global knowledge by sending students abroad. Many of the students stay after finishing their studies to get practical work experience. Some never return; however, China very early on developed programs specifically designed to reattract students and nationals living abroad.

Leveraging the Knowledge and Experience of Their Diasporas

China and India have benefited enormously by drawing on their respective diasporas. China's first export processing zones were set up opposite Hong Kong and Taiwan, as most foreign investment came from those two economies. More than one-half of the FDI in China has come from Taiwan, Hong Kong, and Singapore. These are market economies with much experience operating in global markets. They were already well plugged into global supply chains. They initially moved their more labor-intensive operations into China, but as China moved up the technology ladder, they have been moving into more technology-intensive operations. This is particularly true for Taiwanese companies, which are now putting some of their most advanced production facilities in China. In addition, China has set up special high-technology parks specifically targeted at attracting back experienced overseas Chinese to set up high-tech companies in China. Several of the more than 100 high-tech parks in China cater specifically to this diaspora. Furthermore, China has also made a sustained effort to attract back professors and former foreign students to staff the rapid ramp-up of its tertiary education sector.

India was much slower than China to take advantage of its diaspora. It was joked that NRIs (nonresident Indians) stood for "not required Indians." However, India eventually learned the importance of harnessing its diaspora and since then has made special efforts to attract it back by offering special tax breaks and other fringe benefits.[59] However, even today, its efforts and policies to encourage the return of its diaspora are not as well developed as China's. Indian success in the ICT-enabled export services industry, nevertheless, has been due to a large extent to the linkages to its diaspora in the high-tech areas of the United States and Europe. India has had less success than China in bringing back professors to help with its faculty shortage in popular fields because it is more constrained by regulations that prevent its universities from paying them competitive salaries and places other limits on the number and employment terms of foreigners.

Speeding Up Technological Catch-Up Through Copying, Reverse Engineering, and Intellectual Piracy

Copying and reverse engineering have been very important for the swift catch-up in developing countries. For China, greater access to foreign knowledge through all the formal channels listed earlier, higher levels of human and technological capital, and a policy (now changing) of not enforcing intellectual property rights laws have given it an advantage in copying and reverse engineering foreign technology.

Industrial espionage has been another important way of accessing foreign technology. There have been many examples of industrial espionage where Chinese nationals have been caught stealing technology from U.S. and European companies. One of the early cases in the United States was the theft of the proprietary source code by a Chinese employee of a small firm called Ellery Systems in Denver, Colorado. Although the employee was arrested, he eventually had to be released because there was no explicit law to charge him with industrial espionage. Ellery Systems went out of business. This case led the U.S. Congress to pass the Economic Espionage Act of 1996, which made theft of trade secrets a federal crime.[60] There have been dozens of other cases of industrial espionage involving the transfer of military and private technology to China by employees in U.S. companies. However, with the advances in Internet technology, cyberespionage has become the easiest way to acquire all sorts of technology and trade secrets from the government as well as firms. One of the best-known cases is the cyberattack on Google and more than 30 other high-technology companies (including Adobe, Dow Chemical, Northrop Grumman, and Symantec) in December 2009.[61] Cables made public by WikiLeaks indicated that U.S. embassy personnel were told that the attack had been authorized by a high-level Chinese government official.[62] It is likely that cyberespionage will continue to be used by China as well as other countries to access valuable military and civilian technology.

Conclusion: Both Countries' Growth Is Largely Driven by Technological Catch-Up and Participation in the International System

This chapter has examined the very dramatic rise of China and India, the main factors explaining their ascent, and the similarities and

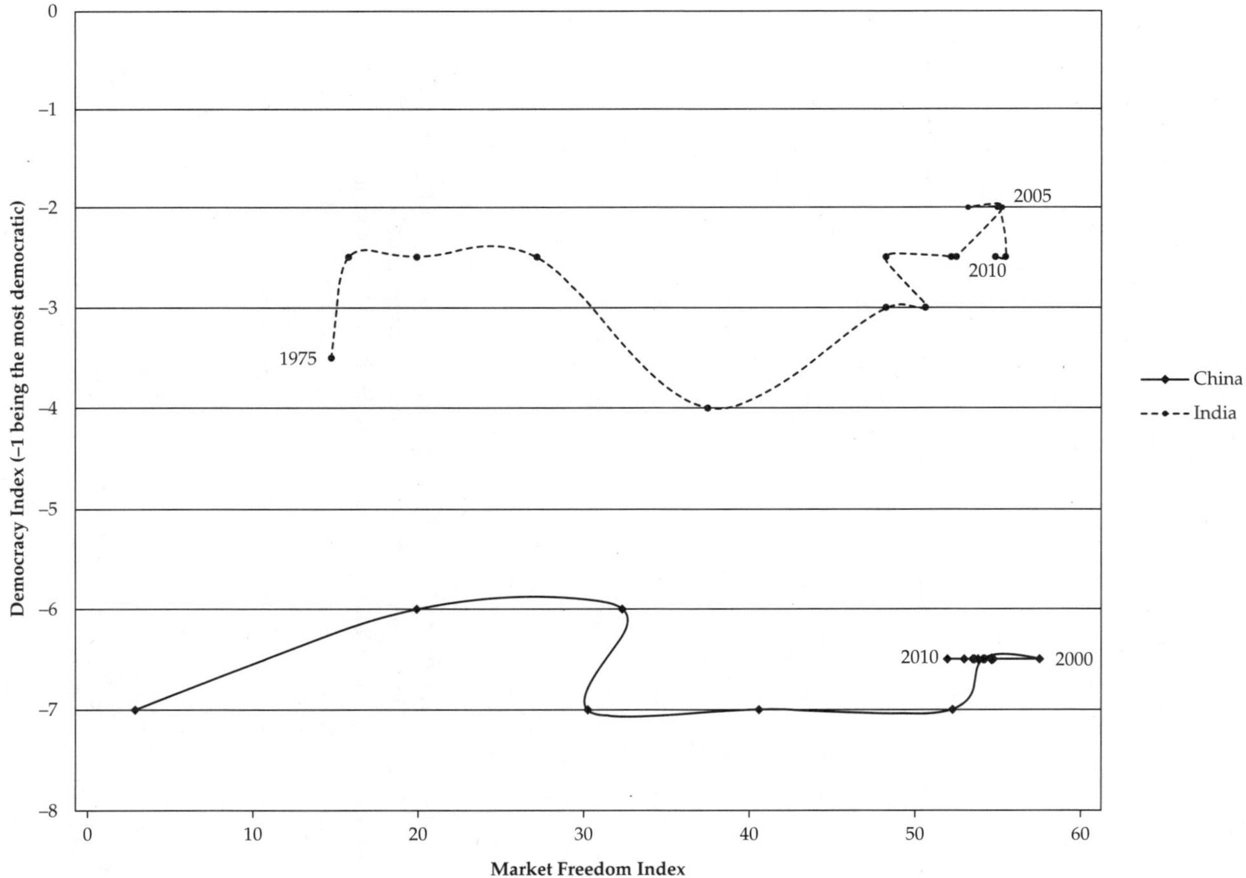

FIGURE 3.2 Evolution of democratic versus market freedom, 1975–2010

SOURCES: Index of economic freedom on horizontal axis, taken from Heritage Foundation, available at http://www.heritage.org/index. Accessed May 25, 2010. Index of democracy on vertical axis taken by averaging index for civil liberties and for political rights taken from Freedom House, freedom in the world historical data, available at http://www.freedomhouse.org/template.cfm?page=439. Accessed May 25, 2010. Because indices were scored from one as best to seven as worst, the negatives of the numerical scores were used so that best would be on top. Graph created by

differences in their development strategies. The key point to emphasize is that, despite their very different governance systems, starting places, and many other nuances, their rises—through a movement toward the market and integration into the international system—actually have much in common. Interestingly, China, the Communist country, started this integration more than a decade before India and moved much more quickly and through its own concerted strategy. India pursued its autarky policy much longer and was forced to move more toward the market and greater global integration as part of conditionality imposed by the IMF in exchange for assistance during the country's 1991 financial crisis. Although it is not possible to quantify, it is clear that both countries have benefited very much from greater integration with the world market and that their rapid growth has been driven in large part by the ability to access existing global knowledge through formal and informal means for technological catch-up.

Figure 3.2 graphs the evolution of these two economies over time as expressed by the degree of democracy[63] and of economic freedom.[64] It is remarkable that, in spite of starting from very different positions and while maintaining two very different systems of government, both countries have moved systematically toward greater market freedom. According to the Heritage Foundation's measure of economic freedom, by 2007–2008, China and India were within two points of each other on a scale of one to one hundred.

As will be developed in the next chapter, there has been some slight retrogression from the movement toward economic freedom not just in China and India but also in most of the world because of the severe market failures associated with the 2008–2009 economic and financial crisis. However, the expectation is that both countries will continue to move toward greater economic freedom once the crisis subsides. The evolution of their systems of government is less clear, particularly in the case of China. However, China's successful authoritarian regime is likely to remain in place as long as it can continue to deliver high growth rates. To the extent that it does, it will continue to have a governance model at odds with the democratic system of most advanced countries, a situation that will exacerbate geopolitical tension.

CHAPTER 4

Positive Growth Prospects for China and India

NOW THAT WE HAVE some understanding of why China and India have been growing so fast, this chapter will focus on their growth prospects. The first section examines why the wrenching 2008–2009 economic and financial crisis, which slowed the growth of developed and developing economies alike, affected China and India less than the rest of the world. The second section makes some simple projections of their growth prospects based on historical trends.[1] It shows that if the past trends were to hold, within 10 years China would become larger than the United States. Within 15 years India would become the third largest economy if measured in PPP and the fourth largest if measured in nominal exchange rates. However, simple historical extrapolations may be too optimistic. The third section of the chapter examines major challenges China and India face. Some are common to both countries; others are more country specific. Nevertheless, after examining these challenges, the conclusion is that although China and India may not continue to grow as fast as they are now, they are still likely to continue to grow much faster than the rest of the world for the next two decades, if only because there is ample room to continue to improve productivity based on technologies that already exist. The fourth section of the chapter examines China's and India's competitiveness. It focuses on two key areas, which both countries are significantly strengthening: higher education and innovation capability. Building up capability in these two areas is making China and India more formidable competitors and increasing their potential to maintain higher growth.

The Impact of the 2008–2009 Financial Crisis on China and India

Initially, many thought that the financial crisis was just a phenomenon affecting advanced industrial countries and that developing countries were not linked to it. By the end of 2008, however, it was clear that there was a great degree of interdependence, even though the financial systems of most developing countries were not directly involved in subprime lending or credit-default swaps. The interdependence occurred through two channels.

The first was the pullback of international finance from developing countries because advanced country institutions needed their capital to cover their precarious financial positions. There was a flight to quality—ironically back to the United States and to U.S. Treasuries in particular—as the safest asset. This outward flow from developing countries was also strengthened by the security umbrella of different guarantee systems put in place by governments in advanced countries. As a result of the large flows back to the United States, there were foreign exchange crises as the currencies of many advanced and developing countries (with the significant exceptions of China and Japan) suffered depreciation versus the U.S. dollar. Both these effects hit the Indian economy, which experienced capital flight and a devaluation of the rupee.

A second channel was the contraction in demand for imports from developing countries as the financial crisis hit the real economy. Imports by advanced countries fell from growth of 4.7 percent in 2007 to only 0.6 percent in 2008 and then declined by 12.0 percent in 2009. Since advanced countries are the major markets for emerging and developing countries, their exports fell by 8.2 percent in 2009.

Faced with rapidly falling GDP, major countries put in place fiscal stimulus packages to try to revive economic activity. The size and speed with which these packages were put into place and implemented varied across countries. The United States saw the need first, but Congress took a long time to pass the stimulus package. Even though it was hit by the global recession later and not as hard, China reacted quickly and started implementing its package faster.

There have been some additional measures, such as government takeovers of the banking, insurance, and auto industries in the United States and other advanced countries. Monetary expansion measures have also been as important as the fiscal stimulus. In China, there was a sevenfold expansion of bank credit. In the United States, there was a major expansion of the monetary supply as well as purchase by the Federal Reserve of many troubled assets from banks and other financial institutions.[2]

The net result of all these interventions has been to avoid a 1930s-type depression. However, as will be developed in Chapter 7, there are still risks that the recovery may stall, and there are also concerns about the long-term fiscal soundness of the United States because of reduced tax revenues from slower growth, continued high fiscal deficits, and rapidly expanding future costs for entitlement programs.

China and India were not as severely affected by the crisis because they were less directly exposed to the financial instruments underlying it. China's exposure to troubled subprime mortgages is estimated to have been very low and to have been quickly reduced early in the crisis.[3] The U.S. Treasury Department estimates that China was not among the top 10 global investors in U.S. corporate-backed securities.[4] The negative effect came from flight to safety (mostly for India) and in fall in demand for exports from both China and India. Furthermore, China quickly mounted a massive fiscal stimulus and expansion of bank lending.

Both countries maintained positive growth rates, higher in fact than what was estimated by the IMF in April 2009.[5] The estimates then for growth in China were for 6.5 percent in 2009 and 7.5 percent in 2010. For India, they were 4.5 percent and 5.6 percent, respectively. The rates estimated in October 2010 were more than 2 and 2.5 percentage points higher for China and 1 percent and 2 percent higher for India, respectively. The higher rates for China are the results of China's massive and quick response to the global economic crisis.

Long-Term Projections for Growth of China and India

The outlook for both China and India for 2011–2015 is positive. China is expected to grow at 9 to 10 percent a year, India at 7 to 9 percent, the United States at 2 to 3 percent, and the euro zone at 1 to 2 percent. China is in an especially strong position. It has $2.9 trillion in foreign exchange reserves and a high domestic savings rate. It is a net capital exporter, unlike most other developing countries and the United States. Therefore, on the supply side, China is not as constrained by the higher

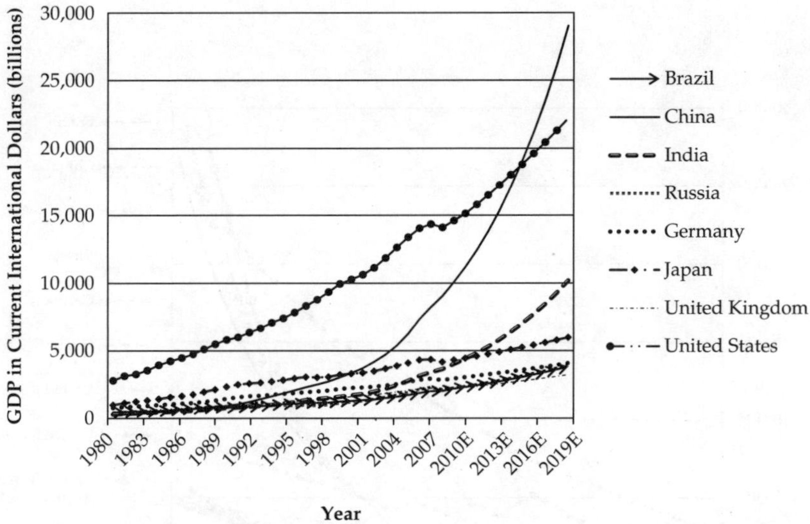

FIGURE 4.1 GDP: Actual (1980–2009) and projected (2010–2019)—largest economies in purchasing power parity

SOURCE: IMF data available from IMF data mapper, available at http://www.imf.org/external/datamapper/index.php. Accessed November 28, 2010.

NOTES: Historical data through 2009. IMF projections for 2010–2015. Projections for 2016–2020 based on using average IMF rate for 2010–2015.

cost of international capital and lower investment mentioned earlier as longer-term implications of the crisis. Its problems will be more on the demand side, as will be discussed in Chapter 7.

Longer-term growth projections are very risky given uncertainty about the future and the poor record of past projections. However, for illustrative purposes of what the differential growth rates imply, Figure 4.1 projects the growth of the world's eight largest economies in 2009 measured in constant 2005 PPP dollars. By this measure, China had already become the second largest economy when it surpassed Japan in 2002, and India became the third largest when it surpassed Germany in 2008. Projecting forward, China will surpass the United States by 2017, and India will surpass Japan by 2013. This is quite a dramatic shift.

Figure 4.2 makes the same projections based for the eight largest countries in 2009 based on constant-year 2000 U.S. dollars. China

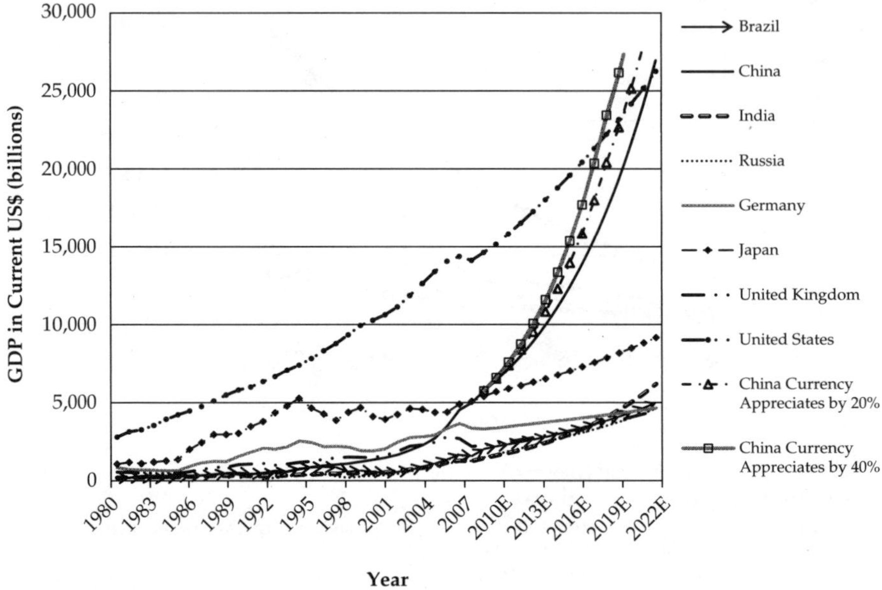

FIGURE 4.2 GDP: Actual (1980–2009) and projected (2010–2022)—largest economies in nominal U.S. dollars

SOURCE: IMF from IMF data mapper, available at http://www.imf.org/external/datamapper/index.php. Accessed November 28, 2010.

NOTES: Historical data through 2009 and projections through 2015 taken from IMF. Projections beyond 2016 based on average IMF rate for 2011–2015. Projections also assume one assumption that currency appreciates by 20 percent by 2020, another that it appreciates by 40 percent by 2020.

actually surpassed Japan to become the second largest economy in the middle of 2010. By this measure, China will surpass the United States in 2024, and India will surpass Germany in 2022 to become the fourth largest economy. As the Chinese renminbi is widely regarded as undervalued, the dashed line shows the projection assuming that the renminbi appreciates by 20 percent or 40 percent over the next 15 years. Using the 40 percent appreciation assumption, China will surpass the United States by 2020.

However, history is not linear. There are many surprises, such as the 2008–2009 economic crisis. In addition, China and India face major challenges, which could slow down or even derail their growth.

China and India Face Daunting Challenges

Before assuming that China and India are going to take over the world, we must realize that they face very real challenges that could make them unravel, or at least slow their growth. Some of these challenges are shared by both countries; others are more country specific.

Similar Challenges

Both countries face three similar challenges: rapidly growing inequality, corruption, and the environment, although the severity of each differs.

Growing Personal Income and Regional Inequalities. In China, the Gini coefficient[6] has increased from 30 in 1990[7] to 41.5 in 2005, which is more unequal than the United States (Gini of 40.8 in 2000).[8] There is also rising inequality between the rapidly growing coastal provinces and Beijing and the poor western provinces. Inequality is also rising between urban and rural dwellers. These inequalities are likely to become an explosive social issue unless they are controlled. The Hu Jintao administration is very aware of this risk. As a result, it has been undertaking several measures to address the problem, including eliminating taxes on farmers, as they are the group that has been most left behind. Health and education benefits have been extended to migrant workers in the city, who had been denied those benefits because they did not have residence permits. In addition, the central government started to transfer education funds directly to the poorest primary schools. The previous policy of fiscal decentralization had created hardship because the poorest regions did not have the tax base to support primary-education costs.[9]

In India, the Gini coefficient increased from 29.7 in 1994[10] to 36.8 in 2005.[11] Inequality has not increased as fast as in China because of India's slower rate of economic growth. Historically, there is a tendency for inequality to increase during periods of rapid economic growth. However, income and regional inequality are increasing rapidly and could become an explosive social issue. India is an extreme example of a dual economy: only 11 percent of the labor force is in the modern sector, and 76 percent of the population continue to live on less than $2 a day.[12] The incomes of those in the modern sector are rising rapidly, but those of the bottom three-quarters are hardly rising at all. Perceptions of inequality also have effects on elections. The electoral loss of the Bharatiya Janata Party (BJP) government in India in 2004 has been attributed to a disgruntled rural electorate. Although the BJP government had steered the country toward a higher growth path and made many economic achievements under its "India Shining" program, it was defeated by the "common man" slogan of the opposition, which represented the rural poor, who had not benefited from the economic progress.[13]

Corruption. Although not among the worst in the world, corruption is a serious problem in both China and India (see Table 4.1). Moreover, according to some indicators, such as the World Bank's Corruption Index, corruption in both countries seems to have become slightly worse over the last decade. Corruption undermines confidence in public officials and the government. Moreover, if it becomes too blatant, it could lead to social instability. Chinese history offers examples of corrupt emperors overthrown by populations that became fed up with corruption. Chinese President Hu Jintao has stated: "Resolutely punishing and effectively preventing corruption bears on the popular support for the Party and on its very survival, and is therefore a major political task the Party must attend to at all times."[14]

TABLE 4.1 Governance indicators for China, India, and the U.S.: Percentile ranks from 0 (worst) to 100 (best)

Governance Indicator	Year	China	India	U.S.
Voice and Accountability	2009	5.2	60.2	86.3
	2004	7.2	61.1	89.9
	1998	9.6	58.2	90.9
Political Stability	2009	29.7	13.2	59.0
	2004	38.9	23.6	51.0
	1998	38.5	21.2	78.4
Government Effectiveness	2009	58.1	54.3	89.0
	2004	54.9	55.3	92.2
	1998	44.7	51.9	90.3
Regulatory Quality	2009	46.2	44.3	89.5
	2004	46.3	42.0	93.2
	1998	39.0	34.1	95.6
Rule of Law	2009	45.3	55.7	91.5
	2004	41.4	56.7	91.4
	1998	40.0	60.0	92.4
Control of Corruption	2009	36.2	46.7	85.2
	2004	31.1	45.1	92.7
	1998	47.1	43.7	92.7

SOURCE: World Bank, *Governance Indicators* (2010).

The Chinese government is fully aware of this problem, and it periodically launches major anticorruption campaigns. Governors of provinces found guilty of corruption have even been executed to send a strong message to government officials. However, the possibilities for corruption abound in governments that place strong regulations on most activities.[15]

Environmental Degradation. Two sets of issues concern the environment. The first is pollution in terms of contamination of air, water, and soil; the second is the sustainability of resource use.[16] Both sets of issues place a constraint on the development of these two giant economies. As will be discussed in Chapter 6, both countries are poor in environmental resources per capita and face issues of environmental sustainability. This also has implications for global sustainability and a possible global backlash against China and India due to their growing CO_2 emissions. This section focuses on environmental pollution and its domestic impacts.

Both countries are suffering from air and water pollution and soil contamination as by-products of their very rapid growth. In both countries, there have been some improvements over time, as highly contaminating stoves and charcoal and coal furnaces have been replaced by gas, oil, or electric units. Governments have also regulated coal mining and use. In China, average particulate matter concentration per cubic centimeter of air in large urban areas has been reduced from 114 particles per cubic meter in 1990 to 73 in 2006. In India, the reduction has been from 112 to 65. However, the average world reduction over the same period has been from 80 to 50 (from 30 to 21 in the United States).[17] These countries still have many air pollution problems, and China is worse off than India. Among the world's 25 most polluted cities in 2006, 17 were in China and 4 were in India. On another air-quality measure—sulfur dioxide—China had 16 of the 25 worst cities and India had none in 2005.[18] This is related to the high percentage of coal as a source of electricity (81 percent in China vs. 68 percent in India)[19] and the greater use of total energy in China because of its higher per capita income and the large share of industry in its GDP.

High levels of air pollution are linked to an increased incidence of deaths from respiratory problems in both countries. The World Bank has developed a green accounting methodology that estimates pollution damages from particulate emissions in terms of human health. Effects include death and illness from cardiopulmonary disease and lung cancer in adults and acute respiratory infections in children.[20] The estimate for 2008 is that this air pollution damage was equivalent to 0.8 percent of gross national income for China and 0.5 percent for India.[21] In addition, air pollution flows across borders and has negative impacts on other countries. It is reported that smog from China floats across to Korea and Japan and even all the way to Canada and the northwestern United States.

Swift economic growth, besides requiring large amounts of water for agricultural, industrial, and household use, also leads to water pollution, which is perhaps an even more serious problem than air pollution. This includes contamination from runoff of fertilizers used in agriculture and industrial and municipal waste. A study of the water quality of China's eight main river systems indicated that, on average, 30 percent of the length of these rivers was so toxic that the water could not be used for irrigation or purified for human use.[22] In India, the rivers are also polluted from agricultural, industrial, and municipal waste, plus the custom of floating corpses onto rivers. In addition, both countries are experiencing water shortages, which will only be exacerbated by global warming (see Chapter 6).

One of the reasons these problems of pollution are not dealt with more effectively in both countries is that environmental concerns have taken a backseat to growth and employment. This is particularly true in China, where government officials are promoted based on the levels of economic growth they can achieve. People in both countries are literally dying from various forms of pollution, which has led to much social unrest. In China, it is estimated that a majority of 90,000 cases of social unrest per year are related to air, water, or soil contamination.[23]

China's Special Challenges

China's main long-term challenges are heavy dependence on the rest of the world for exports and imports, a weak banking system, rising dependence from an aging population, tension between the centralized authoritarian state and a decentralizing economy, and the risk of war with Taiwan.

Heavy Dependence on Exports and Imports. As a result of its successful export-oriented strategy, China is second only to Germany among the world's largest economies in trade as a percentage of GDP (66 percent in 2008). While this has paid high dividends in growth and industrial employment, it is also a key vulnerability. As will be developed in Chapters 5 and 7, there is an increasing risk of a strong protectionist backlash against China, particularly if border taxes for carbon are added to the already growing trade pressures.[24]

Weak Banking System. Although China now has four of the world's ten largest banks, its banking system had traditionally been ranked as relatively weak by international organizations such as the International Monetary Fund, the World Bank, and the World Economic Forum. China's system looks much better in light of the financial meltdown in the United States and other developed countries. The Chinese authorities recognize, however, that China needs to improve the sophistication of its financial market.[25]

In 2005, there was a concern that China's banks held too many nonperforming loans. Their balance sheets have been cleaned up since then, but China's banks are still subject to much administrative guidance by the government and are used to direct credit to state-owned enterprises. As part of the stimulus package to fight the 2008–2009 crisis, bank lending has expanded rapidly. There is a risk that many of these loans could become nonperforming if there is a slowdown in growth. Thus, the weakness of China's financial system remains a concern, although currently it is in much better shape than those of most advanced economies. Also, the incremental capital output ratio in China (the increase in investment necessary for an increase in GDP) has been rising over time and is higher than in most countries, indicating that there are inefficiencies in the allocation of credit.

Growing Population Dependency Ratio and Unbalanced Gender Ratio. Because of China's rapid economic and informal government policies to reduce population growth, total fertility fell from 5.8 children per woman of childbearing age (15–49 years) in 1970 to 2.7 in 1978. With the introduction of the one-child policy in 1979, total fertility rates have declined further to 2.1 percent, which is less than the replacement rate of the population.[26] Because of the one-child policy as well as rapid development,[27] China's population growth for 1990–2008 was 0.9 percent annually and is expected to slow further to 0.6 percent from 2008 to 2015. The reduction in total fertility and population growth rates has given China the benefit of low dependency ratios.[28] Its dependency ratio has in fact fallen from 50 percent in 1980 to 40 percent in 2007 and is likely to stay at that level until 2015, after which it will start to rise. It will pass 50 percent as the first cohort born during the population boom of the early 1960s starts to retire. Thus, China has benefited from a window of low dependency ratios since 1990, which has contributed to its economic growth. Dependency ratios will continue to be very low until 2030, after which they will start to increase rapidly as a lagged result of the one-child policy. The higher than world average dependency ratio after 2035 will start to be a drag on the Chinese economy (Figure 4.3). By contrast, India is just beginning to see its dependency ratio fall below the world average and will reap the gains for the next 30 years.

Thus, China will grow old before it grows rich because of the special population dynamics that led to lower population growth earlier than is typical for developing countries. This is a challenge because China has not yet put in place a social security or pension system to cover the needs of the large share of the population that will be retiring. The government is aware of this problem and has begun to expand the country's social security and pension system. It has also begun to relax the

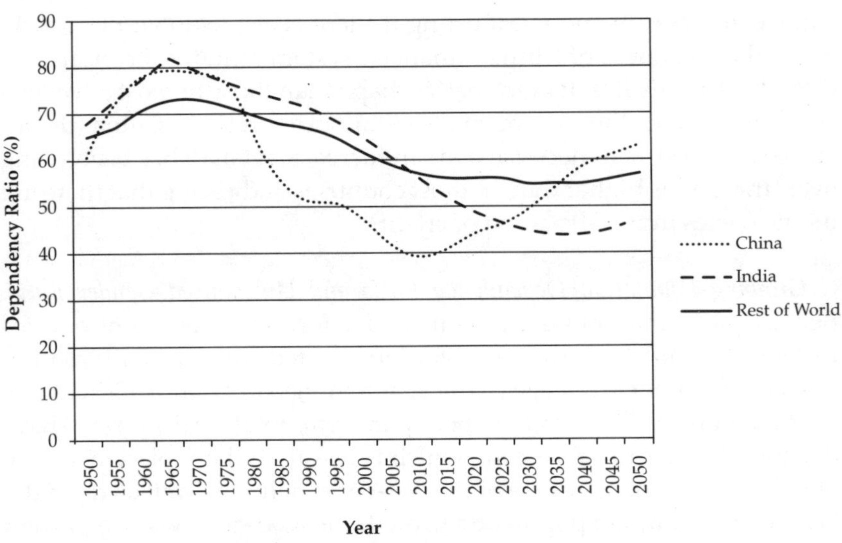

FIGURE 4.3 Changing dependency ratio: China, India, and the rest of the world, 1950–2050

SOURCE: Created by author with data from UN Population Division databank, available at http://esa.un.org/unpp/index.asp. Accessed November 26, 2010.

one-child policy to slow the premature aging of its population structure. Furthermore, it can reduce the problem by extending retirement beyond the current mandatory age of 60.[29] Thus, this problem may not be as big a constraint as some analysts have made it out to be, and in any case, it will not have a significant impact for another 20 years.

Another problem resulting from China's one-child policy is an unbalanced gender ratio. The ratio between male and female births has increased from 106 boys per 100 girls in 1980 to 115 boys per 100 girls in 2008. This is in part a cultural preference for male children in both China and India. However, in China, it has been exacerbated by the one-child policy and advances in medical technology that allow parents to know the gender of the fetus. As a result, selective abortions have increased. The implication of this unbalanced gender ratio is that there are now many more men of marriage age than women in China, perhaps a shortage of as many as 30 million women.[30] The competition for women leads to the sale of women from rural areas as brides to wealthier urban men and increased prostitution. It is also putting pressure on other countries, including trafficking in women. Chinese men are looking to neighboring Asian countries for brides. In addition, some Chinese workers on foreign projects are settling down abroad rather than returning home.

Tension Between Centralized State and Decentralizing Economy. Many analysts have pointed out that there is a growing tension between China's authoritarian regime and its increasingly decentralized economic system. They argue that as a country becomes richer, its citizens will demand more voice and accountability. In the World Bank Governance Index, China ranks low on international comparisons of voice and accountability (see Table 4.1, which also has the rankings for India and the United States for comparison).[31] Moreover, if the surveys on which these rankings are to be believed, it appears that voice and accountability have decreased over the last decade.[32] It is not clear to what extent this reflects Chinese citizens demanding more voice and accountability or an overall global trend in this direction.

In either case, it is clear that over time, people in China have been demanding greater voice and accountability from their government.[33] This has included making more use of the Internet to comment on current events and criticize the government. However, the government has maintained strong control over the Internet, monitoring and arresting those who speak out too loudly and banning politically oriented Web sites. Censorship has also been imposed by forcing foreign Internet companies such as Google to block popular sites and turn over the e-mails and identity of dissidents.[34]

However, the Chinese government and the Communist Party have been quite effective in managing the economy and providing political stability. Table 4.1 shows that government effectiveness and regulatory quality are ranked higher in China than in India. In addition, China is ranked higher on political stability than democratic India, although its index is much lower than the United States.[35] The Communist Party's aim is to stay in power, and it is keenly aware that it must modernize to do so. There are more than 3,300 party schools throughout the country, and their role is to upgrade the technical and administrative capability of the party cadres to enable them to manage a more complex economic and political system. Shambaugh argues that, rather than atrophy, the party has sought to adapt, modernize, and educate its members. This has included more consultative approaches (the People's Political Consultative Congress), more democratization within the party, experiments with democracy at the village level, and modernization of its ideology. Shambaugh cautions that the party's capacity to see future challenges and adapt accordingly should not be underestimated.[36]

Some analysts have argued that the government has earned a "mandate from heaven" from the masses: the right to rule by consistently delivering economic performance.[37] In this implicit social contract, the government maintains a monopoly over political power in exchange for delivering economic growth and increased welfare. The government has also been able to co-opt key interest groups. A significant recent example is President Ziang Zemin's development of the new doctrine of the "Three Represents" in 2002, in which he added entrepreneurs and businessmen to the traditional productive forces of farmers and workers.[38] Although bringing the capitalists into the fold was in contradiction to orthodox Marxist and Maoist theory, Ziang's plan was approved at the 16th Communist Party Congress in 2002. He even placed it into the Chinese Constitution before stepping down from power. This was an effective way to co-opt businesspeople into becoming stakeholders within the party.[39]

Some analysts argue that the Chinese government has attributes of the East Asian development state, blending authoritarian rule with market-oriented policies, and will eventually evolve to democratization. Others, such as Minxin Pei, disagree. While admitting that the government has been successful at co-opting business and the middle class, he argues that China is trapped in an "incomplete transition." Rather than a development state, it has become a "decentralized predatory state." Pei warns that sustained economic growth will not lead to further political liberalization and democratization but to "illiberal adaptation." He argues that the most likely outcome is that elites will limit political liberalization and democratization because of pervasive corruption and breakdown of accountability.[40]

Thus, there is much disagreement on the future evolution of governance in China. In spite of some arguments to the contrary,[41] there seems to be a broad consensus that China is not about to fall apart. The Pew Global Attitudes Survey Project tracks the views of people around the world on a set of common questions. On the question "How satisfied are you with the future direction of your country?" China has the highest positive index, with 87 percent of the respondents in 2010 approving the direction of their country. This was 37 percentage points higher than the next country, which was Brazil, with 50 percent responding positively. Positive responses were 45 percent in India compared with just 30 percent in the United States.[42] Therefore, in spite of the 1989 Tiananmen revolt, when the citizens of Beijing rose in protest against the government and paralyzed the attempt to crush the revolt for three weeks, it is not clear that the government will have trouble with concerns about stability in the next decade unless there is a major exogenous shock to the economy or an unforeseen political crisis.[43]

Taiwan and Other Asian Flashpoints. The relationship between the People's Republic of China and Taiwan has been tense from the beginning. Mao drove Chiang Kai-shek from mainland China to the island of Formosa, now Taiwan, as part of the long march that eventually led to the Communists' victory and the establishment of the People's Republic of China in 1949. The United States has sided with Taiwan since the beginning of the conflict. Although the people of Taiwan elect their own congress and president, China has always maintained that Taiwan is a province. This has led to very high tensions over time, which escalate whenever a Taiwanese president makes a strong statement about Taiwan's independence.

Tensions were exacerbated under Taiwanese President Chen (president from 2000 to 2008), but the current administration has taken a less confrontational approach with China. Business and commercial relations between Taiwan and China have grown and strengthened over the last 60 years. During the early phase of China's opening up in the late 1970s through the 1990s, Taiwanese businessmen off-shored their more labor-intensive operations to the Chinese mainland. After China's entrance into the World Trade Organization in 2001 and the explosive growth in China's trade, Taiwanese business has moved even high-technology plants and research centers onto the mainland to exploit economic and commercial opportunities not just for export but also for the booming Chinese domestic market. Furthermore, in 2010, the two countries reached a historic free trade agreement.

Thus, there has been very strong economic integration between Taiwan and China. China became Taiwan's largest export partner in 2005. However, there still remain strong tensions between the two countries. China has explicitly said on many occasions that it would invade Taiwan if Taiwan were to declare independence. Most of China's military buildup and war games are directed at Taiwan. Therefore, this flashpoint still remains a risk that could lead to war.

Other Asian flashpoints include North Korea and disputes over the islands in the East and South China Seas. The North Korean flashpoint is not that China will have a war with North Korea but that North Korea may trigger a war with South Korea, which could drag China in. There is also a risk that continued North Korean belligerence and threats of the continued buildup of its nuclear program may provoke a surgical strike by the United States, which could also pull China into a military conflict. Finally, China's aggressive claim to the various islands in the East and South China Seas could lead to military conflicts with its neighbors.

India's Special Challenges

India's major special challenges are governance, basic education and health, labor market efficiency, infrastructure, and flashpoints.

Weak Governance. As was seen in Table 4.1, India scores very low on political stability, regulatory quality, government effectiveness, and corruption. Many well-informed analysts rate governance as India's greatest challenge. A Goldman Sachs report on improving India's economic performance puts improved governance at the top of the list of 10 key things India needs to do to improve its growth.[44] Similarly, an excellent report sponsored by the Asian Development Bank, which analyzes the prospects of India to the year 2030, also cites governance as India's key challenge.[45]

As noted, India is a very peculiar democracy. Impressively, it has remained a democracy since its first constitution in 1949 despite major economic and political upheavals (the assassinations of Indira Gandhi in 1984 and Rajiv Gandhi in 1991) and wars (with Pakistan in 1947, 1965, 1971, and 1999; with China in 1962). However, because of its diversity of languages, religions, and culture, its strong caste divisions, and the divisive nature of its local politics, India is a challenging country to govern. This is compounded by the large number of political parties in the country and high levels of illiteracy among the population. There is also the burden of federalism, which places much power in the hands of states, resulting in a very fractious political system. After the end of what was basically one-party rule in 1989, no party won a majority until the 2009 election. It is very difficult for policy makers to pass critical reforms because they are blocked in Parliament by coalitions of multiple opposition groups, which constantly regroup along different opportunistic lines.

A well-known Indian political economist, Pranab Bhardan, has distinguished between procedural democracy, based on democratic institutions and parties, and the substantive results of democracy, such as liberty, economic equality, and redistributive justice. He argues that although India seems to have a participatory democracy, it is actually elitist, serving the interests of the dominant classes made up of professional bureaucrats, industrial capitalists, and rich farmers.[46] Because of fragmentation and localization, the votes of the poor are manipulated by local leaders, who put their own personal and local interests above the larger public good. In addition, although there is nominally rule of law, the judicial system is very corrupt. Trials take a decade or more to decide and are influenced by powerful interest groups. Furthermore, there is little accountability of elected leaders. It has been claimed that up to one-third of members of Parliament have criminal records.[47]

Thus, it is clear that democracy in India does not function in an ideal manner. While it does provide the benefits of voice, as there is a very active free press and many channels for expressing dissenting views and opinions, it also makes it difficult to govern effectively and to pass reforms for the public good if they affect vested interests.[48] Nevertheless, although there are many obstacles to overcome, most Indians are optimistic that the country will not only manage but also improve its system of government over time. The relative success of China's authoritarian regime stands in stark contrast to the constraints of India's democratic government, but many would argue that India's system is more resilient than China's in the long run.[49]

Poor Health and Primary Education. Poor health conditions in India are reflected in high infant mortality rates and low life expectancy. The latter is only 64 years compared to 73 years in China.[50] India's low educational level is its Achilles heel. Illiteracy is 49 percent among women and 25 percent among men. The average educational attainment of the adult population in 2000 was five years. Low education levels constrain the effective functioning of India's democratic system (see below). They are also a constraint on transitioning the population to higher value added jobs. India did not industrialize rapidly partly because of policy (Chapter 3) but also because it did not have an attractive low-cost skilled labor force as a site for export-oriented foreign investment, as was the case in the NIAEs and China.

The low level of education is also related to the problem of caste in India. Members of the lower castes have great difficulty gaining access to quality education, so they remain trapped in lower economic strata. Even when they do gain access to education, they still face much discrimination. Higher educational levels of the population as a whole could help break some of the traditional caste constraints, but there are still strong caste biases, even among highly educated Indians. This is a cultural problem that will take a long time to resolve, even with affirmative-action programs. Therefore, it is likely to continue to be a drag on India's progress.

Rigid Labor Mobility and Market Reservation for Small Firms. Labor market regulations that make it onerous to fire workers are another major constraint on India's development. This helps explain why there has been very little employment growth in the modern manufacturing sector. The constraints of labor market legislation were compounded by the reservation of 1,500 products for exclusive production by very small enterprises. Even after two decades of liberalization, today there are still around 600 products reserved for very small scale industries. This was done with the good intention of promoting small industry, but it has led to inefficient scale, low productivity, and low-quality manufacturing, all of which have constrained the competitiveness and expansion of manufacturing in India.[51]

Underdeveloped Infrastructure. Poor infrastructure—including poor electric power supply and underdeveloped roads, airport, and port facilities—has also been a major constraint on India's development. India's infrastructure is much less developed than China's. Electric power supply interruptions are common and losses are large. Consumption in 2007 was only 542 kilowatt hours (kWh) per capita and transmission and distribution losses were 25 percent compared with 2,332 kWh and 10 percent transmission and distribution losses in China. Power failures force companies to install expensive, less energy-efficient backup supplies. In communications infrastructure, the number of fixed phone and mobile phone lines per capita was one-third that of China in 1995. By 2008, the penetration ratio was almost half that of China.

The road system, while almost as extensive as China's in length, is of very poor quality. India only recently completed a "golden quadrilateral," a turnpike that encircles the country. Only 47 percent of the roads are paved, compared with 71 percent in China.[52] Its rail system is as extensive as China's, and it carries a similar number of passengers a year. However, it is slow and inefficient and carries only one-fifth of China's cargo tonnage per year.[53] Its airports have less than one-third the number of international flights, only 26 percent the total number of passengers, and 11 percent the number of airfreight ton-kilometers a year as China's.[54]

China's comparative advantage in manufactured exports is due in part to its relatively efficient port and transport infrastructure and its lack of bureaucracy in goods exchange. India's higher infrastructure costs and bureaucratic import and export procedures make it less competitive in trade of manufactured products. The International Finance Corporation (2010) cost of doing business report ranks China 50th and India 100th among 183 economies in the ease of doing business across borders.[55] The ICT infrastructure has been built up very rapidly in both countries, but China is still considerably ahead of India.

The poor infrastructure and high cost of getting goods into, around, and out of India are one of the main complaints of foreign companies looking to invest in the country. The physical infrastructure constraints compared with the relatively good fiber-optic and satellite infrastructure are part of the reason India has developed a comparative advantage in information-enabled services rather than in labor-intensive manufactured exports, which require the movement of physical goods.

Pakistan, Kashmir, and Other International Flashpoints. India has deep-rooted tensions with Pakistan. There have already been four wars between the two countries, three of them over the region of Kashmir. The first was the India–Pakistan War of 1947, in which the two countries disputed control over the princely state of Kashmir. The UN intermediated and gave control of the northern portion to Pakistan and the southern portion to India. The second war was the Indo–Pakistan War of 1965, fought again over control of Kashmir. The third was the Indo–Pakistan War of 1971, fought not over Kashmir but for the independence of East Pakistan, which seceded from Pakistan and became, with India's help, the independent country of Bangladesh. The fourth was the Indo–Pakistan War of 1999, when Pakistan infiltrated the Indian side of Kashmir but was turned back. Kashmir has also been a constant area of violent clashes and political unrest.

There have also been continuing skirmishes over time. Ten bombs in Mumbai between November 26 and 29, 2008, killed more than 170 people. They were attributed to Lashkar-e-Taiba, a Pakistan-based terrorist group with purported links to the Pakistani military.[56] This exacerbated tensions, and for a while, there was concern it could spark a war with Pakistan. However, the Pakistani government actively pursued the terrorist organization and jailed some members, which calmed tensions.[57]

India had a war with China in 1962 over disputed areas of their Himalayan border. China captured territory but eventually declared a ceasefire and returned most of it. There were also two border skirmishes between the two countries in 1967 and in 1987. Tensions subsided for some time after that. In 1993 and 1996, China and India signed peace agreements, and in 2006, they reopened the Silk Road, which passes through both territories, pledging peaceful cooperation.[58] However, tensions still continue over the disputed territories, with both countries reiterating their claims and remaining wary of each other. And new tensions are appearing over China's water diversion in the Himalayan glaciers (see Chapter 7). Such tensions could escalate into significant confrontations.[59]

India also has internal security issues linked to a Maoist movement called the Naxalites, which has been operating in India, mostly in the poorest provinces, for more than 10 years. In 2007, the Naxalites already controlled areas in 220 districts, accounting for 40 percent of India's territory.[60] They have been escalating their sabotage efforts, and in April 2010, they ambushed and killed more than 160 Indian police officers. In May 2010, they were suspected of being behind a train derailment that killed 71 civilians and injured more than 140.[61] In the short run, the Indian government needs to clamp down on these activities. However, the problem appears to be not so much foreign-supported terrorism as a reaction to India's lack of economic opportunity and increasing inequality. Therefore, the solution requires more inclusive growth.

In conclusion, both China and India face daunting challenges, any of which could spin out of control and slow down the rate of growth of either country. However, barring any major disruption, both countries can be expected to continue to grow faster than the rest of the world for the next few decades. The main reason is that they are still behind the technological frontier in many areas, so there is much room for productivity improvement by moving workers out of low-productivity agriculture and menial services to higher-productivity jobs throughout the economy. China's rate of growth will probably slow a couple of percentage points over the next decade and maybe another couple the following decade, as it catches up more and the dependency ratio turns against it. India is likely to continue longer at its current rate of growth if it can improve its governance and invest more in education and infrastructure. As noted, its demographic structure will give it an advantage similar to the one China has had, and it is just entering this favorable situation. However, it needs to implement a development strategy that productively absorbs the rapid expansion of its labor force. This is likely to require a strong export push in manufacturing, which will bring it into more direct competition with China.

Nevertheless, some of the challenges that have been discussed, such as environmental pollution and inequality, are likely to worsen over time and may eventually slow their growth or lead to some instability.[62] The flashpoints may also flare up and cause social and economic disruption, which could slow growth. In addition, China may face much stronger pushback from the rest of the world against its very strong export-oriented strategy supported by exchange-rate manipulation, intellectual property piracy, and industrial policy, which could slow its growth. Thus, although the precise outlook is uncertain, both countries have strong growth potential and are likely to continue to grow quite rapidly for the next 10 years. In addition, both are making investments in higher education and R&D, which will make them stronger international competitors and prolong their growth prospects.

Both Countries Are Increasing Their Competitiveness

An aggregate assessment of the growing international competitiveness of China and India is available through the World Economic Forum (WEF).[63] It has developed a detailed methodology for calculating the international competitiveness of countries that includes both quantitative and qualitative variables collected through international surveys. Between 2004 and 2010, China has improved its ranking from 46 of 104 countries to 27 of 133. India has improved its ranking from 55 to 51. Both countries are ahead of the other two BRICs,[64] Brazil and Russia, which ranked 58 and 63, respectively, in 2010.

Table 4.2 presents the rankings, including subindices, for what the WEF calls the 12 pillars of competitiveness. The table includes the BRICs and the NIAEs (newly industrialized Asian economies: Hong Kong, Singapore, South Korea, and Taiwan)[65] along with the United States as comparators to put China and India in context. In this assessment, China's main weaknesses are technological readiness,[66] higher education and training, financial market development, and infrastructure. Its greatest strengths are market size, macrostability, innovation, and labor market efficiency. India's greatest weaknesses are health and primary education, followed by macrostability, labor market efficiency, infrastructure, and technological readiness. Its strengths are market size, financial market development, and innovation.

Thus, the two countries have similarities in both strengths (market size and innovation) and weaknesses (technological readiness and higher education). There are also major differences. The largest are in macrostability, health, basic education, and labor market efficiency, where China is strong and India is weak; in financial market development, the opposite is the case. Both countries need to improve the quality of their institutions, anticorruption, the rule of law, transparency, and property rights.

Looking forward, besides improving the quality of their institutions and maintaining macroperformance, the two key areas that will strongly affect China's and India's competitiveness and growth prospects are education and innovation. These are the focus of the sections to follow.

Part of Their New Competitive Advantage Is Their Growing Critical Mass in Higher Education

Both countries came out poorly in the WEF rankings for education because the rankings were based on values normalized by population. However, both have been increasing their tertiary enrollment rates, and they actually now have a large critical mass of tertiary-educated persons. India and China have the largest educational systems in the

TABLE 4.2 Rankings of China, India, U.S., BRICs, and NIAEs by World Economic Forum's 12 Pillars of Competitiveness, 2010

	Overall Ranking	Institutions	Infrastructure	Macrostability	Health & Primary Education	Higher Education & Training	Goods Market Efficiency	Labor Market Efficiency	Financial Market Development	Technological Readiness	Market Size	Business Sophistication	Innovation
U.S.[a]	4	40	15	87	42	9	26	4	31	17	1	8	1
Singapore	3	1	5	33	3	5	1	1	2	11	41	15	9
Hong Kong	11	8	1	10	28	28	2	3	1	5	28	17	29
Taiwan	13	35	16	21	11	11	15	34	35	20	17	13	7
Korea	22	62	18	6	21	15	38	78	83	19	11	24	12
China	27	49	50	4	37	60	43	38	57	78	2	41	26
India	51	58	86	73	104	85	71	92	17	83	4	44	39
Brazil	58	93	62	111	87	58	114	96	50	54	10	31	42
Russia	63	118	47	79	53	50	123	57	125	69	8	101	57

SOURCE: Created by author from data in World Economic Forum (2010), *Global Competitiveness Report 2010/2011*. Geneva: WEF.

[a]The surprisingly low rankings of the U.S. on macrostability and financial market sophistication are the result of negative evaluations following the 2008–2009 financial and economic crisis. They were much higher in prior years.

world, including a number of elite higher education institutions. In addition, they have benefited from sending students abroad for foreign education and then tapping these students and their large global diasporas to return to their countries to contribute to their development. As a result, education has become the foundation of the labor forces in these nations. It is the key to turning these nations' abundant human resources into a strategic asset for competitiveness.

Although both countries' educational systems are growing, China's is larger and more robust. China has already implemented universal primary education, and it plans to increase compulsory education through the 12th grade by 2015. It is rapidly increasing its focus on tertiary education, with special attention to engineering, science, and technology. Between 1980 and 2009, the tertiary enrollment rate rose from 2 percent to 25 percent. In 2008, China had the largest number of students at the postsecondary level in the world (27 million), followed by the United States (18 million), India (15 million), Russia (9 million), and Brazil (6 million).[67] Forty percent of Chinese students are in engineering, math, and science, which is considerably higher than the other countries. In addition, the Chinese educational system is quite open to the foreign provision of educational services. Chinese universities have set up hundreds of formal and informal associations with foreign education and training providers.

While expanding the number of universities and tertiary enrollment rates, China has also been focusing on increasing the quality of tertiary education. There are various rankings of the quality of universities. One of the most rigorous, because it is based on quantitative factors, has been produced by the Shanghai Jiatong University of China since 2003. As expected, the United States has dominated the rankings since the start. In 2010 rankings, the United States had 17 of the top 20, 51 of the top 100, and 154 of the top 500 universities. In 2010, the United States was followed by Germany and the United Kingdom with 39 and 38, respectively, in the top 500. China was fourth worldwide, with 34 in the top 500. Although China did not have any in the top 100, it had four in the top 200 and had more than doubled the number in the top 500 compared with 2004. India had only two in the top 500, which was one fewer than in 2004.[68]

Although the total number of students in India is rising, including at the tertiary level, India's educational system is less developed than China's, mostly due to a history of excessive governmental regulation.[69] In 2008, the government began to ease its restrictions in an effort to create significant reforms, resulting in the creation of additional elite institutions of higher education.[70] However, India has failed to establish as many associations with foreign educational and training providers as China has.[71] In this regard, it lags behind in its development of advanced educational pedagogies, curriculum content, and education management, all of which would improve the quality and effectiveness of its educational system. Nevertheless, some education and training institutions are starting to go global, such as the National Institute of Information Technology (NIIT), with operations in 40 countries.

At approximately 70 million, China has the largest absolute number of adults with some level of university education in the world. It is followed by the United States, with about 60 million. India is ranked third at about 53 million.[72] China has more graduates in the natural sciences and engineering than any other nation, roughly four times those of the United States[73] and an even higher multiple than India. Some analysts have speculated that such inflated numbers suggest a problem with the data. In light of this, a team from the Pratt School of Engineering at Duke University conducted an extensive analysis of the data for engineering degrees. Their methodology included the analysis of published sources and travel to China and India for interviews with education authorities, certification and accreditation offices, and foreign and domestic hiring enterprises.[74] Although there are still some concerns about the Chinese data, the results of the study confirmed the rapid scale-up of the educational system in China and concluded that China and India now award more four-year engineering bachelor's degrees than the United States.[75]

More broadly, the U.S. National Science Foundation (NSF) estimates that the number of first university degrees in the natural sciences and engineering in China increased from about 239,000 a year in 1998 to 807,000 by 2006, which is roughly four times the number in the United States.[76] More impressive is a more than tenfold increase in the number of doctoral degrees in the natural sciences and engineering granted in China. The NSF estimates that in 2006 China was graduating 21,000 a year, nearly the same number as the United States (Figure 4.4). This is particularly telling because in the United States roughly half the students earning these doctorates are temporary or permanent visa holders (31 percent from China, 14 percent from India). In engineering, the percentage of doctorates by temporary or permanent visa holders was even higher, at 68 percent, and almost three-quarters were from East Asia or India.[77]

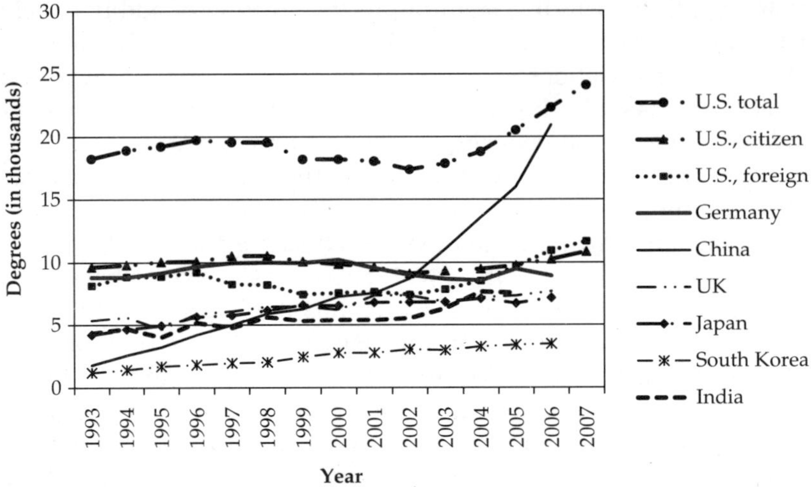

FIGURE 4.4 Doctoral degrees in the natural sciences and engineering, selected countries, 1993–2007

SOURCE: Created by author from data taken from Excel files for Figure O-9 of National Science Board. 2010. *Science and engineering indicators 2010.* Arlington, Va.: National Science Foundation (NSB 10-01). Overview chapter.

China and India have the largest number of tertiary students studying outside their home country. Of the 3.0 million tertiary students worldwide, China accounts for 14.9 percent and India for 5.7 percent. The importance of study-abroad programs is more significant for China than for India, with 1.7 percent of its tertiary students studying abroad (compared with 1.0 percent for India). The main destinations for Chinese students are the United States (110,000), Japan (78,000), Australia (58,000), the United Kingdom (45,000), and Korea (31,000). China hosts 51,000 foreign tertiary students. The main destinations for Indian students are similar: the United States (95,000), Australia (27,000), the United Kingdom (26,000), and Germany and New Zealand (3,000 each).[78] A recent study in the United States found that an increasing number of the foreign students from China and India return to their home countries after the completion of their academic work. The "five-year stay rate" had been 92 percent for Chinese students and 85 percent for Indian students. However, interviews with students in 2008 found that 40 percent of students of Chinese origin and 55 percent of Indian origin wanted to return to their home countries within five years of graduation. Although problems with visas were a common concern, most desired to return because they felt there were better opportunities in their home countries than in the United States.[79]

In sum, China and India started from very far behind, but both have made impressive gains and have a growing critical mass of highly educated professionals, engineers, and scientists.[80] This is especially true of China, although there are still problems of quality in its educational system. A recent book by Simon and Cao (2009) has done extensive analysis of China's increasing investment in higher education. It concludes that although there are still many bottlenecks and challenges to improving the quality of higher education and to making efficient use of the large number of graduating scientists and engineers for innovation, China's tertiary education graduates and their managerial base constitute a critical source of competitive advantage for the country. This advantage can be expected to grow stronger over time as policy makers continue to focus on getting more out of these important assets.[81]

They Are Also Moving from Imitation to Innovation

In addition to acquiring knowledge from abroad, China and India are also increasing their capacity for innovation. The main actor in the creation of basic knowledge is the government or university research lab. However, the main actor in the creation of applied, commercialized knowledge or innovation is the productive enterprise. Research outputs are scientific and technical papers, which generally reflect advances in basic knowledge. Patents represent more applied knowledge that is believed to have some commercial value. Table 4.3 compares the R&D efforts of China and India in terms of two inputs (R&D and scientists and engineers) and two outputs (scientific and technical publications and patents in the United States[82]).

China has made major strides in increasing its R&D efforts, as can be seen from its more than doubling its number of researchers in R&D (Table 4.3), the dramatic increase in spending on R&D in the last 15 years, and the corresponding increase in the number of world-recognized scientific and technical articles.

There is much evidence for China's strong technological capability. It has been a nuclear power since 1964. It is one of only three countries to have launched men into space. It has demonstrated its missile capability by shooting down one of its low-orbit satellites. It has very strong

TABLE 4.3 China and India: R&D inputs and outputs

Indicator	China	India
Researchers in R&D		
1995	531,997	145,115
2007	1,419,075	156,180
R&D Researchers (per million population)		
1995	445	157
2007	1,071	137
Spending on R&D		
U.S. $ billion nominal 2007	48	9
U.S. $ billion in PPP 2007	118	27
Spending on R&D (percentage of GDP)		
1995	0.55	0.80
2007	1.49	0.80
Scientific and Technical Journal Articles		
1995	9,261	9,591
2007	56,806	18,194
Scientific and Technical Journal Articles (per million population)		
1995	7.7	10.3
2007	43.1	16.17
Patents Granted by U.S. Patent Office		
Average 1991–1995	56	36
Average 2006–2010	1930	723
Patent Applications Granted by U.S. Patent Office (per million population)[a]		
Average 1991–1995	0.05	0.04
Average 2006–2010	1.44	0.62

SOURCE: Created by author based on data in World Bank *World Development Indicators* database and the USPTO General Patent Statistics Reports. Accessed April 11, 2011.

[a] The 2010 population was projected using the five-year average population growth rate ending in 2009.

construction capability, as is evident from the massive projects it has undertaken successfully. It has very strong manufacturing capability, as is evident from the strong competitiveness of Chinese enterprises in the global market. It recently developed the fastest supercomputer in the world.[83] It has strong software capability, as is evident from cyber-attacks which have been traced to China. Finally, it is strong in alternative energy technologies, including wind and solar power.

India has also increased its R&D spending and output, although not as much as China (Table 4.3), and it also has strong technological capability. It has been a nuclear power since 1974. It has a strong space program. It has strong manufacturing capability, particularly in pharmaceuticals and auto parts. It is also very strong in software and alternative energy technologies, particularly wind power. Like China, it is producing electric cars.[84]

Ramping Up Research and Development Expenditures

On the global scale, both nations are already major research powers. The bubble graph in Figure 4.5 presents the relative positions of the main global R&D spenders. The horizontal axis represents R&D expenditures as a percentage of GDP, and the vertical axis shows the number of scientists and engineers per million of population. The size of the bubble represents the absolute expenditures on R&D in each of the countries in PPP terms. The absolute scale is particularly significant in the area of knowledge because, unlike other goods, it is not consumed during use. Once knowledge is produced, it is potentially available for dissemination to all.[85]

China has been very effective at assimilating global knowledge and is now beginning to generate its own. By the end of 2010, China was second only to the United States in spending on R&D (measured in PPP terms). This is the result of an explicit strategy by the Chinese government to move beyond copying, reverse engineering, foreign direct investment, and technology licensing to start investing in domestic innovation.

In 2006, the government announced a National Medium and Long Term Plan for the Development of Science and Technology (2006–2020) to increase expenditures on R&D to 2.0 percent by 2010 and to 2.5 percent by 2025 (the average level of more advanced developed countries).[86] By 2006, China had already increased R&D to 1.42 percent of GDP, whereas most other countries (except South Korea) had shown very little increase, and some even experienced decreased numbers. In addition, the distribution of R&D effort between the government and the productive sector is already close to that of developed countries, with about two-thirds produced by the productive sector.[87]

The Medium and Long Term Plan has targeted 16 key megaprojects for development. Thirteen of these are public, and three are classified and believed to be military related. The first four are related to electronics, the next three are related to energy and environment, the next

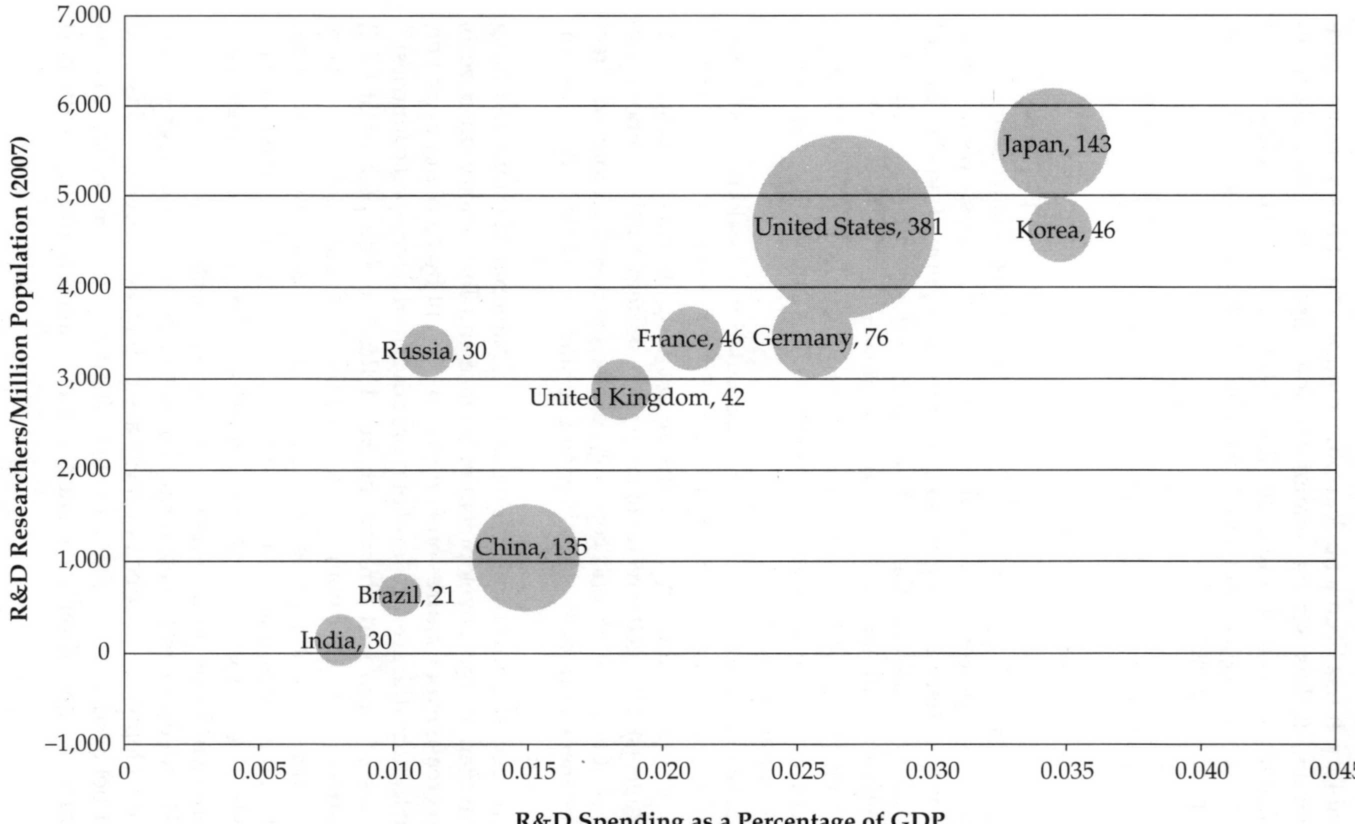

FIGURE 4.5 Relative R&D expenditure and scientists and engineers per million population (expenditures in 2009 in billions of PPP dollars)

SOURCE: Created by author from data from WDI database. Accessed November 10, 2010.

three to biotechnology and health, and the last three to aeronautics and space. The thirteen projects are:

1. Core electronic components, high-end general use chips, and basic software products
2. Large-scale integrated circuit manufacturing equipment and techniques
3. New generation broadband wireless mobile communication networks
4. Advanced numeric-controlled machinery and basic manufacturing technology
5. Large-scale oil and gas exploration
6. Large-scale nuclear reactors
7. Water pollution control and treatment
8. Breeding new varieties of genetically modified organisms
9. Pharmaceutical innovation and development
10. Control and treatment of AIDS, hepatitis, and other major diseases
11. Large aircraft
12. High-definition Earth observation system
13. Manned spacecraft and lunar probe programs

India was very technologically autarkic until reforms in 1991. Until that point, the public R&D infrastructure was mostly invested in the development of technology for large state-run enterprises. As a result, little new or cutting-edge technology was developed. Since then, its public research infrastructure has been redirected toward more commercially relevant research. Recently, the private sector, particularly the pharmaceutical and information technology industries, has begun to invest more in R&D. As a result, R&D expenditures have increased to over 1 percent of GDP, and half of total R&D is carried out in the private sector.[88]

In addition, as part of the global outsourcing trend, many multinational corporations (MNCs) are increasing their own R&D in these developing countries. By 2006, there were more than 750 MNC R&D labs in China and over 250 in India.[89] It is estimated that the foreign share of spending in business R&D in China is 25 percent as a result of the rapid increase of R&D in China by foreign firms.[90]

Globally, roughly two-thirds of all R&D is done by private firms. A 2008 study by Booz Allen Hamilton[91] found that the thousand largest global companies actively involved in R&D were responsible for $492 billion of an estimated total worldwide R&D expenditure of $982 billion in 2007[92] and that 91 percent were conducting their R&D activities outside their country of headquarters. On average, 55 percent of R&D was being done abroad. Based on surveys of 184 firms accounting for $350 billion of R&D spending, Booz Allen Hamilton found that the two countries whose hosting of foreign R&D exceeded spending by their own MNCs abroad ("net R&D importers") were China and India. China's "net imports" of foreign R&D were $24.7 billion, and India's were $12.9 billion. The study also found that between 2004 and 2007, global multinationals increased the number of R&D sites by 6 percent and that 83 percent of the new sites were located in China and India. Staff also increased by 22 percent, and 91 percent of that increase occurred in these two countries.[93]

In their interviews, the Booz Allen Hamilton researchers found that the initial impetus for handling R&D abroad was the lower cost of personnel. However, due to this emerging trend, foreign labor costs abroad rose rapidly. For example, in India, the wage for a highly skilled employee was 53 percent of the U.S. equivalent in 2005, but it rose to 65 percent in 2008 and is expected to rise to 77 percent in 2012, eventually reaching 90 percent in 2020. Beyond labor costs, the growing talent pool in developing countries across different stages of the value chain, from ideation to research and strong product development and testing, made it attractive to do more R&D abroad. In addition, greater competition made it important to locate their R&D operations closer to the growing markets to tailor their products to the specific needs of those markets.[94]

Expanding Researchers in R&D

Various other measures besides R&D expenditures show the increasing scientific and technical capabilities of China and India. As noted in Table 4.3, China has significantly increased its number of researchers. Figure 4.6 puts this on a global scale: by 2007, China had almost reached the same number of researchers as the United States, and by 2010, China led the world in number of researchers.

Growing Scientific and Technical Publications

Another measure of R&D capability is the number of internationally recognized publications in scientific and technical fields. The absolute

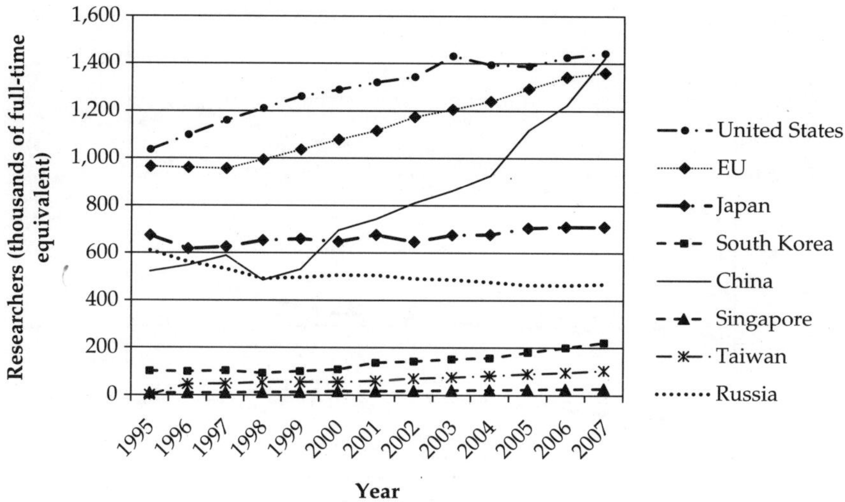

FIGURE 4.6 Researchers in R&D, selected countries, 1995–2007 (thousand full-time equivalents)

SOURCE: Created by author from data taken from Excel files for Figure O-10 of National Science Board. 2010. *Science and engineering indicators 2010.* Arlington, Va.: National Science Foundation (NSB 10-01). Overview chapter.

amount is more relevant than the number per capita because knowledge is not consumed in its use. China's recent rapid increase is very impressive. Between 2005 and 2008, China passed Germany and Japan in the number of internationally recognized scientific and technical publications to become second only to the United States (Figure 4.7).

Exploding Intellectual Property Registration in China

There has been a general trend toward increased patenting and other forms of intellectual property across all countries.[95] As shown in Figure 4.8, China has had the fastest rate of increase over the last 10 years. By 2008, the number of patents registered in China was the third highest globally (289,838 compared with 456,321 in the United States and 391,006 in Japan).[96] Technologies in which there is relative specialization in China include digital communications; telecommunications; audiovisual technology; computer technology; thermal processes and apparatus; electrical machinery, apparatus, and energy; furniture; games; and microstructural and nanotechnology.[97] Thus, it is clear that

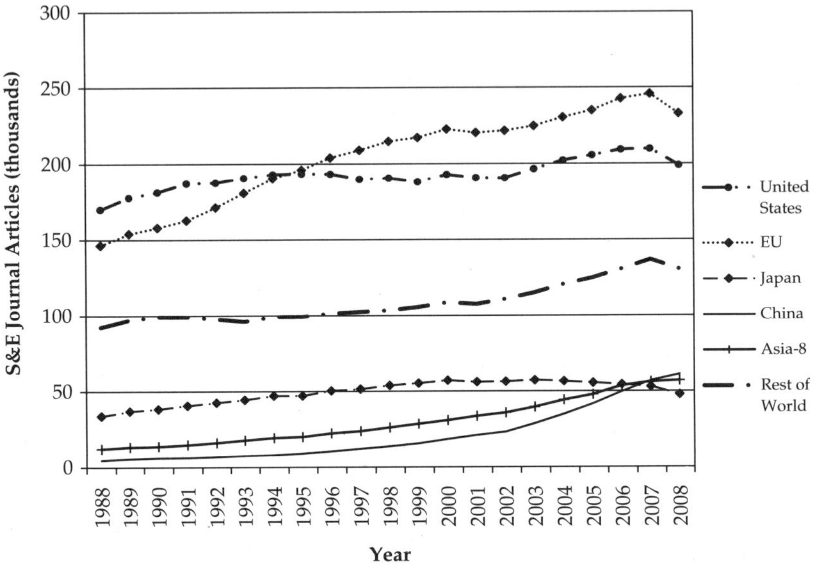

FIGURE 4.7 Scientific and engineering journal articles, selected regions and countries, 1988–2008

SOURCE: Created by author from Excel files for Figure O-13 from National Science Board. 2010. *Science and engineering indicators 2010*. Arlington, Va.: National Science Foundation (NSB 10-01). Overview chapter.

China is very strong in electrical engineering. India, on the other hand, exhibits its strength primarily in chemicals, particularly organic fine chemistry, pharmaceuticals, and food chemistry.[98]

As domestic patent legislation varies across countries, it is useful to briefly examine triadic patents, or those that are filed simultaneously in the U.S. Patent Office (USPTO), the EU Patent Office (EPO), and the Japan Patent Office (JPO). These are a good indicator of patents with worldwide importance and provide a fairly standardized measure of patenting around the globe. In 2005, China and India had the 12th and 22nd highest share of triadic patents, at 0.80 percent and 0.25 percent, respectively. Although their total shares were still relatively low, China exhibited the highest annual growth rate (36.7 percent) between 1995 and 2005, while India showed the second highest (27.6 percent).[99]

In addition to the provisions of the triadic patent, there is also a patent cooperation treaty that allows a country to register a patent once with the World Intellectual Property Organization (WIPO) and receive

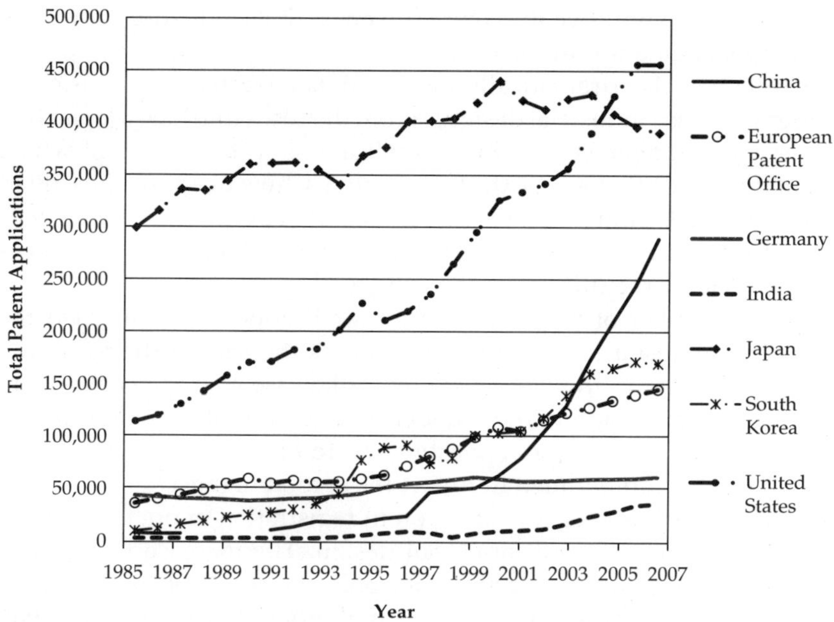

FIGURE 4.8 Trends in patent filings by country, 1985–2007

SOURCE: Created by author from data from World Intellectual Property Organization patent database, available at http://www.wipo.int/ipstats/en/statistics/patents. Accessed December 12, 2010.

subsequent recognition from national patent offices in different countries. In 2009, there were 155,900 patent cooperation treaty applications. Of those, China accounted for the fifth highest share, with a 33 percent increase over 2008.[100] In 2009, Panasonic had the highest number of patents with 1,871 applications. The Chinese company Huawei Technology had the second highest number of applications with 1,847. Another Chinese electronics company, ZTE, was number 22 with 517.[101]

As a result of its ramp-up in R&D efforts, China has a very high patent intensity whether measured by unit of GDP or spending on R&D. In 2008, China ranked third in the world, after Korea and Japan, in the number of patents registered by its residents per billion of GDP. The United States was fourth. In that same year, China was also ranked third (after Korea and Japan) in terms of resident patent filings per million of R&D expenditures. The United States ranked twelfth.[102] India has not yet become a major power in patents; however, like China, it is also increasing spending on R&D and focusing on more applied technologies to improve the competitiveness of its industries. It will be a stronger competitor in the future.

China has also dramatically increased as a location for registering trademarks and industrial designs. From the 1950s until 1995, Japan had the largest number of trademark applications in the world, at which point the United States took the lead. In 2001, China overtook the United States. In 2008, China filed 669,088 trademark applications, which was more than twice as many as the United States and almost five times as many as Japan, the third largest in filings.[103]

In the number of industrial design applications, Germany led the world for almost a century until Japan took the lead in the 1950s, followed by China in the late 1990s. As in the case of trademarks, there has been an explosion in the number of industrial design applications in China. In 2008, 312,904 applications were filed in China, more than five times the number filed in Korea, the second highest.[104]

Thus, there has been an explosion in registration of not just patents but also trademarks and industrial design. The increase in all these forms of intellectual property is not only the result of foreign firms filing in China to protect their intellectual property. Two-thirds (in patents) to 99 percent (in utility patents) of the filings for different types of intellectual property are by residents rather than foreigners (Table 4.4). In addition, the vast majority of IPR suits currently in Chinese courts are domestic ones.

There is an apparent paradox of China's weak record on IPR enforcement and the increase in Chinese patenting activity. A recent study argues that only part of the increase in patenting corresponded to the increase of Chinese R&D expenditure.[105] Other factors seemed to have a more significant impact. Increased foreign direct investment contributed to increased patenting for domestic firms, presumably because it

TABLE 4.4 Total number of applications for different types of intellectual property in China and percentage by domestic residents, 2008

	Total	Percentage by Domestic Residents
Patents	289,838	67.1
Utility Patents	225,586	99.3
Trademark Applications	669,088	88.3
Industrial Design Applications	312,904	94.4

SOURCE: Created by author based on data from World Intellectual Property Organization, *World Intellectual Property Indicators 2010.*

raised awareness of the strategic value of patenting in a competitive environment. The privatization of many state-owned enterprises also led to a clarification of property rights, which may be associated with the increase in patent applications. The largest effect, however, came from reforms in Chinese patent legislation in 2000–2001, which made the patenting process simpler and more user friendly. Thus, it appears that the importance of protecting intellectual property is being rapidly internalized by Chinese firms as they face greater foreign competition and as the domestic intellectual property system becomes more accessible to applicants.

As China and India continue to improve their innovation capability, they will become even stronger competitors. Some analysts are concerned about the rapid rise in technological capability of these two countries. Preeg, for example, wrote a book in 2005 titled *The Emerging Advanced Chinese Technology Superstate.* He followed with a book in 2008 titled *India and China, the Advanced Technology Race and How the United States Should Respond.*[106] Both books are somewhat extreme and credit the two countries with swifter advances than they have actually achieved. As documented in this chapter, both countries still have fairly low levels of technological capability. However, they are certainly building on this capability rapidly and will become much stronger over time. China, in particular, is well on its way to becoming a major innovative power. It has the critical mass of high-level human resources and research expenditures. As seen in this chapter, it is also investing further in higher education and R&D. In addition, it is investing in improving the quality of both and beginning to show some innovation leadership in several areas, including green technology.

Both Countries Are Likely to Continue to Grow Much Faster Than the World Average for the Next Two Decades

The analysis of this chapter has four major implications. First, the 2008–2009 economic crisis has had a differential impact on advanced and emerging economies. China and India, in particular, are coming out of the crisis stronger relative to the developed economies. They also appear set to continue growing faster than the rest of the world for the next few years.[107] They face major challenges that could slow their rapid advance or even lead to major social and economic turmoil. Based on history, almost anything could happen, so forecasting is hazardous. However, the trajectory appears to be that economic power will continue to shift to these to countries for the next decade or so.

Second, India and China are strengthening the advantage of their large populations and labor forces through education and training. They have the largest and second largest educational systems in the world and are well on their way to creating strong competitive advantage in educational services. In terms of higher education, they have the largest (China) and third largest (India) number of tertiary students in the world. As these education and training systems enhance the capability of new entrants into the labor force, China and India will be able to scale the technology ladder, producing more sophisticated products and delivering more specialized services. Both countries are still net importers of educational services, as they send more students abroad for education and training than they host. However, as they continue to strengthen their educational systems, they are likely to become large net exporters. This will give China and India a greater global profile that will allow them to export their culture and world philosophies, including their alternative political and socioeconomic models.

Third, the combination of this increasingly educated labor force with the quick reduction in transportation and communications costs and a reduction in policy barriers affecting the flow of goods and services across borders is leading to a global rebalancing of relative wages between developed and developing countries. It is already evident in developed countries that wages for unskilled workers with only a high school education in industries where products can be traded internationally are rising more slowly than wages for workers with college educations or higher. This is because there is a rapidly rising global supply of unskilled workers. What is new is that wages for knowledge-intensive work that can be accomplished digitally and remotely may not be rising as quickly as wages for service work that requires physical interaction.[108] Virtually anything that can be done digitally and that does not require physical or face-to-face interaction can be done more cheaply by skilled persons in China, India, and other low-wage developing countries that leverage their labor forces through education.

Finally, it can be expected that both countries will continue to put strong restructuring pressure on global economic activity as they continue to improve their innovative capability through large investments in R&D. In the short run, this is being led by China. Its large investments in higher education and R&D will continue to strengthen the capabilities and competitiveness of its industries. Of course, China cannot have a comparative advantage in everything. As its wages increase, other countries with low wage costs, including India and others such as Vietnam and Indonesia, will move in to produce labor-intensive goods as China moves further up the technology ladder. However, because China still has large reserves of underemployed workers in agriculture, it is likely to continue to exert strong pressure even in labor-intensive industries.

In short, the large labor forces and rapidly increasing skills and technological capabilities of these two countries will continue to place very strong restructuring pressure on the world. The next chapter surveys some of the positive and negative economic impacts that are already evident from the two countries' swift development.

CHAPTER 5

Growing Economic and Geopolitical Impact

THE SWIFT ASCENT AND GROWTH of China and India have a strong economic impact on the rest of the world. Their growing size and economic interactions with other countries also have increasing geopolitical impact. These nations have become additional growth poles for the world economy. This change is particularly important because of the 2008–2009 recession and the expectation that recovery will be slow in the developed world. The results of such quick growth are evident primarily in trade.[1] The first section of this chapter examines the positive and negative effects of their trade on other countries. The positive aspects are the reduction in prices of the goods and services they export as well as the large market for imports they provide. The negative aspects are the strong competition to other producers of the goods and services they export. A second impact, the contribution of China to global imbalances, is covered in the following section. China has the world's largest trade surpluses, and the United States has the largest trade deficits. China uses part of its trade surplus to buy U.S. Treasuries, creating a strong symbiotic link between the two countries. This helps keep the Chinese renminbi from appreciating and helps the United States finance its foreign debt. However, it also undervalues the Chinese currency and gives China an unfair advantage in exports, which has negative impact on other countries and is leading to growing trade tensions not only with the United States but also with the rest of the world.

A third important economic impact, the link through foreign direct investment (FDI), is analyzed in the next section. Both countries are attracting large volumes of FDI that might have gone elsewhere.

In addition, both countries, especially China, are becoming large foreign investors. Much of this investment is going to buy natural resources and high-technology companies as well as to enter new markets. However, it also reflects both countries' growing capability and increasing competitiveness in many areas. A fourth economic impact, the complex issues of unfair competition through intellectual piracy and restricted access to domestic markets, is covered in the following section. As noted in Chapter 3, China's and India's swift development can in part be explained by the fact that they are tapping global knowledge by formal and informal means, including reverse engineering and stealing foreign technology. This is compounded in China by the government's using access to China's booming domestic market to demand greater technology transfer as well as giving preferences to domestic firms at the expense of foreign firms. The last section covers the geopolitical implications of China's growing influence on other countries. This is the result of the impressive performance of its economy, which has grown at about 10 percent per year for the last 30 years and weathered the economic crisis of 2008–2009 better than any other. In addition, its development model is looked on favorably by other authoritarian states. More broadly, it is also gaining influence because it has become the key trading partner for most countries in the world. Furthermore, it is becoming a magnet for most multinational corporations (MNCs) because of its large, booming domestic market. In a sense, it has turned the MNCs into its key ally in accelerating its development. Finally, given its rising economic strength and its dependence on imported resources, China is strengthening its military capability. This creates concerns about the changing balance of military power and leads to traditional spirals of arms buildup and the search for new counterbalancing alliances.

Positive and Negative Impact Through Increased Trade

China has increased its share of global merchandise exports from 0.9 percent in 1980 to 10 percent in 2010 (Figure 5.1), and this share will likely continue to grow. No other country has had such a massive increase in world export share in such a short time. In 2009, Indian merchandise exports were just under 2 percent of the world's. In fact, the value of the increase in China's exports between 2006 and 2007 alone was larger than India's total merchandise exports in 2007.

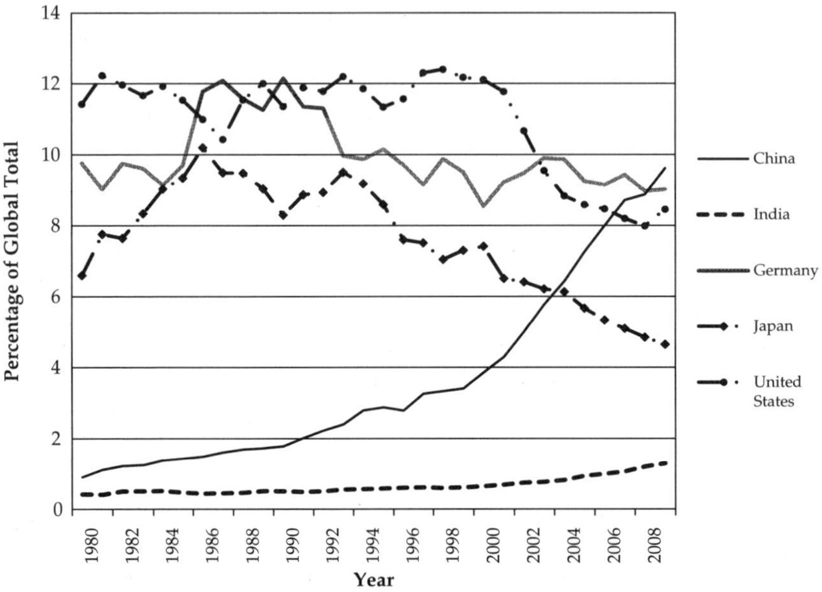

FIGURE 5.1 Rising shares of China and India in world's merchandise exports, 1980–2008

SOURCE: Created by author from data in UNCTAD international trade data, available at http://unctadstat.unctad.org/ReportFolders/reportFolders.aspx?sCS_referer=&sCS_ChosenLang=en. Accessed December 5, 2010.

Both countries have also been increasing their service exports. India, in particular, has been rapidly increasing its service exports since 1996. These now account for 3.5 percent of the world's total. Although the total remains lower than China's, the gap is swiftly closing (Figure 5.2). The driving force has been India's exports of computer and information services, and India's exports in 2008 were almost eight times China's.[2] Initially, India entered at the low end of this market, primarily with the establishment of technology-related call centers. However, it swiftly expanded to include higher-end services, such as software development, animation, and new information-technology tools and applications. Many service workers in knowledge-intensive industries that can be operated remotely worry that their jobs may be outsourced to India. Both countries can be expected to continue to make significant inroads into the service export market as they invest in knowledge workers and provide more information-enabled service exports.

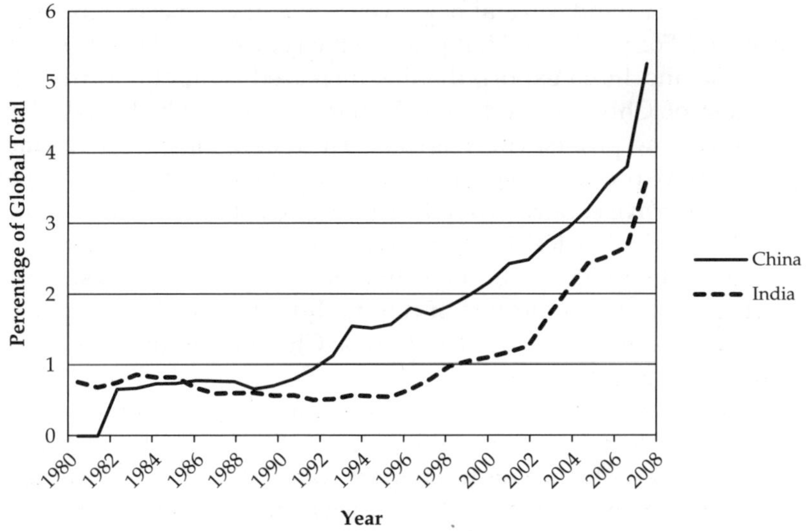

FIGURE 5.2 Rising share of China and India in commercial service exports, 1980–2008

SOURCE: Created by author from data in UNCTAD international trade data, available at http://unctadstat.unctad.org/ReportFolders/reportFolders.aspx?sCS_referer=&sCS_ChosenLang=en. Accessed December 5, 2010.

This swift increase in trade from both countries has both positive and negative impacts on others in the global system. On the positive side, increased manufactured exports from China result in lower-priced manufactured goods for consumers abroad. Given the very large expansion and competitiveness of manufactured exports from China, their low prices have helped keep global inflation low. For exporters of commodities, this also means windfalls from higher commodity prices (see Figure 6.1 in Chapter 6), which rose quickly from 2003 until the global crisis in 2008. This escalation was caused by increased demand from China and India, largely because both countries are poor in per capita resources.[3] For exporters of components and high-technology goods and services imported by China and India, the rapidly growing markets of these nations are an additional benefit. More than 60 percent of China's merchandise imports are manufactured products. These are mostly capital goods and components. Only slightly more than one-third of India's imports are manufactured products. Both countries have also become important markets for services, and they import more commercial services than they export.

On the other hand, several negative results have emerged as causes for concern. For producers that provide the type of goods and services that China and India export, there is increased competition from the lower cost of Chinese goods and Indian services, which may drive down prices and profits. This has caused a "hollowing out" of the most labor-intensive production in developed countries, and negative impact on labor-intensive exports from developing countries has been significant.[4] One of the hardest-hit sectors has been textile exports, particularly due to the removal of quotas that had restrained Chinese textile imports in 2005. For importers of commodities (especially energy), the price increases that result from additional Chinese and Indian demand equate to higher costs.[5]

The very swift expansion of China into different export markets can be seen in Table 5.1. Because both level of development and geography have some influence on trade (particularly the strong intra-Asian production networks), the world has been divided into four import markets: developed economies (excluding Japan), developed Asian economies (Japan, Hong Kong, Korea, Singapore, and Taiwan), Asian developing economies, and all other developing economies.

Between 1995 and 2009, the greatest expansion of Chinese market share occurred in other developing economies markets, where it increased 10.3 percentage points of their total imports. The second largest increase was in developed East Asian economy markets (10.2 percentage points), followed by developing Asia (8.6 percentage points), and lastly, developed economies excluding Japan (7.5 percentage points). This indicates that, overall, the competition from China is particularly strong in products imported by developing economies. However, the largest total share of any of the regional markets, at 23.6 percent, is developed Asia, reflecting the importance of the Asian production networks.[6]

In terms of specific sectors, China's greatest share in all four markets is in miscellaneous manufactured products (where its share of the region's imports of that category is an impressive 53 percent in developed Asia and 28 percent in developed economies). However, the category in which China has been expanding its share the fastest over this 15-year period is machinery and transport equipment.[7] The change in its share in other developing economies is a remarkable 1,500 percent, followed by 1,200 percent in developing Asia, 680 percent in developed economies, and "only" 280 percent in developed Asia. (But its share there started the highest and ended the highest among the four regions, at 33 percent of the imports of that category.)

TABLE 5.1 Changing share in world imports from China and India divided by region, 1995–2009

SITC	DEVELOPED			DEVELOPED ASIA			DEVELOPING ASIA			OTHER DEVELOPING		
Disaggregation of Imports from China	1995	2009	% Change	1995	2009	% Change	1995	2009	% Change	1995	2009	% Change
1+0: Food, beverages, & tobacco	1.1	2.8	146.8	18.5	22.3	20.4	7.1	8.4	18.5	1.3	4.1	207.9
2+4: Materials (excluding fuels) oils, & fats	1.5	3.2	113.9	14.1	9.6	–31.9	2.3	1.6	–29.5	0.8	2.4	220.4
3: Mineral fuels, lubricants, and related materials	1.4	0.1	–91.3	4.2	2.8	–35.1	1.8	1.1	–41.4	0.7	0.3	–51.9
5: Chemicals and related products	1.1	2.7	151.9	5.3	12.0	124.7	2.7	7.5	179.8	1.0	6.4	517.0
6: Manufactured goods classified chiefly by material	2.0	9.9	390.5	15.9	27.5	73.4	4.2	12.8	207.6	2.0	14.5	638.0
7: Machinery and transport equipment	1.8	14.2	680.2	8.5	32.8	283.5	1.3	17.3	1216.7	1.1	17.0	1498.2
8: Miscellaneous manufactured articles	11.3	27.5	143.2	41.0	52.6	28.4	5.0	17.4	249.8	4.2	25.3	497.5
9: Commodities and transactions not elsewhere classified	0.6	2.2	247.4	2.6	5.6	112.9	1.4	7.6	443.0	0.2	4.4	2175.7
Total China	**2.9**	**10.4**	**258.6**	**13.4**	**23.6**	**76.1**	**2.3**	**10.9**	**356.1**	**1.4**	**11.7**	**730.0**
Total India	**0.6**	**0.9**	**50.0**	**0.8**	**1.4**	**75.0**	**1.2**	**2.8**	**124.4**	**0.6**	**1.8**	**212.1**

SOURCE: Created by author from trade data in UNCTAD Comtrade database.

NOTES: SITC = Standard International Trade Classification. World imports divided into four regions: Developed is developed countries minus Japan; Developed Asia is Japan, Hong Kong, Korea, Singapore, and Taiwan; Developing Asia includes East, Southeast, South, and West Asia. Other developing countries are developing countries in the rest of the world excluding those in Asia.

Table 5.2 shows the top 10 product groups[8] in which China has a revealed comparative advantage (RCA)[9] in 1995 versus 2009. Five of the ten groups in 1995 still appear, although with lower RCA, among the top ten in 2009: travel goods, apparel, footwear, yarn, and miscellaneous manufactured products—all labor-intensive manufactured products. The other five product groups, which were natural resource or raw industrial commodities (coal, animal/vegetable materials, inorganic chemicals, crude fertilizers, and fish), drop out of the top ten by 2009. Instead, two high-technology categories (office machines and computers and telecommunications and sound recording equipment) and three other labor-intensive manufactured products (furniture, prefabricated buildings, and metal manufactures) replace them. This shows the speedy movement out of natural resource–based exports into labor- and technology-intensive manufactures.

India's share in the different markets of the world increased less than 1 percentage point on average across the four markets. The largest increase was in developing economies (1.6 percentage points in Asian

TABLE 5.2 China's revealed comparative advantage (RCA), 1995 versus 2009

Product Groups	RCA
1995 (SITC two-digit level of disaggregation)	
Travel goods, handbags, etc.	6.34
Articles of apparel and clothing accessories	4.81
Footwear	4.68
Textile yarn and related products	2.85
Coal, coke, and briquettes	2.58
Crude animal and vegetable materials	2.37
Inorganic chemicals	2.36
Crude fertilizers other than division 56 and crude minerals	2.24
Miscellaneous manufactured articles	2.23
Fish, crustaceans, mollusks, and preparations thereof	1.99
2009	
Travel goods, handbags, etc.	3.90
Footwear	3.45
Office machines and automatic data processing machines	3.25
Articles of apparel and clothing accessories	3.19
Telecommunication and sound recording apparatus	2.76
Textile yarn and related products	2.72
Furniture and parts thereof	2.58
Prefabricated buildings, sanitary, heating, and lighting fixtures	2.31
Manufactures of metal	1.57
Miscellaneous manufactured articles	1.54

SOURCE: Created by author from trade data in UNCTAD Comtrade database.

developing economies and 1.2 percentage points in other developing economies; bottom line of Table 5.1).[10] In India's case, there has not been any major change in the sophistication of its exports over time at the broad two-digit SITC level of disaggregation (Table 5.3).[11] Six of the top ten products with the highest RCA in 1995 were still among the top ten in 2009. The new ones in the top ten are still natural resource based or labor intensive.

Moving Up the Technology Ladder

It was generally thought that developing countries compete only through natural resource–based or labor-intensive and low-technology products. However, a more detailed analysis of the exports of China and India shows that they are moving up the technology ladder quite quickly, particularly China. When exports are classified according to technology intensity, a recent study found that among products in which China has a revealed comparative advantage, the share of products with

TABLE 5.3 India's revealed comparative advantage (RCA), 1995 versus 2009

Product Groups	RCA
1995 (SITC two-digit level of disaggregation)	
Nonmetallic mineral manufactures	7.64
Feedstuff for animals (excluding unmilled cereals)	5.47
Coffee, tea, cocoa, spices, and manufactures thereof	4.69
Cereals and cereal preparations	4.46
Textile yarn and related products	4.24
Leather, leather manufactures, and dressed fur skins	4.05
Articles of apparel and clothing accessories	3.91
Fish, crustaceans, mollusks, and preparations thereof	3.33
Travel goods, handbags, etc.	3.25
Crude fertilizers other than division 56 and crude minerals	3.02
2009	
Coin (other than gold coin), not being legal tender	8.04
Nonmetallic mineral manufactures	5.98
Textile fibers and their wastes	3.82
Crude fertilizers other than division 56 and crude minerals	3.06
Textile yarn and related products	2.94
Articles of apparel and clothing accessories	2.54
Miscellaneous manufactured articles	2.51
Leather, leather manufactures, and dressed fur skins	2.29
Feedstuff for animals (excluding unmilled cereals)	2.29
Metalliferous ores and metal scrap	2.17

SOURCE: Created by author from trade data in UNCTAD Comtrade database.

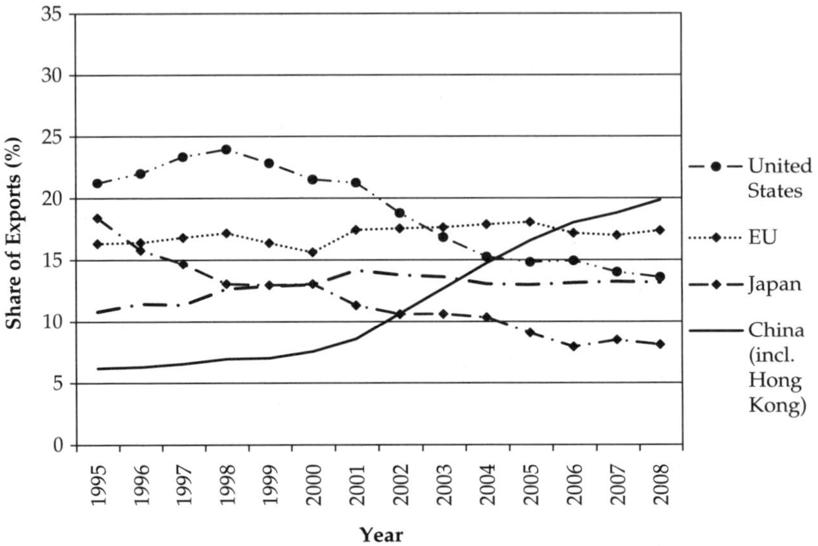

FIGURE 5.3 Share of global high technology exports by region/country, 1995–2008

SOURCE: Created by author from Excel files for Figure O-30 in National Science Board. 2010. *Science and engineering indicators 2010*. Arlington, Va.: National Science Foundation (NSB 10-01). Overview chapter.

higher technology intensity grew significantly between 1984 and 2006.[12] The same was true for products in which India has a revealed comparative advantage, although the increase in the share of higher-technology products was not as high as in China.[13] Another study found that in the key main developed markets—the United States, the European Union, and Japan—the biggest increases in market share of imports from China between 1990 and 2000 was in labor-intensive products, but between 2000 and 2007, it was in high-technology products. In the high-technology categories that consisted mainly of electronics and transport, the changes in market share were very large. In the United States, it was 24 percent, in Japan 19 percent, and in the European Union 13 percent. The changes in market share for India were all less than 1 percentage point in all technology categories in the three markets. The small changes for India are consistent with the more general findings reported in Table 5.1.[14]

As can be appreciated from Figure 5.3, China has rapidly become the largest exporter of high-technology products in the world. This category includes aerospace, scientific instruments, and information technology (IT). China's lead in high technology is based largely on its exports of IT products, including data processing and telecommunications equipment. In this subcategory of high-technology products, China is not only the largest exporter but also the largest producer in the world.[15] This has been possible due to its strategy of attracting foreign companies to produce in China. But China is also developing capability in its own companies, which are becoming globally competitive, as will be seen in the section on Growing Foreign Direct Investment (FDI). Here it is worth noting that both countries have taken advantage of the IT wave, although China has done this primarily in the production and export of hardware, whereas India has done it mostly in the export of information-enabled services.

Information and Communications Technology (ICT)

For some time, China has shown strength in hardware production, and it is now working to expand its software market. It is already the largest exporter of ICT products in the world, and it has developed a strong innovation capability in electronics (see Chapter 4). The ICT service sector in China is actually larger than India's in total size, but it is not very export oriented, so it is not known as well on world markets. India's situation is the opposite of China's: it has strong capability in software and is now attempting to expand its hardware capability. Although India still has a small share of the global market in IT-enabled services, it has become a major hub among developing countries. Also, its large IT service companies, such as Infosys, Tata Consulting Services, and WIPRO, are going global.[16]

Automobiles and Auto Parts

Another sector creating additional competition from China and India is automobiles and auto parts. In 2009, China became both the world's largest automobile producer (surpassing Japan) and largest consumer (surpassing the United States). Because of very large growth in domestic demand for cars, foreign firms have not been very interested in exporting cars to foreign markets, which they can supply from production facilities in other countries.[17] However, Chinese car producers have been eyeing foreign markets and have begun exporting. Most of these exports have been to other developing countries; exporting to developed markets has proven difficult because of higher quality and safety standards. Chinese auto-parts producers, for their part, have succeeded in penetrating foreign markets in both developing and developed nations. In 2008, the United States imported $5.5 billion in auto parts from China, thus illustrating its emerging and increasingly important presence in the global market.[18]

India has also become an exporter of cars and trucks to developing countries and auto parts to both developing and developed countries. Moreover, since its purchase of Jaguar and Rover in 2008, Indian-owned Tata is exporting kits to make the popular MG roadster from India for assembly in the United Kingdom. In addition, Tata has announced that it will start exporting its low-cost Nano. Currently, however, domestic demand is very strong, with waiting lists in excess of one year. The feasibility of exportation is best viewed as a long-term goal.

Global Economic Restructuring

Major global economic restructuring is in process as a result of the entry of new players into world export markets as well as two major technological changes. The reduction in transportation and communication costs combined with the digitization of information has led to the physical "unbundling" of production. Because of lower transaction and transportation costs, different components of a final product are now often manufactured in several different countries.[19] The product may then be assembled into its completed form in yet another country and then distributed worldwide. The same is true for some services. The consequence of such unbundling is that to get products or services to market, it has become increasingly important to tap into global supply chains and distribution systems. To some extent, even research and development is being commoditized, as it is now outsourced to specialized centers in places like India and China.

It is helpful to distinguish between the two types of unbundling because they have different trajectories and implications.[20] The first involves the end of the need to produce goods close to their consumers. For centuries, production has attempted to move away from this logistical requirement, but the process has been accelerated in the last four decades by the rapid decline in transportation costs, particularly with the widespread use of containers and bulk carriers. Much manufacturing production, especially of more standardized and labor-intensive goods, is now being transferred to developing countries with lower labor costs, particularly China.

The second type of unbundling is characterized by the end of the need to perform services near the user of those services. This has been made possible by the swiftly decreasing cost of telecommunications and the possibility of codifying and digitizing tasks. Many service tasks, including those that support manufacturing, are now being transferred to countries with lower knowledge-service labor costs, such as India and, more recently, China.[21]

Growing Export-Oriented Labor Force

As the previously inward-oriented economies of China, India, the former Soviet Union, and other developing countries have increased their participation in the international trading system, the global labor force has effectively quadrupled between 1980 and 2008.[22] This has had strong implications for developed as well as developing countries. Developed countries are now facing competition from much lower cost workers, which places pressure on their labor-intensive industries. This growth in the global labor force has increased the marginal productivity of capital. As a result, the share of profits in value added has increased, but that of labor has decreased.[23] The principal beneficiaries of this globalization and rebalancing of relative wages are the multinational corporations, which are the most effective agents at intermediating and taking advantage of differences in global factor prices.

The implication of these developments is that there are greater opportunities for countries to position themselves to take advantage of the unbundling. China has been the major beneficiary of the first type of unbundling, as it is becoming the world's manufacturing workshop. India, on the other hand, has significantly capitalized on the second type of unbundling, thanks to its critical mass of higher-educated, English-speaking technicians, engineers, and scientists. Other economies with a critical mass of highly skilled workers, such as the Philippines, Vietnam, and the former Soviet republics, along with some of the English-speaking Caribbean island economies, are also benefiting from the digital trade made possible by this second unbundling. Most other developing countries without critical mass in skills, English language, or advanced telecommunications and other physical infrastructure (including most of Latin America) have not benefited as much and are having trouble competing.

The first unbundling is more in keeping with the expectations of the traditional trade and product cycle theory, which postulated that labor-intensive manufacturing would move to labor-abundant countries.

Under this theory, it was also expected that developed countries would stay ahead by moving into more skill- and technology-intensive sectors. The second unbundling is a newer phenomenon not foreseen by traditional trade theory. Until the development of advances in information technology, it was not anticipated that services could be traded virtually.

Various economists, including Alan Blinder (2006) and Gene Grossman et al. (2006), are beginning to focus on this phenomenon. Blinder has even gone so far as to call off-shoring the third industrial revolution. Off-shoring's most significant characteristic is that the dividing line between jobs that can be outsourced versus those that cannot is unrelated to skills. Many highly skilled and knowledge-intensive jobs can now be outsourced. Blinder further estimates that the total number of U.S. jobs that are potential candidates for off-shoring range from 30 to 40 million out of a U.S. labor force of 160 million.[24] The challenge of off-shoring service jobs is an important new consideration not anticipated by economic policy in developed economies. It is no longer sufficient for developed countries to invest in higher education to stay ahead. Instead, they will need to focus on exploiting advantages in nontradable services, transforming their educational systems to prepare workers for those jobs, strengthening innovation and creativity, and enacting adequate trade-adjustment mechanisms.[25]

It is not clear how well the world will handle the high adjustment costs of the rapid entry of China and India into the global trading system. Both have large labor forces working at wages that are a fraction of those prevailing in developed economies. As both countries educate their workers and increase their technological capability, they will increase their competitiveness and continue to expand their exports of goods and services. Even though there is not perfect labor mobility across countries, a global rebalancing of wages between developing countries like China and India and those in developed countries is occurring through trade.[26] This move toward convergence of wages is accelerated by the continued high unemployment in developed countries resulting from the financial crisis versus the rising wages in developing countries. The latest global wage report issued by the International Labor Office confirms this trend.[27] However, even if trade continues to expand significantly, it will take a very long time to arrive at wage convergence because both China and India still have hundreds of millions of underemployed workers in low-productivity agriculture, industry, and service jobs who can be brought into export industries at very low costs.

The growing populations of these two countries create correspondingly large labor forces. China's economically active population in 1980 was already as large as that of the developed countries combined (27 percent). Because population growth in developed countries has fallen, the share of their populations in total world population is decreasing. In Japan and some European countries, the absolute size of their populations is shrinking. This is not the case in China, however. In spite of the one-child policy instituted in 1979, the economically active population continues to grow. This growth is slower than for the world as a whole, however, so China's share of the world's economically active population has been declining slightly. In 2008, it fell to 25 percent, while that of developed countries fell to 19 percent because of their much lower population growth rates. In 2007, the economically active population of China was 796 million, with an average educational attainment level in 2000 of 6.4 years.

India, on the other hand, has an economically active population that has been steadily growing at the same level as the world average, which has allowed it to maintain its global share of 14 percent. By 2020, it will increase its share slightly to 15 percent (almost equaling the combined share of developed countries, which will fall to 17 percent), and China will continue to decline to 22 percent. Other developing countries will increase their combined share from 32 percent in 1980 to 45 percent in 2020 because of their much higher than world average population growth rates.

India has an economically active population of 438 million,[28] but the average educational attainment level for the adult population in 2000 was only 5.1 years. More than 70 percent of India's labor force is still in the traditional nonformal sector, living at or near subsistence levels. The share of the labor force in the modern sector (roughly defined as organizations with more than 10 workers) is a mere 11 percent, two-thirds of whom work for the government at the federal, state, or municipal level.[29] Another 15 to 20 percent work in small-scale industry. The small share of the work force employed in the modern sector is illustrated by the fact that in 2005, 76 percent of the Indian population earned less than $2 PPP a day.[30] The average cost of labor in India is even lower than in China, but this is because India has not developed through a labor-intensive export strategy. Instead, the recent acceleration of its growth has been based largely on more education-intensive service exports (such as software and medical transcription) and skill-intensive manufactured exports (such as pharmaceuticals and auto parts). Its success in these areas is due to early investments in elite quality higher education.

The average cost of labor for the manufacturing sector in China is only 3 percent that of the U.S. worker. The average cost of labor in India is even less. Although labor costs can be expected to rise gradually over time, both countries still retain large numbers of underemployed workers in agricultural jobs that can be transitioned into export-oriented industries. As they educate these workers and as the countries improve their technological capabilities, they will be putting greater pressure on the global system through exports of goods and services. This will continue to put downward pressure on wages in developed countries not only for low-skilled workers but also increasingly for high-skilled knowledge workers. India and China are moving up the technology ladder in manufactured goods while also competing in high-skill, knowledge-intensive service areas, where the work can be done at a distance through the Internet.

From China's Trade Surpluses to Global Imbalances

There is a strong interdependence globally among trade imbalances, current account surpluses, exchange rates, and concerns about the U.S. dollar as the international reserve currency. Moreover, as discussed in Chapter 2, these issues are points of tension that reflect shifts in the global distribution of economic power.

Current Account Surpluses

As a result of its increased ability to compete, China has been running a trade surplus that has grown from $35 billion in 2002 to $436 billion in 2008. In 2009, it fell to $297 billion because of the contraction in imports by the rest of the world that resulted from the global economic crisis.[31] This surplus increased every year, from 1.3 percent of China's GDP in 2001 to 10.6 percent in 2006, before decreasing to 9.6 percent in 2008 with the beginning of the world economic crisis and then to 6.0 percent in 2009. The IMF estimates it will be 5.2 percent in 2010 and then rise again every year to 7.8 by 2015.[32]

In the U.S. Congress, it is often argued that the nation's large trade deficits are due to China's surpluses.[33] However, the situation is much more complex. The trade deficit in the United States started in the early

1990s and rapidly increased through 2006, while a substantial Chinese surplus did not emerge until the late 1990s. See Figure 5.4 for the current account balances of the main countries and regions of the world, including IMF projections through 2015. Before 2004, the countries and regions with large current account surpluses that counterbalanced the U.S. deficit were Japan, the NIAEs, and the oil exporters in the Middle East. Germany also had a surplus after 2002, which grew steadily from 2004 to 2008, surpassing even Japan's.

China's trade surpluses are not the sole cause of U.S. deficits, but the two are closely related. China's trade surplus with the United States increased steadily from $69 billion in 1999 to $268 billion in 2008, before decreasing slightly to $227 billion in 2009 as a result of the contraction in U.S. imports following the global economic crisis. China's share of the U.S. total trade deficit has increased from just 21 percent in 2000 to 70 percent in 2009. This is one of the reasons there is so much concern about China's trade policies in the United States.

Global Imbalances and Symbiotic Interdependence

China's large surpluses drove its international reserves to a record $2.3 trillion at the end of 2009, estimated to rise to $2.7 trillion by the end of 2010.[34] This is more than twice the second largest foreign exchange reserves, held by Japan.[35] China uses these reserves to buy U.S. Treasury bonds and other securities. In July 2010, China and Hong Kong were estimated to hold $982 billion in U.S. Treasury securities, which makes China the largest foreign creditor of the U.S. government. This was approximately one-quarter of all foreign-owned U.S. publicly held Treasuries, or about 12 percent of the total of $7.5 trillion publicly held U.S. Treasury securities.[36] The amount held by China could actually be double if purchases of bonds of Fannie Mae and Freddie Mac and unregistered purchases of Treasuries through Caribbean tax havens and the London currency market were taken into account.[37] This does not include Chinese purchases of private U.S. bonds or corporate equities.

In view of the foregoing, it is clear that there is a strong interdependence among China's large trade surpluses and foreign exchange reserves, purchases of U.S. Treasury bonds and securities, China's exchange rate, and the U.S. interest rate.[38] Chinese purchases of U.S. Treasury bonds and other securities help China keep its currency from appreciating and therefore make its exports more competitive. Investing in U.S. Treasuries and securities also helps finance the U.S. trade

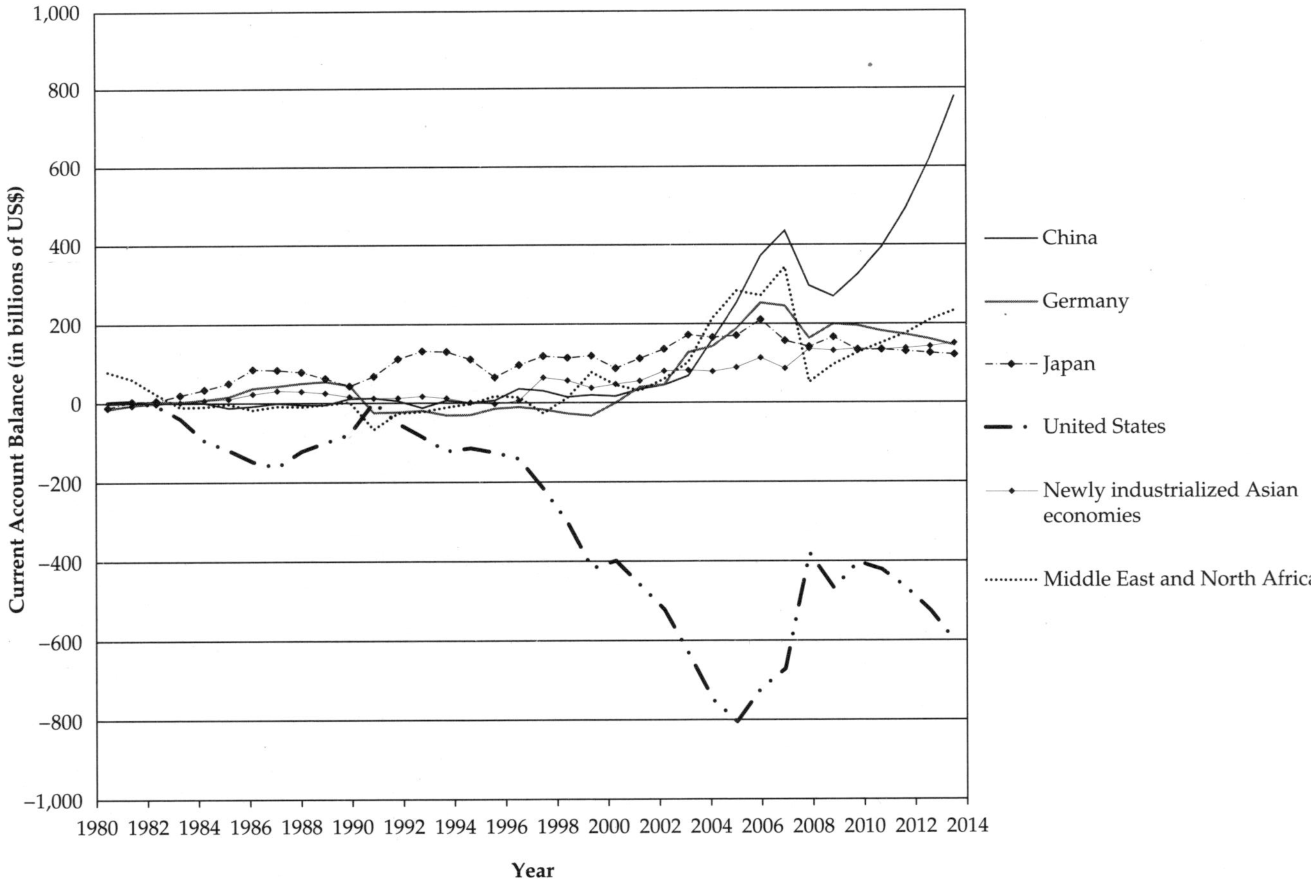

FIGURE 5.4 Current account balances and projection, 1980–2014

SOURCE: Created by author with data from IMF. IMF data from IMF data mapper, available at http://www.imf.org/external/datamapper/index.php. Accessed November 28, 2010.

and fiscal deficits and keep interest rates low. This has allowed U.S. consumption to exceed its savings and to continue running large trade deficits with China—a complex symbiotic relationship.

A key concern among some U.S. policy makers is that China may use its large holdings of U.S. securities, particularly its Treasury assets, as a political tool against the United States.[39] Rapid disinvestment of U.S. Treasuries could force an increase in interest rates as well as a faster depreciation of the dollar. It could also result in increased inflation in the medium term. However, most analysts do not expect such drastic actions. If China were to suddenly sell a significant amount of its U.S. Treasury securities, their value on global markets would be reduced, thus reducing the value of China's remaining holdings. Further, there would also be a depreciation of the dollar, which would impact remaining U.S.-denominated assets held by China. The rise in interest rates would reduce growth in the United States and other countries, inevitably leading to a reduction of demand for Chinese exports. This shows the complex interdependence between China and the United States and is one important reason both countries carefully manage these sensitive issues.

China is concerned by the current weakness of the U.S. economy and the possible increase of anti-Chinese sentiment because of its rapid rise in the global economy. From a narrower financial perspective, it is worried that its large holdings of U.S. Treasuries are poor investments, as they pay low interest rates and lose value as the dollar depreciates. Many economists agree.[40]

To mitigate such problems, China is seeking to diversify its foreign exchange reserves. In September 2007, it created the China Investment Corporation (CIC), financed with $200 billion from its foreign exchange reserves, with an expectation that it will receive additional funding if it shows productive financial returns. The CIC's stated objectives are to improve the rate of return on China's large foreign exchange reserves and to absorb some of China's excess liquidity. It has already invested the bulk of its money in strengthening domestic financial institutions in China. However, it has made large foreign acquisitions. The most visible of these was the purchase of a 9.9 percent share of the U.S. financial firm Morgan Stanley for $5 billion in December 2007 to help the struggling corporation overcome a balance sheet weakened by the write-off of billions of dollars in losses on bad subprime loans.[41]

The creation of the CIC has caused some concerns in the United States that have been brought to the attention of Congress. These include the adverse effects of its investment activities on the U.S. financial markets and economy, compromised national security, and the fear that China may use the CIC to pursue geopolitical objectives.[42] China has pledged not to use the CIC to harm the United States, but there have been calls for greater oversight and regulation of the activities of the CIC and other Sovereign Wealth Funds (SWF). These include calls for the IMF and World Bank to develop guidelines for SWFs. Moreover, some U.S. experts argue that Congress should review its current laws and regulations and possibly implement special restrictions on proposed investments by SWFs. These would include special reporting requirements, limits on ownership, and restrictions on equity investments in U.S. companies.[43]

The Exchange Rate

China's very quick export expansion since 2000 is also related to its exchange-rate policy. The Chinese renminbi (RMB) was pegged to the dollar until 2005. The value of the renminbi stayed consistent at 8.24 RMB to the dollar from 1994 until July 21, 2005. This includes the period during the Asian financial crisis of 1997 when China held the value of the RMB stable despite external pressures for its devaluation. China was subsequently praised for keeping its currency consistent because this helped speed the Asian recovery.

Since 2004, the United States has pressured China to revalue, particularly as both the U.S. trade deficit with China and China's overall current account surplus (Figure 5.4) have steadily grown. In July 2005, China announced it would adjust its currency in line with a basket of currencies;[44] it revalued the RMB against the dollar by 2.1 percent and gradually let the value of the RMB rise. From 2005 to 2008, roughly until the beginning of the 2008 crisis, the RMB appreciated against the dollar. However, when the financial crisis hit in 2008, China stopped appreciating its currency. The regions most negatively affected by the slow-moving renminbi are the United States and the European Union, and their exporters are feeling the competitive pressure the most.

When the European Union confronted China with this issue at a November 2009 economic summit, President Hu Jintao replied that China reserved the right to manage its own currency as it saw fit. China has been particularly concerned to defend the renminbi against foreign investors speculating on its appreciation. In the first half of 2010, the euro depreciated against the other main currencies because many European banks were exposed to fear of a default by Greece. This has helped countries in the euro zone gain some competitiveness. On the other hand, it is making China more reluctant to appreciate its currency against the dollar because the euro's depreciation against the dollar is reducing China's competitiveness against euro markets.[45]

The Peterson Institute, a private Washington think tank specializing in international trade issues, has long argued that China's currency is undervalued. Fred Bergsten, its president, has argued that in the short run the renminbi will have to appreciate not only with respect to the dollar but also against the euro and the yen. In the medium and longer run, there will need to be something approaching freely floating exchange rates. However, the financial imbalances are related not just to the exchange rate but also to structural imbalance.

Here there is some relevant historical experience worth remembering. At the beginning of the 1980s, Japan was running large surpluses with the United States, and there were very strong concerns that Japan was putting too much pressure on U.S. jobs and industries. The United States, with the help of Germany and France—through what came to be known as the Plaza Accord—met with Japan and agreed to depreciate the dollar against the yen. The dollar fell by 51 percent against the yen from 1985 to 1987.[46] The intervention helped reduce the U.S. deficit with European countries but not with Japan, which increased its productivity. A relevant lesson for the United States is that exchange-rate realignment alone may not be sufficient to reduce a trade deficit.[47] It also requires reducing consumption in the deficit countries like the United States and increasing consumption in the surplus countries like China.

In the United States, both private and government savings have been negative, so exports have been lower than imports. In China, private net savings are positive, so exports were larger than imports to the tune of 10 percent of GDP in 2007. In the United States, although private saving has begun to increase as households rebuild savings in response to the loss of wealth caused by the financial crisis, the government deficit increased from less than 2 percent of GDP in 2006 to more than 10 percent of GDP in 2009 and 2010. It is expected to run about 4 percent of GDP through 2019.[48]

Challenges to the Dollar as the Principal Global Reserve Currency

The reserve currency is tied to global power. During the nineteenth century, when Britain was globally dominant, the pound sterling was the most common medium of international exchange. It was the de facto major reserve currency, although the German mark and the French franc also served as less important reserve currencies. Britain and the other major countries were on the gold standard, meaning that their currencies were backed by gold at a predetermined price.

After World War II at the Bretton Woods meeting, it was decided to make the U.S. dollar the new international reserve currency. All currencies were then pegged to the dollar at fixed exchange rates.[49] This gave the United States an important role in international finance.

The United States ran large current account surpluses as European countries were using U.S. imports to rebuild their war-torn economies. However, to serve as a reserve currency, the United States had to run current account deficits to provide dollars to increase the liquidity of the international system. The United States also realized that the limited balance of payments funding provided through the IMF and the lending for reconstruction provided by the World Bank were insufficient for the reconstruction of Europe. Therefore, it put together the Marshall Plan, which transferred $17 billion as grants rather than loans toward the reconstruction effort to 16 European countries between 1948 and 1954. By 1950, the United States started to run current account deficits.

Being the world's reserve currency created a problem for the United States that has yet to be solved. To provide liquidity for the global system, the United States needs to run a current account deficit. However, if the United States continuously runs a current account deficit, the countries holding the U.S. dollar as the reserve currency may begin to lose confidence in its value.[50]

By the mid-1960s, Japan and the European Economic Community had recovered and had higher levels of growth, trade, and reserves than the United States. The United States was playing the role of central banker to the world and injecting liquidity through its current account deficits. This arrangement worked as long as other countries had confidence in the dollar, relied on the United States for defense against the Soviet Union, and generally agreed with U.S. foreign policy. However, by the early 1970s, fear of the Soviet Union started to decline as the policy of détente was appearing to work. In addition, many countries opposed the U.S. war in Vietnam. Economic tensions between the former allies rose, and there was speculation against the U.S. dollar because of the large fiscal deficits resulting from President Johnson's Great Society programs and large trade deficits because of the escalating costs of the Vietnam War.

The United States began to lose gold rapidly as other countries asked to have their dollars converted to it. In August 1971, President Nixon unilaterally terminated conversion into gold.[51] In December 1971, through the Smithsonian Agreement, the main developed countries agreed to devalue the dollar from $35 to $38 per ounce of gold and to adjust exchange rates to the dollar with 2.25 percent trading bands. However, gold prices rose to more than $70 per ounce in 1972, and countries began abandoning the pegged exchange rates. By March 1972, most countries had switched to floating exchange rates, thus bringing the Bretton Woods monetary system to an end. Since then, the U.S. dollar has continued to be the world's main reserve currency but without the gold convertibility obligation. In 2000, the dollar accounted for roughly 70 percent of global reserves. By 2008, this had fallen to 62 percent.[52]

There are two primary concerns associated with maintaining the dollar as the principal global reserve currency. First, by having the reserve currency, the United States has benefited from seigniorage (profit from the difference of the cost of printing money and the value of the money). Estimates are that in 2007 there were $829 billion in circulation and that more than half were being held abroad as currency.[53] This implies that the United States has benefited from printing its money and exchanging it for foreign goods without having to provide any tangible product in return (beyond the cost of printing). Although this is true of the operations of all central banks, it is of particular concern with respect to the United States because of the dollar's supremacy in both international and domestic markets. The United States also saves by not having to pay any fees for currency conversions because the loans are denominated in dollars.

The second, more important concern is that the United States has become a major net world borrower, and the bulk of its debt is denominated in U.S. dollars. As a result, if the dollar loses value, those who have loaned money or purchased other assets denominated in dollars lose on the value of their investment when they convert it back to their own currency. Their loss is in proportion to the depreciation of the dollar. This is of special concern to the Chinese because they are the world's largest holders of U.S. Treasury bonds. Currently, these bonds yield a very low interest rate, which makes them a poor investment because of the exchange risk. Traditionally, people have chosen to invest in Treasury bonds because they were presumed to be one of the soundest investments available, but that assumption is starting to change.

In addition, it is estimated that up to 70 percent of China's foreign exchange reserves are denominated in U.S. dollars.[54]

Reflecting these worries, in March 2009, the governor of the People's Bank of China, Zhou Xiaochuan, called for the replacement of the U.S. dollar as the international reserve currency with a new global system controlled by the International Monetary Fund.[55] He called attention to the United States' continuing fiscal and trade deficits and the prospect of their increasing. He was also concerned that the United States might inflate its way out of its international obligations. He proposed that the IMF take a more active role in controlling U.S. deficits and use Special Drawing Rights (SDRs) as the global reserve currency.[56]

The Chinese government had developed various currency swap arrangements in RMBs for other currencies. It is also trying to negotiate contracts in RMBs rather than in dollars. This has included trade deals and currency swaps in RMBs with several countries, including Brazil, Russia, Malaysia, and other ASEAN countries. However, this still accounts for less than 1 percent of its trade. In addition, for the RMB to become an international reserve currency, it needs to have full convertibility, which is something the Chinese government is not ready to do. Furthermore, the idea of switching to the SDR as the new global reserve currency was not endorsed by the G-20.[57] In any event, reserve currencies are not dictated by governments but rather evolve from market transactions. Although the U.S. dollar is losing some power as the principal reserve currency, it will take a long time for markets to switch because of the lack of good alternatives. The most viable alternative until recently was the euro, but the crisis of that currency in 2010 has greatly dimmed that option.

These worries about the dollar as the reserve currency have also been exacerbated by the program launched by the U.S. Federal Reserve to buy long-term bonds toward the end of 2010. In addition, the extension of the Bush tax cuts for 2011 and 2012 imply greater fiscal deficits that will need to be financed. With growing U.S. fiscal deficits and the extra liquidity that the U.S. Federal Reserve has been pumping into the economy, many foreign investors fear that there will be a greater risk of inflation in the future. If U.S. inflation rates were to exceed those of the rest of the world, the dollar would further depreciate, thereby causing greater losses for holders of dollar-denominated assets.

The IMF was supposed to monitor flexible exchange rates as well as country foreign debt ratios, and it does hold periodic meetings with China and the United States, but in practice, the Fund has no power to discipline either. The United States became a net debtor again in 1986.[58] Its major net creditor is China, which has accumulated $2.4 trillion in reserves. Despite achieving an unfair advantage by manipulating its exchange rate, China has not been disciplined by the IMF. Part of the problem is that the IMF has no leverage against a country running a surplus that does not need to borrow from it. It can only impose conditionality when countries want to borrow from it.

Growing Foreign Direct Investment (FDI)

Attracting FDI Because of Their Lower Production Costs and Expanding Markets

It was previously thought that developing markets were marginally attractive compared to those of developed nations as markets. However, China and India are becoming magnets not only for trade but also for foreign investment. In the current recession, their markets have become critical for global growth and recovery. This increased importance has forced multinational companies (MNCs) to develop strategies specific to China and India. Multinational companies are moving key production and service components to these countries, including the relocation of corporate headquarters as well as significant portions of their R&D. This increased focus and reliance on these previously marginalized economies illustrates the changing landscape of global economic power.

Foreign direct investment into China and India is attractive both to the foreign investor and to the host country. Both the rapidly growing domestic markets of these countries as well as their low-cost production advantages for exporting to third markets are attractive to foreign investors. From the host-country perspective, China and India gain access to foreign technology and management as well as to foreign markets through the distribution networks of the foreign firms. However, there is concern from the home countries of the FDI as well as from other potential host countries that China and India may be siphoning off investments that otherwise would have created jobs in their economies.

To date, China has been more attractive than India because it has maintained a consistent rate of growth of about 9–10 percent per year for the last 30 years. Although the average per capita income in 2008 was just $6,010 in PPP terms, the average per capita income of the richest 10 percent of the population (132 million people) was $18,865. China enjoys, therefore, a richer and larger market than India.

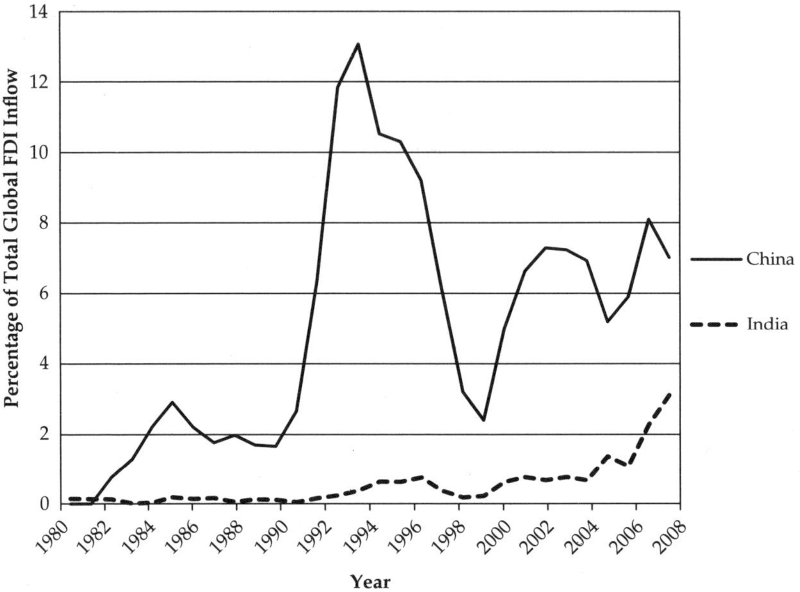

FIGURE 5.5 China and India: Percentage of world FDI inflows, 1980–2008
SOURCE: Created by author from data in UNCTAD foreign direct investment data, available at http://unctadstat.unctad.org/ReportFolders/reportFolders.aspx?sCS_referer=&sCS_ChosenLang=en. Accessed December 5, 2010.

Figure 5.5 shows that in the mid-1990s there was a surge of FDI into China. This peaked in 1994 at 13 percent of global FDI and then fell to about 4 percent in 2007 before rebounding to 8 percent in 2008. The actual value of FDI inflows into China was $72 billion in 2005 and 2006 and $84 billion in 2007. In 2008, they reached their highest point at $108 billion before falling slightly in 2009. However, since global foreign investment fell from $2,100 billion in 2007 to $1,114 billion in 2009 because of the economic crisis, China's share of the world total increased significantly.[59]

Benefits to foreign investors in China include access to great production capability, scale, and skills. This is leading to global restructuring of production from developed countries to China. Numerous U.S. corporations have relocated operational processes to China, which offers increased production capability, scale, and low-cost skilled labor.

General Motors, for example, has already closed several of its U.S. plants in favor of new plants in China for China's domestic market, and it is currently exploring similar possibilities for exports. In 2009, GM was the largest automobile producer in China, with a market share of 13.4 percent. According to corporate data, GM sold 1.8 million vehicles in 2009, which accounts for a 67 percent increase over 2008.[60] It had nine joint ventures and more than 32,000 employees. In July 2009, GM announced the relocation of its international operations from Detroit to Shanghai, giving the Shanghai office worldwide functional and geographic control of the company outside the U.S. market. GM joint ventures in China are already exporting to other developing countries. In May 2009, GM announced it was planning to build a new small car in China for export to the United States. This drew strong opposition from the United Auto Workers union; as a result, the plan appears to have been abandoned in favor of producing these automobiles domestically.[61]

Despite the clear benefits of foreign investment in China, there are also several important concerns. U.S. investors in China worry that the Chinese government's tougher stance on FDI may affect the feasibility of future investments. The Chinese government recently revoked the favorable tax treatment that foreign investors enjoyed over their domestic counterparts.[62] Surveys conducted by the U.S.–China Business Council also indicate that U.S. companies are concerned that there are signs of slowness in the opening of additional sectors of FDI as part of China's WTO commitments.[63]

India got a late start in attracting FDI. Foreign direct investment into India averaged about one-third of 1 percent of global FDI prior to 1991. Annual inflows have grown since the liberalization of the economy and controls on FDI in 1991, and in 2008, India accounted for 3 percent of global FDI (Figure 5.5). Foreign direct investment inflows into India increased from $20 billion in 2006 to $40 billion in 2008 despite the global economic crisis, but they fell to $35 billion in 2009.[64] The quick growth of the Indian market is attracting the attention of foreign exporters who want access to the market. Foreign investors are also relocating to India to utilize relatively low-cost skilled labor. IBM, for example, has hired tens of thousands of workers to handle its increasing global workload, and it holds its annual procurement meeting in Bangalore, India, rather than in the United States.

Although there are many advantages to moving production to China and India, workers and policy makers in developed economies remain concerned about the shutdown of domestic production facilities. Policy makers also worry that as MNCs relocate regional corporate headquarters and R&D to these nations, their countries lose linkages and positive interactions with other domestic agents that are key sources of their competitive strength. Further, it is perceived that as MNCs become more engaged in foreign markets, they become less concerned with the activities and well-being of their home countries. Other developing countries worry that China and India have captured investments that otherwise would have gone to them. In 2008, China and India accounted for 24 percent of all FDI going to developing and transition countries.[65] This degree of concentration in just two countries does legitimize the fear of other developing countries, particularly given that overall global foreign investment flows have decreased.

Investing Abroad to Secure Natural Resources and Acquire Foreign Brands and Advanced Technology

In addition to receiving increased amounts of FDI, both China and India are becoming significant direct foreign investors abroad. China began investing abroad in the early 1980s with tens of millions of dollars a year, growing to hundred of millions by the end of 1980 and increasing to $2 to $4 billion per year in the late 1990s. Starting in the early 2000s, the government's "go global" policy led overseas investments to more than double to $12 billion in 2004 and then nearly double again to $22 billion in 2006 and 2007. They doubled again to $52 billion in 2008 while worldwide FDI investment as a whole fell. In 2009, China's foreign investments were down slightly to $48 billion, but since the world's fell faster, China's share increased to almost 4.5 percent of the world's (Figure 5.6).

Of $246 billion in stock at the end of 2009, two-thirds were in Hong Kong. This involved some Chinese investment going to Hong Kong and then back into China to get special incentives for foreign investment. Therefore, Chinese outward foreign investment statistics need to be interpreted with caution. Most of China's outward foreign investment is by large state-owned companies, which are required to register and get approval. On other hand, many nonstate companies invest abroad without registering, so the real total is higher than officially recorded.[66] Of the total official stock, slightly more than three-quarters were in services (with 19 percent in financial services and 15 percent in wholesale and retail trade). Seventeen percent was in the primary sector, virtually all in mining and petroleum. Only 6 percent was in manufacturing.

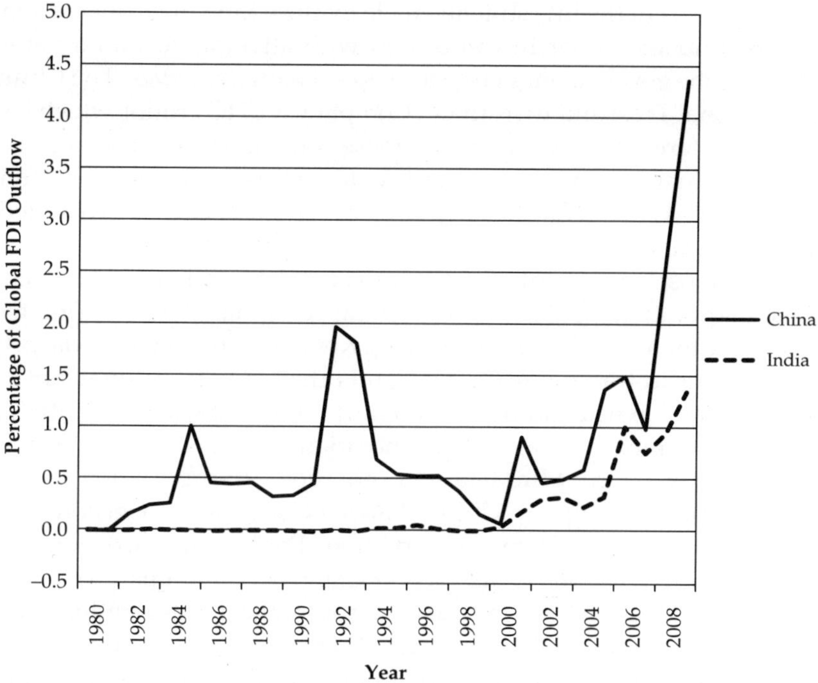

FIGURE 5.6 China and India: Percentage of global FDI outflows, 1980–2008
SOURCE: Created by author from data in UNCTAD foreign direct investment data, available at http://unctadstat.unctad.org/ReportFolders/reportFolders.aspx?sCS_referer=&sCS_ChosenLang=en. Accessed December 5, 2010.

Thus, the picture that emerges from Chinese outward foreign investment is somewhat different from the stereotype that China is investing abroad primarily to secure natural resources. The large share of investment in services is explained by three main factors. One is that a large part consists of investment in services that support its trade. A good example of this is investments by COSCO (China Ocean Shipping [Group] Company). In 2007, COSCO had the second largest foreign assets among Chinese firms.[67] COSCO is one of the world's largest shipping companies and operates in more than 100 harbors. Recently, it has been very active investing in ports in Greece and Italy to increase the cargo capacity of ports in those countries. A second is investment in the depressed financial sector in developed countries. This has accounted for a large part of the investments made by the China Investment Company mentioned earlier in connection with attempts to find a better return on the government's large foreign exchange reserves. The China International Trust and Investment Company (CITIC group), which has the largest foreign assets among Chinese companies, has also been investing in finance and financial services as well as in commercial activities. The third reason for the large investment in services is investment in foreign real estate.

In the most recent ranking of the 100 largest nonfinancial transnational corporations (data for 2008), Hong Kong has the most (16), followed by China (13). Although the Hong Kong transnationals are largely private firms in trading, real estate, and other services, China's are almost all state-owned companies in natural resources (China National Petroleum Company, Sinochem Corporation, China National Offshore Oil Company, China MinMetals Corporation), transportation (China Ocean Shipping Company, China Railway Construction Corporation), construction (China State Construction Engineering Corporation, China Communications Construction Company), and one investment company (CITIC, the second largest nonfinancial corporation from developing and emerging countries). There are a few manufacturing companies, including Lenovo (computers), ZTE (telecommunications and networking), and TPV Technology Limited (computer monitors).

There are four motivations for China's outward FDI. The first has been to promote China's modernization and support its growing trade. Examples include CITIC (set up by Deng Xiaoping in 1979), trade-supporting companies such as COSCO, and other transport- and retail-supporting companies. A second motivation has been to secure access to natural resources. This has intensified in the last five years and is carried out mostly by the large state-owned natural resource companies.

Some of the biggest Chinese greenfields are in energy and mining. A significant share of these are in rogue states, where China has an advantage in that many other countries are not allowing their companies to invest there.[68] The largest greenfield investments during 2008–2009 include $4.5 billion in Vietnam, $2.2 billion in Turkmenistan, $1.8 billion in Iran, $1.7 billion in Oman, $1.7 billion in Sudan, $1.6 billion in Chad, $1.6 billion in Niger, $1.5 billion in Syria by the China National Petroleum Company, $4.0 billion in Brazil by the Wuhan Iron and Steel Company, $2.9 billion in Afghanistan by the Chinese Metallurgical Company, $2.4 billion in Nigeria by the Shenzhen Energy Group, $2.6 billion in Liberia for metals by China, $2.2 billion in India by Xinxing Group Union,

$2.2 billion in Peru by the Aluminum Corporation of China, $1.7 billion in Saudi Arabia, $1.4 billion in Peru by Jiangxi Copper, and $1.2 billion Iran by the China Petroleum and Chemical Company.[69]

A third motivation has been to make better use of China's growing foreign exchange reserves, such as investments made by the China Investment Corporation (CIC). Many of these investments have been in the financial sector, which explains why finance figures so prominently in China's outward FDI.

The fourth and newest motivation is to exploit technological and management capabilities acquired domestically. Among the largest greenfield investments in 2008–2009, they include $3.0 billion in India for engines and turbines by Shanghai Electric Power, more than $2 billion in various developing countries by SAIC Cherry Automobiles, and $1.0 billion in the United States by Tianjin Pipe.[70] They also include Haier, a producer of domestic appliances with factories in 24 countries and sales outlets in more than 160.[71] There are also many investments in auto parts by China's other swiftly growing domestic auto companies as well as by other electronics firms. These manufacturing investments include the acquisition of foreign companies to access superior technology and brand names. A good example of one in electronics is Lenovo's purchase of the personal computer division of IBM in 2005, which gave Lenovo a global brand name and more advanced technology. In 2010, Geely bought Volvo from Ford.[72]

These examples are the largest and most visible. Chinese outward FDI is very diversified and growing. Already in 2007, there were more than 7,000 Chinese entities involved in more than 10,000 foreign enterprises in 173 countries.[73] These investments can be expected to continue to grow rapidly given China's large foreign exchange reserves. The financial difficulties of many companies in the rest of the world also provide excellent opportunities for Chinese investors to buy natural resources, brand names, and companies with more advanced technology.

Unlike China, outward FDI in India was virtually nonexistent during the 1980s and only in the tens of millions of dollars in the 1990s. From 2001 to 2005, it rose to between $1 and $3 billion. In 2006, it jumped to $14 billion and then to $18 billion in 2008 before declining to $15 billion in 2009 with the world recession.[74] Indian outward FDI is driven much more by the private sector than by the government. The Indian economy, and thus the investing companies, was affected significantly by the credit crunch brought about by the global financial crisis, which caused a marked depreciation of the Indian rupee against the U.S.

dollar in 2008 and a global contraction of economic activity.[75] This was not the case in China due to its $2.3 trillion in foreign exchange reserves, a very high domestic savings rate, and its steadily expanding outward FDI, primarily at the hands of large state-owned enterprises.

Indian greenfield investments are more diversified than China's both by sector and by region. The largest Indian greenfield investments in 2007–2009 include $5.2 billion in Iran by the National Thermal Power Corporation, $4.2 billion in chemicals in Saudi Arabia by GAIL, $3.5 billion in metals in Vietnam, $900 million in Argentina by Tata, $3.0 billion in Iran, $1.5 billion in Iraq by the Oil and Natural Gas Company, $1.8 billion in oil and natural gas in Zambia by Era, $1.7 billion in Malaysia in software services by Mahindra Satyam, $1.7 billion in Poland and $1.6 billion in Italy by Videocon (consumer electronics), $1.7 billion in Kenya and $1.4 billion in the United States by the Essar Group, and various other large investments in metals.[76]

Four of the five Indian companies on UNCTAD's list of the 100 largest transnational corporations from developing and transitioning countries are private.[77] They are Tata Steel, Tata Motors, Hindalco (aluminum), and Zuzlon (windmills for electricity). The public enterprise is the Oil and Natural Gas Corporation. Other important Indian foreign investors include Reliance, Vardhman Polytex, and Bharti Airtel (cellular phone service). Their main motivation is to exploit the managerial and technological capabilities they have developed from their operations in India. A good example is the spread to 40 countries of India's National Institute of Information Technology (NIIT). NIIT provides not only information technology training but also management training to leading Fortune 500 companies in the United States.[78] However, some investments are also motivated by acquisition of brand names and more advanced technology that can complement the skills of the Indian company. Tata's purchase of Land Rover, Jaguar, and the Corus Steel Company and Hindalco's purchase of Novelis are recent examples of such efforts.[79]

The increasing strength of these multinationals from both countries suggests that they can be expected to continue to expand overseas to exploit their managerial and technological assets as well as to secure natural resources and to buy advanced technology. The latter two types of FDI cause concern in other countries. They worry that China and India may be preempting access to natural resources and strengthening their competitiveness through the purchase of high-tech companies. This could cause strong nationalist reactions against both types of FDI, particularly in the case of China, given the rapid growth in its foreign exchange reserves. There is also fear in many countries that the Chinese government may begin to use its vast assets to make strategic investments in their national companies, particularly in the high-technology and national security sectors. For example, there was a very strong negative U.S. reaction to China National Offshore Oil Company's $18.5 billion bid to purchase the Union Oil Company of California (UNOCAL) in 2005. Most analysts did not consider this investment to be of any strategic significance, given the very small share of global oil supplies involved, but the U.S. government was nevertheless concerned about the implications of the proposed transaction for national security. As a result, the sale did not go through. As another example, in 2007, Huawei (a Chinese computer and telecom equipment firm) attempted to buy a stake in 3Com (a U.S. technology company) but was again opposed on the grounds of national security risks after being reviewed by the U.S. Committee on Foreign Investment.[80] In 2009, Chinalco, the third largest aluminum producer in the world, made a $19.5 billion bid to increase its holding in the Australian mining company Rio Tinto. However, it was rejected by the Australian government and the firm's stockholders, who were concerned about too much Chinese influence.

In short, both China and India are becoming more important in international capital markets. There will be increasing FDI from China and India over time not only to secure raw materials and energy supplies but also to purchase technology-rich companies in developed countries. Additional purchases will occur as these developing nations use their increased global positioning to buy firms that give them access to more global markets. Further, FDI will increase with regard to the exploitation of their existing technology and management assets abroad. The exponentially high increase in FDI from China, in particular, places it in a similar position to that of Japan in the 1980s when it, too, caused concern by purchasing major U.S. companies.[81]

A Tilted Technology Playing Field

Intellectual Property Piracy

India, and even more so China, have advanced rapidly by taking advantage of existing knowledge through trade, FDI, technology licensing, foreign education and training, copying, and reverse engineering. Both countries have been improving their intellectual property right regimes and have strengthened their IPR legislation to become WTO compliant. India finally complied with WTO IPR rules in 2005, when it extended patent protection to pharmaceutical products not previously protected as part of industrial policy.[82]

In the World Economic Forum's qualitative ranking of IPR protection, on a scale from 1 (worst) to 7 (best), China's score has increased from 3.6 in 2004–2005 to 4.0 in 2010–2011. India's has increased over the same period from 3.4 to 3.6.[83] However, foreign companies and governments remain concerned about weak IPR and copyright rules in China and India. For example, in its 2009 and 2010 annual reports, the Office of the U.S. Trade Representative (USTR) still lists China and India on its priority watch list.[84]

Eighty-one percent of the IPR-infringing product seizures at the U.S. border in 2008 were of Chinese origin. These included primarily pharmaceuticals, electronics, batteries, auto parts, industrial equipment, and toys. The U.S. copyright industries (movies and other mass media) estimated losses of $3.5 billion for Chinese-pirated music recordings and business software.[85] Weak enforcement is due to the high value and volume thresholds required for offenders to trigger criminal prosecutions.[86] The U.S. trademark and copyright industries (luxury goods, DVDs, software, etc.) argue that "the fines are too low and irregularly awarded to provide an effective deterrent, and as a result infringers continue to consider administrative seizures and fines as a cost of doing business."[87]

The USTR supports concerns from U.S. companies that Chinese laws and policies in many industries are being used to favor domestic over foreign companies in issues related to IPR. One example is the use of procurement preferences for domestically innovative products. Another is forced sharing of patented technologies on a royalty-free basis or mandatory requirements to register for patent pools to participate in the standard development processes. A third is compulsory licenses for foreign IPR. Finally, import restrictions on wholesale and retail distribution of movies, video games, and books are believed to lead consumers to the black market, where pirated versions of these products are widely available.[88]

Regarding India, the biggest area of concern is the counterfeiting of pharmaceutical products and a lack of adherence to copyright laws, particularly in the case of movies, music, and software.[89] Both countries are also accused of unfair commercial release and use of undisclosed tests and other data generated to obtain marketing approval for pharmaceutical and agrochemical products.[90]

These issues have led to several IPR-related suits against China. In 2005, Cisco sued the Chinese corporation Huawei for violating at least five of its patents. Huawei admitted copying some of Cisco's source code, and the two companies reached a settlement. Huawei has had joint ventures with other foreign companies including Siemens, Qualcom, and Symantec and has invested a lot in its own R&D. As a result of these efforts, in 2009, Huawei overtook Alcatel-Lucent to become the world's number three mobile network gear maker. Later, it overtook Nokia Siemens Networks for the number two spot. In addition, 75 percent of Huawei's revenue in 2009 was derived from oversea sales, making it one of the truly global Chinese companies and one of the world's top patent seekers. Currently, Huawei has strong sales to governments ranging from Brazil to Germany, where it competes head to head with some of the world's top equipment manufacturers.[91]

Most recently, in January 2010, Google threatened to leave China over alleged cyberattacks on its servers that involved violations of its intellectual property. The attacks were said to have also occurred against at least 20 other large MNCs in the finance, media, chemicals, and defense industries. The attackers were after "source code," the most valuable form of intellectual property because it underlies the firms' computer applications.[92] This made front-page news in the United States and has raised the issue of IPR piracy to a heightened level. The issue of intellectual property is likely to become even more contentious as China and India become stronger competitors in international markets and in more technology-intensive goods and services.

Restricting Access to the Chinese Market to Develop National Champions

A related concern is what has been labeled the indigenous innovation focus of the Chinese government that started around 2004 when China began preparing its ambitious medium- and long-term science and technology plan to promote innovation by domestic firms. This has led the government to use access to its market as an explicit strategy to help its firms acquire technology. A good example is the development of the high-speed train.

Chinese state-owned train builders, while gaining technological abilities very rapidly over the past decade, still produced trains whose operation safety was not up to international standards. As a result, the State Council turned to advanced technology abroad to develop its own high-speed train building capacity through technology transfers. Consequently, the State Council, Ministry of Railways (MOR), and state-owned train builders, the China North Car (CNC) and China South Car (CSC), used China's large market and competition among foreign train makers eyeing China's potentially huge market to induce the entrance of high-quality foreign firms and technology transfers.

In June 2004, the MOR solicited bids to make 200 high-speed train sets that can run 200 kilometers/hour to comply with China's new high-speed railway plans launched in 2005. Kawasaki of Japan, Alstom of France, Siemens of Germany, and Bombardier Transportation of Germany all submitted bids. All but Siemens were awarded portions of the contract. All had to adapt their HSR train sets to China's own common standard and assemble units through local joint ventures.

Of the bidders, Kawasaki got the highest portion of the deal, securing over U.S. $100 billion worth of deals in the future for high-speed trains. However, the company failed to recognize the speed with which their Chinese joint venture, the CSR Sifang, was able to replicate Kawasaki's technologies. Essentially, by 2008, all the trains (the CRH2) modeled after the initial Kawasaki technology transfer (the E2-1000 series used in Shinkansen) were manufactured by Sifang without any help or technology updates from Kawasaki. As one of Sifang's executives stated, the new trains are only Shinkansen in look but are Chinese in the interior. Kawasaki is no longer involved with CSR and has backed off from further deals with the Chinese firm.[93]

With the newly acquired technology, Chinese producers are rapidly gaining an international audience previously open only to European and Japanese firms by leveraging their home market size and strength and going abroad. In a sign of how much Chinese railway companies have become internationally competitive, Siemens has abandoned a bidding war against a Chinese consortium for a railway linking Mecca and Medina in Saudi Arabia in March 2010 and joined the Chinese instead. Furthermore, while Chinese firms still lag their European competitors in advanced technology and quality, they are able to beat their counterparts with low prices and cheap financing. In addition, domestically and internationally, the Chinese Ministry of Railways is able to coordinate tenders so Chinese producers don't bid against each other and encourages foreign companies to join Chinese consortia by holding out the prospect of greater access to an enormous market in the future (both within China and abroad).

Chinese companies are already very active in bidding for projects in Middle Eastern countries, such as Saudi Arabia and Iran, and Latin American countries, including Argentina, Brazil, and Mexico. They are also targeting projects in Australia and the United States and have made significant inroads in their own region, with contracts in Thailand and Hong Kong.[94]

An annual survey of 500 European companies investing in China reported that 36 percent of the respondents thought that Chinese government procurement policies had biased foreign companies. They complained they were losing market share in China because of poor protection of intellectual property and selective enforcement of laws and regulations.[95] The chairman of BASF and the chief executive of Siemens both complained at a meeting with Premier Wen Jiabao that their companies were being forced to disclose their technology to do business in China.[96]

In the U.S.–China Business Council's 2010 survey, eight of the top ten concerns raised by respondents were about unequal access to the Chinese market. They were, in order of importance, administrative licensing, business and products approval, competition with state-owned enterprises, intellectual property rights enforcement, market access in services, transparency, protectionism risks, government procurement, and standards and conformity assessment.[97]

The U.S. Chamber of Commerce has produced an excellent report which summarizes the problems that result from China's strong indigenous innovation strategy.[98] This strategy was announced in 2006 as part of the Medium and Long Term Science and Technology Plan discussed in Chapter 4. Although the plan proposed an openness to foreign technology, including joint research and development, it also had strong elements of technonationalism. In 2009–2010, there has been a strong perception among foreign firms that the balance has shifted much more toward technonationalism. A key element of this has been mandates to replace foreign technology with domestic technology in banking and telecommunications, "product testing and approval regimes . . . geared to delay the introduction of foreign imports to China, and to study foreign designs and production processes before the products cross the border," continuation of Chinese state monopolies, along with the enactment of antimonopoly laws aimed at foreign companies, "government procurement block products not designed and produced in China," and development of Chinese and industrial standards that "serve as market barriers to foreign technology."[99]

The last point has to do with the development of standards as an instrument of industrial policy. This concern stems from China's attempts to promote its own national wireless authentication and privacy infrastructure (WAPI) interface in wireless communications in 2003. This created a conflict with the U.S. producers, who claimed the standard was a ploy to provide an unfair advantage to domestic companies. Only 11 Chinese companies received access to the encryption code, and foreign companies were encouraged to work with those companies to produce products for the Chinese market. The United States complained that this gave Chinese companies an unfair advantage in accessing the Chinese market. The Chinese government eventually backed off the standard,[100] but the issue of the use of standards as an instrument of industrial policy still remains.

The basic issue is that as China acquires greater technological capability, it wants to use its large market to develop its own standards, which it hopes will eventually become global. This is part of a Chinese strategy to change from being standards followers to standards creators by 2020. Many foreigners see this as a new technonationalist strategy on China's part. This is a complaint heard from an increasing number of foreign companies, particularly in the United States. Suttmeier,[101] however, points out that there have long been two camps in China: those who favor more self-reliance (the technonationalists) and those who accept heavy reliance on foreign technology. The latter recognize that China has greatly benefited by drawing heavily on imported technology. Suttmeier explains that both strands are alive and well in China and that their relative strength depends on the specific sector that is being considered as well as on cultural preferences. He anticipates that China's large market, increasing technological capabilities, cultural preferences, and growing sense of international importance will lead it to take a more active role in setting standards. Successful engagement with China on this issue will require recognizing the diversity of the many interests at stake as well as China's greater technological capabilities and global status.[102] The net result will be China having more clout in setting standards that are in tune with its needs.

Growing Geopolitical Impact of the Rise of China

The Growing Influence of the Beijing Consensus

China represents a different political/economic model than the developed economies. Politically, China is an authoritarian regime that has been successful not because it is authoritarian but because it has focused on economic growth. There are many authoritarian regimes (including many in sub-Saharan Africa) that have not focused on growth and have not performed well. There have also been authoritarian regimes that have performed well economically when the government has focused on growth to gain legitimacy among the population. Examples are South Korea from 1965 to 1980, Brazil during the "Miracle Years" of 1964 to 1980, and Taiwan.

The Economist Intelligence Unit ranks countries into four groups by type of government: fully democratic, flawed democracy, hybrid regime, or authoritarian regime. Roughly half the world's countries and half the global population are ranked as democracies. Only 30 are full democracies (mostly the OECD countries) versus 50 flawed democracies (including Brazil, India, Indonesia, and Malaysia). Roughly one-fifth of the countries, accounting for one-sixth of the world's population, are hybrid systems (including Hong Kong, Singapore, and Russia). And roughly one-third of the countries and of the world's population have authoritarian regimes (including China, Egypt, and Vietnam). There has been some progress toward democracy since the 1970s, particularly after the collapse of the USSR, but it appears to have stalled. Furthermore, countries like Russia have moved backward from flawed democracy to hybrid. Unfulfilled expectations and economic setbacks have seemed to result in a sliding away from democracy.[103]

Economically, China's model also involves much greater government control of the market than is typical of the Washington Consensus. China's development represents a "Beijing Consensus."[104] It is also argued that because of China's superior growth over the last 30 years, and particularly with respect to the 2008–2009 economic crisis, its model is gaining currency in the rest of the world.[105] The frictions also extend beyond governance models into values in international relations such as interactions with states that do not respect norms on human rights and freedom of expression. These include states such as Iran, Myanmar, North Korea, Sudan, Russia, and Venezuela, with which China has extensive trade relationships.

The issue of the role of government in the economy is more complex, as even governments of very capitalist-oriented countries such as the United States and the United Kingdom have had to intervene strongly in their economies as a result of the economic crisis of 2008–2009. This intervention has not been only through large stimulus packages, monetary expansion, and the injection of liquidity by central banks but also through direct government takeover of ailing financial and industrial firms in the United States, the United Kingdom, and several other European economies. These large interventions were sold as temporary measures taken as a means to stabilize economies in free fall. The expectation is that they will be reversed once economies stabilize and private-sector growth resumes.

The Heritage Foundation tracks market freedom over time.[106] Since its Economic Freedom Index began in 1995, there has been a slight movement away from state control and toward markets. However, globally, there was a slight regression in 2008 and 2009 as governments all around the world had to intervene more directly in markets to contain the financial and economic crisis. As developed in Chapter 3, China and India are nearly identical in their overall rating regarding degree of market freedom (53.8 for India, 50.1 for China in 2010; the difference was only 1 percentage point in 2009).[107] China's rapid growth over this period and India's more rapid growth since 1991 have been due more to reduction of state intervention and movement toward the market, including greater integration into the global economic system, than from increased state control.[108] However, the difference between their political systems remains quite strong.

The contrast between China's authoritarian governance model and India's democratic model will probably persist. China is not likely to democratize in the near future.[109] Democracy may even make it harder for China to integrate into the world, as a democratic China may become even more nationalistic.[110] It should also be noted that the government enjoys strong support from the Chinese population. In the Pew global surveys, the percentage of the respondents satisfied with the country's direction increased steadily from 48 percent in 2002 to 87 percent in 2010. In contrast, in the United States, it has gone down from 39 percent in 2003–2004 to 23 percent at the height of the financial crisis in 2008 and moved back up to just 30 percent in 2010.[111]

For its part, India's flawed democracy faces many challenges. These include capture by strong interest groups, deadlocks, and difficulties in addressing key reform agendas compared with the greater capability of an authoritarian regime like China's to pass and implement critical reforms. Although India's problems with democracy are much severer, the United States is also facing some problems of fractious politics and capture by strong lobbies and ideological divides, which are making it difficult to address critical long-term issues. Thus, there is likely to be continued competition among the various political/economic models for some time to come.

Deepening Economic Ties and the Leverage of China's Booming Domestic Market

China is also gaining geopolitical strength because it has become an important trading partner for so many countries. It is the largest trading export market for Australia, Argentina, Brazil, and many African and Middle Eastern countries. It is the second largest export market for Japan and the second largest non-European market for the European Union. It is the third largest market for the United States and India. This gives China a lot of influence on countries that depend on it for exports.

More broadly, China's and India's large and growing markets are a key source of strength. China and India currently account for 37 percent of the total world population. In 2008, the population of each country was larger than the total population of high-income countries. Moreover, their populations will continue to grow faster than those of high-income countries, and they will increase their share of global population over the next 20 to 30 years, while that of high-income countries will continue to fall. These two countries have also been growing faster than average for the world. Thus, these nations will become even larger players in the global economy in terms of population, economic size, demand for natural resources, and CO_2 emissions.[112]

In economic size, China accounted for 8.3 percent of global national income at nominal exchange rates in 2009, and India accounted for 2.3 percent. Although this is still small compared with the United States (24.5 percent) or the European Union (28.1 percent), both countries account for a much larger share of market growth because their economies have been growing at two to three and a half times the average rate of growth of the world. Moreover, both economies are projected to continue to grow much faster than the high-income countries for the next decade or two.[113]

China's growth is particularly striking when we look at global growth at PPP exchange rates. While the growth of the United States was the largest contributor to global growth between 1980 and 2000, that distinction has shifted to China since around 2000. Most impressively, since the onset of the global economic crisis of 2008, China has contributed to roughly half of total global growth, whereas the U.S. contribution was negative. International Monetary Fund projections are that China will be the largest country contributor to economic growth through 2015.[114] The United States is expected to account only for roughly one-eighth of global growth, much below its historical contribution.

Two key areas where China is using its very large market to attract foreign investment and appropriate foreign technology much the way it did with high-speed trains are aircraft and wind power. In aircraft, there are various estimates that China is the largest market in the world. One of China's megaprojects is to develop its own medium-capacity airplane by 2014 to compete with Boeing and Airbus. It is trading access to its aviation market by foreign companies in exchange for technology transfer and training. In wind technology, it has used access to its large market to obtain technology and training from foreign wind turbine producers such as the Spanish firm Camesa and General Electric. Both these companies have lost market share in China as the domestic companies they helped have expanded. However, even with the loss of market share, the dynamic growth of the market still makes it attractive to participate.[115] In addition, it has been reported that many large multinationals prefer not to discuss problems with China's trade, technology, and market access policies out of fear of retaliation by the Chinese government against their activities in China.[116]

Thus, China and to a lesser extent India have become very critical markets for exporters and MNCs.[117] For most of the large MNCs, the markets outside their home country account for more than 50 percent of their activities. Among foreign markets, none is as large as China's. The size of their growing, unsaturated markets is particularly appealing to Western and Japanese MNCs, which are looking for attractive markets worldwide as the already-saturated markets in their home countries stagnate. The attractiveness of their markets gives China and India great leverage in enticing MNCs. Multinational corporations that venture into these dynamic markets have to bring their best technology because the competition from both local firms and other MNCs is fierce.

In exchange, China and India get advanced technology and management and training for the local staff that work for these companies. Because of weak IPR enforcement, much of the technology leaks out and is copied by domestic firms. In addition, the presence of the MNCs increases domestic competition and puts pressure on local firms to improve their technologies, products, services, and management and business models. The MNCs train the locals, who may later leave to start their own companies or go to work for domestic firms or government institutions. There are also other benefits, such as the development of domestic supplier and distribution networks and access to international networks. All of this helps develop greater domestic technological and management capability in China and India and strengthens the competitiveness of their economies. In short, because of the attractiveness of their markets, they are harnessing the most dynamic player in the global economy, the multinational corporation, to play on their team. As MNCs put more and more of their new investment and R&D into these markets, concerns are raised from their home country governments, who are losing out.

Military Buildup Leads to Increasing Security Concerns

A final issue of geopolitical concern is the growing investment in military power by both China and India. As both countries become bigger economically, they are also investing more in their military capability. India continues to build its military because of its fear of conflict with Pakistan and, down the road, with China. China is building its military capability as part of its general economic growth. However, it has a strategic need to secure not just its borders but also its supply of natural resources from all over the world. Therefore, it is compelled to build up its air and sea power to project its power beyond its borders to secure the safe passage of the oil and other critical natural resources it needs.

As both countries strengthen their military power, neighboring countries worry about their increasing military capability and their future intentions. They then feel compelled to build up their own military power and to seek alliances with other countries, including the United States. This is the traditional spiral pattern of arms buildup in an uncertain world. It is not only regional but global because of the broader balance-of-power implications. As the reigning power, the United States is increasingly concerned about China's growing economic strength, geopolitical projection, and rising military power.

CHAPTER 6

Environmental and Natural Resource Impact

THE GROWTH OF CHINA AND INDIA has major implications for global environmental sustainability. This chapter will cover overall resource use with a special focus on energy and the environment in the context of climate change due to China's and India's impact on the global system.[1] China and India have limited resources per capita. The first section will analyze their endowments in terms of arable land, water, and energy. They also have to import many basic commodities, notably iron ore, other metals, food, and energy. The global impact of their increased demand for primary goods has been an upsurge in commodity prices. The next section takes a broader view of environmental sustainability using a composite index of environmental resource availability and use, including CO_2 absorption. It shows that China and India are already running a net deficit equivalent to 14 and 4 percent, respectively, of globally available sustainable environmental resources. Given their size, the pressure they put on the global system will be unsustainable if they continue to grow at their current rate.

The third section looks at the rising energy demand in absolute levels as well as in terms of energy intensity per unit of GDP and per capita for China and India compared with other major energy consumers. It is projected that their increased energy demand between 2007 and 2035 will be 53 percent of the total global increase.[2] This is due to both their higher growth rates and their lower energy efficiency. This section also examines historical trends of CO_2 emissions as well as the changing intensity of CO_2 emissions per unit of GDP and per capita for the major emitters. The increase in CO_2 emissions from China and India is estimated to account for 91 percent of the increase in global CO_2 emissions between 2007 and 2035.[3] Thus, it is clear that both countries have to take more aggressive action on energy efficiency and CO_2 emissions if the world is to avoid global warming.

The next section examines the current stalemate on efforts to address climate change. The December 2009 Copenhagen Climate Change Summit did not produce any globally binding agreements on limiting CO_2 emissions. Complex issues of cost, equity, efficiency, collective action, and monitoring and enforcement need to be sorted out to address the global warming challenge. The following section focuses on the role of greater technological effort as a way to move beyond the stalemate. The final section points out that the speedy development of China and India is a harbinger of a larger issue: our current growth model is not sustainable. The growth of other developing countries is also going to increase pressure on limited environmental resources. To deal with this broader challenge, it will be necessary to devise more environmentally sustainable economic and social systems.

China and India Are Resource Poor

Low Arable Land per Capita

China and India have one-half and two-thirds, respectively, of the world average arable land per person (see Table 6.1, which provides comparative data for the other BRICs and the United States). Because of land constraints and low rainfall, the irrigation rate of their cropland is roughly twice the world average. The agriculture of both countries is much more labor intensive and less mechanized than that of Brazil, Russia, or the United States.

China is more land constrained than India. To get high yields from its limited arable land, China uses roughly two and a half times the average amount of fertilizer per arable hectare than the world average and roughly twice the average for the United States. Nevertheless, China's cereal yields per hectare are almost as high as those of the United States and 60 percent higher than the world average. India's yields per hectare are about three-quarters of the world average, in part because it uses less fertilizer per hectare, although it has been starting to increase fertilizer use and getting higher yields. The two countries' heavy use

TABLE 6.1 Arable land, inputs, and outputs of agriculture: China, India, and selected countries

	Brazil	China	India	Russia	U.S.	World
Arable land hectares per 100 people						
1990–1992	33.2	10.4	15.6	84.9	61.6	22.8
2005–2007	31.6	10.5	14.3	85.3	57.4	21.0
Irrigation % of cropland[a]						
1990–1992	4.6	36.9	28.3	—	11.3	17.0
2003–2006	4.4	35.6	32.9	3.6	12.5	18.0
Fertilizer consumption per hectare arable land (kilograms)						
1990–1992	66	232	758	42[a]	101	95
2005–2007	156	328	121	11[a]	150	119
Tractors per 100 sq km arable land						
1990–1992	144	64	65	98[a]	236	190
2005–2007	132	124	187	44[a]	259	199
Cereal yield kg per hectare						
1990–1992	1,916	4,307	1,947	1,743	4,875	2,839
2006–2008	3,206	5,388	2,574	2,092	6,578	3,397
Agricultural value added per worker (in constant 2,000 dollars)						
1990–1992	1,611	269	359	1,917	353	801
2005–2007	3,315	459	460	2,914	45,015	959

SOURCES: Compiled from *WDI* (2010), Table 3.1, pp. 154–156; Table 3.2, pp. 158–160; Table 3.3, pp. 162–164.

[a] Taken from *WDI* (2009).

of fertilizers also translates into extensive use of energy and water for agricultural production. Extensive fertilizer use also contributes to water pollution.

Strained Water Resources

China and India are water-poor economies. Their available water resources per capita are, respectively, one-third and one-sixth of the world average and an even smaller fraction of those of the United States, Brazil, and Russia (Table 6.2). India's water withdrawals are already at 51 percent of its available resources, which is more than five times the average world rate. China is withdrawing resources at

TABLE 6.2 Water resources and use: China, India, and selected countries

	Brazil	China	India	Russia	U.S.	World
Renewable Internal Water Resources (cubic meters per capita 2007)	28,498	2,134	1,121	30,350	9,283	6,624
Annual Freshwater Withdrawals (billion cubic meters 2007)	59.3	630.3	645.8	76.7	479.3	3,850.0
% of internal resources	1.1	22.4	51.2	1.8	17.1	9.0
Distribution by Sector						
% for agriculture	62	68	86	18	41	70
% for industry	18	26	5	63	46	20
% for domestic use	20	7	8	19	13	10
Water Productivity (GDP $/cubic meter in $ of 2000)	10.9	1.9	0.7	3.4	20.4	10.3
Access to Improved Water Source 2006						
% of urban population	97	98	96	100	100	96
% of rural population	58	81	86	88	94	77

SOURCE: *WDI* (2010), Table 3.5, pp. 170–172.

two and a half times the average world rate. Both countries face periodic water shortages.

China's Yellow River dries up periodically before reaching the sea. China has a major water diversion project to take water from the more water-abundant southeast region to the drier north. One project is an almost 1,241-kilometer canal from close to Nanjing to Tianjin. A second project is a 1,130-kilometer canal from the Danjiangkou Reservoir to Tianjin and Beijing.[4] However, the water level at Danjiangkou is at historic lows. There are plans to divert water from the Himalayas to several of these river systems.

The Himalayas are the source of water for more than 45 percent of the world's population. They are the headwaters of 20 major rivers, including the Yellow and the Yangtze in China; the Mekong, which provides water for Cambodia, Laos, and Vietnam; and the Indus and Brahmaputra, which provide water for India, Bangladesh, and Pakistan.

This diversion has serious implications for water availability for India and Bangladesh. As has been noted, India is already withdrawing water at more than 50 percent of its available resources. In addition, both China and India make extensive use of wells for irrigation. The water levels for those wells have been falling very quickly. In Beijing, for example, the water table has fallen from 5 meters below the surface in 1950 to more than 50 meters in 2003.[5] Both countries need to improve access to safe water for their rural populations. Both also have very low water productivity in terms of GDP per cubic meter of water used (Table 6.2).

In China and India, from two-thirds to almost nine-tenths of water is used for agriculture, which is a much higher proportion than in the United States and other high-income countries (Table 6.2).[6] In addition, because water for agriculture is free or highly subsidized,[7] there is no incentive to use it efficiently. Charging for water would lead to more efficient water-use management and the use of existing technologies such as drip irrigation. Without prices that reflect the opportunity cost of water, more efficient use is not encouraged. However, it is very difficult to raise prices because most farmers are barely eking out an existence, and many would go under if they had to pay for water. Many of the mass suicides of farmers in India can be traced to problems in making ends meet.[8]

Leaving aside the strategic security advantages of self-sufficiency, it would be much more efficient for water-poor countries such as China and India to import cereals and other water-intensive food crops from other parts of the world such as Brazil, Russia, and the United States, which are water and land rich. In fact, India had been a major importer of wheat before the green revolution made it self-sufficient. However, the productivity increase that came from the green revolution is faltering, since lands have reduced yields because of salinization from irrigation. Thus, there is renewed concern about food shortages, particularly if there are droughts or more pervasive water shortages from climate change or reduced flow from the Himalayan glaciers. These are important concerns for the government, given the continued high rates of population growth and increasing water scarcity.[9]

High Dependence on Imported Energy

China's and India's annual energy growth since 1990 has been two to almost two and a half times faster than the world average and higher than the other BRICs or the United States. Both are also net energy importers but are not as dependent as the United States on foreign energy supplies. China had been a net energy exporter in the 1990s but became an importer in 2001 as its domestic resources became unable to keep up with its swiftly rising demand.

Like the United States and Russia, both countries are heavily dependent on fossil fuels for their energy needs and have lower shares of clean (non-carbon-dioxide-producing) energy in their total energy use. This is significant to the discussion of projected CO_2 emissions below.

Their Large Demand for Natural Resources and Commodities Raises World Prices

Because both India and China are generally poor in most natural resources on a per capita basis (with the exception of coal), they have needed to import many basic commodities.

The share of primary commodities in imports has increased over the last 15 years for both China and India. In China, primary-commodity imports as a share of total imports have risen from 21 percent in 1995 to 35 percent in 2008. In India, they have risen from 46 percent to 56 percent. For both countries, the main commodity imports are fuels and ores. Food makes up a very small percentage. The extraordinary demand of China's need for commodities from abroad can be assessed from its relative intensity in different imports (a revealed import needs indicator similar to the RCA of exports). In 2009, the share of China's imports was above its average imports from the world in 20 of the 63 STIC product categories it imports. Only 6 of these were manufactured products. The other 14 were all natural resources or semiprocessed resource-based products. In the top 5 categories—all of which were primary products—it imported from 21 percent to 40 percent of total world imports. These products were oil seeds (40 percent of total world imports), metalliferous ores (39 percent), pulp and waste paper (31 percent), hides and skins (28 percent), and crude rubber (21 percent).[10] India imported more than its overall share of world imports in 23 SITC two-digit categories. All but 2 of them were also natural resources or semiprocessed resource-based products.[11]

The demand for metals has been particularly strong in China because it has such large and rapidly growing industrial sectors. China is the world's largest producer and consumer of iron, steel, and aluminum.[12] Between 2000 and 2008, China's demand for key metals such as aluminum, copper, lead, nickel, tin, and zinc grew on average by

16.1 percent a year compared with less than 1 percent in the rest of the world.[13]

The demand for natural resources from China and India has already been seen in the quick increase in the price of commodities in the run-up to the global economic crisis of 2008–2009 (Figure 6.1). Some of the increase in commodity prices was due to speculation by hedge funds as well as weather-related problems for some agricultural commodities and mining strikes. However, one of the main drivers was the voracious demand of China and to a lesser extent India. Commodity prices suffered a sharp fall in the second half of 2008 as the economic crisis led to a sharp fall in demand. However, commodity prices are already increasing again as China's and India's growth picks up and the world begins to recover. Although agricultural raw materials, beverage, and food prices are not expected to increase much in 2011–2012, metals and energy prices are expected to rise, although not to their precrisis peaks for some years.

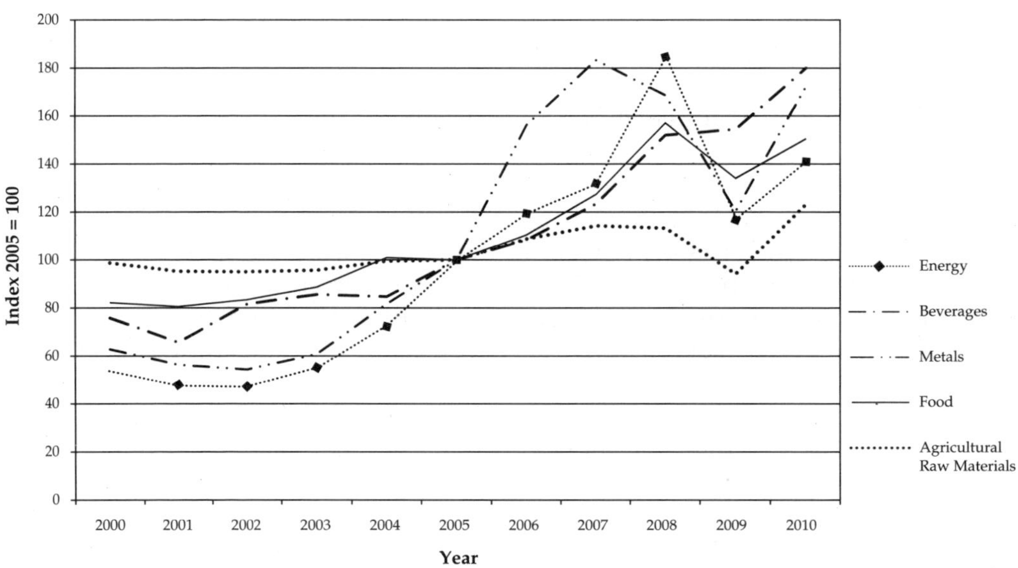

FIGURE 6.1 Commodity prices, 2000–2010

SOURCE: Created by author with IMF data obtained from www.imf.org/external/np/res/commod/table-120910.pdf. Accessed January 5, 2010.

In the short run, there should be stronger attempts to combat price speculation by providing more information about natural resource reserves, stocks, and purchases by major players. In the medium and long run, if the higher prices are seen as sustainable, they will lead to increased supply using existing but more expensive technologies, the development of more efficient technologies for extraction and delivery to the market, and better technologies for industrial and human use of commodities.

The argument about the limits to growth made by the Club of Rome in 1972 proved to be wrong because it assumed exponential growth in demand and only a discrete increase in supply. What actually happened was that as raw materials prices rose, better and new technologies were developed to facilitate extraction and refining of minerals, reduction in use of raw materials in production, recycling, substitution with new materials, and an increase in agricultural productivity. This is testimony to the supply-response capacity of technological innovation and entrepreneurship to respond to new economic opportunities. Thus, technology can be an important part of the solution, as will be developed in the final section of this chapter.

The Rapid Growth of China and India Combined with Their Large Populations Is Creating Global Environmental Sustainability Problems

One way to get a view of the overall environmental resource use of a country is to examine its ecological footprint, which measures the demand of human activity on the biosphere.[14] Figure 6.2 graphs total global biocapacity versus the world's ecological footprint and the 10 countries with the largest footprint. These 10 countries (led by China, the United States, and India) account for half the global footprint. Since the late 1970s, the world's ecological footprint has exceeded its regenerative capacity. This overshoot has been growing and was estimated to have risen to 50 percent above global biocapacity in 2007. The result is water shortages, deforestation, reduced biodiversity, and climate change, which are putting the long-term sustainability of the world at risk.[15]

In 2007, the global ecological footprint was 18 billion global hectares (gha), or 2.7 gha per person. (A global hectare is a hectare with

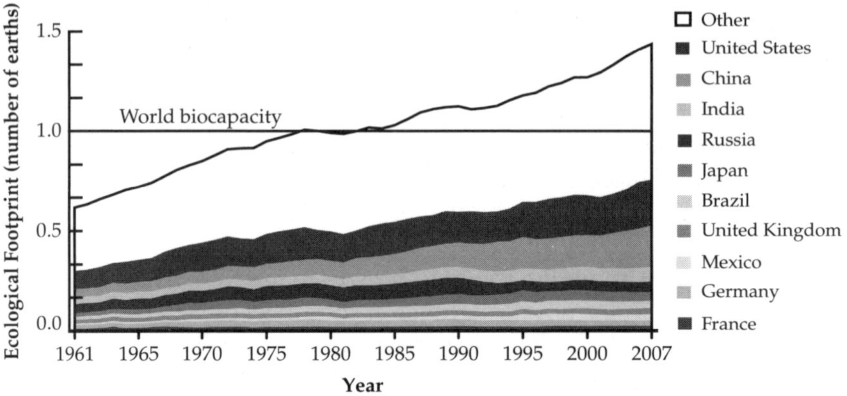

FIGURE 6.2 Ecological footprint, main countries, 1961–2007

SOURCE: From B. Ewing, D. Moore, S. Goldfinger, A. Oursler, A. Reed, and M. Wakernagel. 2010. *The ecological footprint atlas 2010*. Oakland: Global Footprint Network, p. 18.

world-average ability to produce resources and absorb wastes.) On the supply side, the total productive area, or biocapacity, was 11.9 billion gha, or 1.8 gha per person.[16] Brazil has the largest biocapacity, followed by China, the United States, Russia, and India.

Table 6.3 compares the six countries with the largest ecological footprint, plus Europe, with their biocapacity in 2007. It shows the net surplus or deficit of each country compared to the world's total biocapacity. The ecological footprints per capita of China and India are much lower than those of developed countries (2.2 and 0.9, respectively, versus an average of 6.1 for high-income countries) because they are still relatively poor and do not use as many resources per person. However, because of their large population and because they are resource poor on a per capita basis, they have large deficits. Globally, the largest deficits are China (14 percent of the world's total biocapacity), Europe (12 percent),[17] the United States (11 percent), Japan (4 percent), and India (4 percent).[18]

That China and India are growing three to four times faster than the world average means they will be putting increasing pressure on global environmental resources. Thus, it is clear that there will be a global adding-up problem. The swift ascent of China and India shows us that our development models are too resource and environment intensive. We will return to this point in the last part of this chapter.

TABLE 6.3 Ecological footprint versus biocapacity for countries with the largest total ecological footprint, 2007

	U.S.	China	Europe	India	Russia	Japan	Brazil
2007 Population (in millions)	308.7	1,336.6	589	1,164.7	141.9	127.4	190.1
Ecological Footprint per Capita (global hectares) (world average: 2.70)	8.00	2.2	4.77	0.9	4.4	4.7	2.9
Total Country Ecological Footprint (millions of global hectares)	2,469.60	2,940.52	2,810.87	1,048.23	624.36	598.78	551.29
% of World Ecological Footprint (18,013.32 million global hectares)	13.71	16.32	15.60	5.82	3.47	3.32	3.06
Biocapacity per Capita (global hectares) (world average: 1.8)	3.9	0.9	2.23	0.5	5.7	0.60	9.0
Total Country Biocapacity	1,203.93	1,202.94	1310.78	582.35	808.83	76.44	1,710.9
% of World Biocapacity (12,008.88 million global hectares)	10.03	10.02	10.96	4.85	6.74	0.64	14.25
Net Position (in million hectares)	−1,265.67	−1,737.58	−1500.09	−465.88	184.47	−522.34	1,159.61
Net Position as % of World Biocapacity	−10.54	−14.47	−12.49	−3.88	1.54	−4.35	9.66
Net Position on per Capita Basis	−4.1	−1.3	−2.55	−0.4	1.30	−4.1	6.1

SOURCE: Extracted from Global Footprint Network, National Footprint Accounts, 2010 edition. Available at http://www.footprintnetwork.org/images/uploads/2010_NFA_data_tables.pdf. Accessed November 1, 2010.

NOTES: Ecological footprint is cropland, grazing land, forests (including for fuel wood), fishing grounds, built-up land (including areas of dams for hydropower), and global hectares needed to absorb CO_2 emissions (from fossil fuel consumption as well as from products manufactured abroad). Biocapacity includes cropland, grazing land, forests, and fishing grounds.

China and India Will Account for the Majority of Global Increase in Energy Demand and CO_2 Emissions from 2008 to 2035

Rising Energy Consumption per Unit of GDP and per Capita

China's demand for energy has been growing very rapidly. In 2010, it surpassed the United States to become the world's biggest energy user. India became the fourth largest in 2006 when it surpassed Japan.

To put China's extraordinary increase in energy demand in perspective, it is instructive to compare its consumption to that of the European

Union and the United States over time. In 1990, China had roughly half the total energy consumption of the European Union or the United States. By 2020, China's energy consumption is projected to be 83 percent higher than the European Union's and 38 per cent higher than the United States'. By 2035, it is projected to be 116 percent higher than the European Union's and 64 percent higher than the United States' (Table 6.4, new policies scenarios).

Because of the concerns about energy use and global warming and the debate about efficiency and equity, it is useful to look at energy use from the angles of both energy intensity per unit of GDP and per person. For the world as a whole, there has been a slight improvement over time in energy efficiency as measured by the amount of energy necessary to produce a unit of GDP (in constant PPP prices; see Figure 6.3). China has had the most impressive improvement in energy efficiency, from about five times the world average in 1980 to just 50 percent higher than the world average in 2001. However, after 2001, there was a surprising increase in energy intensity per unit of GDP.[19] This occurred because China entered a stage of very energy-intensive growth as it expanded infrastructure and building construction and also increased the share of energy-intensive products such as steel and chemicals in its exports. India's energy intensity, which had been slightly above the average for the world, is converging toward the world average.

From the perspective of energy, emissions, and climate change, it should be noted that the United States' energy intensity per unit of GDP has been much higher than that of the European countries and Japan. Although it has converged toward the world average, energy efficiency per unit of GDP is still about 30 percent higher than that of the other developed countries.

The United States is by far the most energy intensive of the major countries in energy use per capita. It uses over four times more energy per person than the world average and roughly twice that of other developed economies such as France, Germany, Japan, or the United Kingdom (Figure 6.4). India has the lowest energy use per capita among the major energy-consuming countries. In 1980, China's energy consumption per capita was almost as low as India's. However, its per capita consumption has increased rapidly due to industrialization, and by 2009, it was already higher than the world average (Figure 6.4).

Coal has been and is expected to remain one of the major energy sources for the world, and China, the United States, and India still

TABLE 6.4 Population, GDP, energy demand, and CO_2 emissions, selected countries/regions, 1990–2035

	1990	2008	2020 Current Policies	2020 New Policies	2020 450 Scenario	2035 Current Policies	2035 New Policies	2035 450 Scenario
World								
Population (millions)	5,265	6,688	7,614	7,614	7,614	8,497	8,497	8,497
GDP (billion U.S. dollars, current international prices, and PPPs)	24,804	69,947	106,927	106,927	106,927	164,179	164,179	164,179
Energy Demand (million tons oil equivalent)	8,779	12,271	14,896	14,556	14,127	18,048	16,748	14,920
Energy per Capita	1.7	1.8	2	1.9	1.9	2.1	2	1.8
CO_2 (thousand metric tons)	20,965	29,381	35,437	33,739	31,908	42,589	35,442	21,724
CO_2 per Capita	4	4.4	4.7	4.4	4.2	5	4.2	2.6
CO_2 per GDP	0.9	0.4	0.3	0.3	0.3	0.3	0.2	0.1
China								
Population	1,141	1,333	1,411	1,411	1,411	1,434	1,434	1,434
% World	22	20	19	19	19	17	17	17
GDP	910	8,217	20,464	20,464	20,464	36,327	36,327	36,327
% World	4	12	19	19	19	22	22	22
Energy Demand (Mtoe)	872	2,131	3,288	3,159	3,097	4,215	3,737	3,131
Energy per Capita	0.8	1.6	2.3	2.2	2.2	2.9	2.6	2.2
CO_2	2,244	6,551	9,993	9,381	9,030	12,561	10,118	5,164
% Share of CO_2	11	22	28	28	28	28.5	29	23
CO_2 per Capita	1	4.9	7.1	6.7	6.4	8.8	7.1	3.6
CO_2 per GDP	0.5	0.8	0.5	0.5	0.4	0.4	0.3	0.1
India								
Population	850	1,140	1,317	1,317	1,317	1,469	1,469	1,469
% World	16	17	17	17	17	17	17	17
GDP	750	3,390	7,895	7,895	7,895	18,080	18,080	18,080
% World	3	5	7	7	7	11	11	11
Energy Demand (Mtoe)	319	620	934	904	869	1,535	1,405	1,243

(Continued)

TABLE 6.4 *(Continued)*

	1990	2008	2020 Current Policies	2020 New Policies	2020 450 Scenario	2035 Current Policies	2035 New Policies	2035 450 Scenario
Energy per Capita	0.4	0.5	0.7	0.7	0.7	1	1	1
CO_2	591	1,428	2,300	2,162	2,027	4,089	3,371	2,316
% Share of CO_2	3	5	6.5	6	6	10	10	11
CO_2 per Capita	0.7	1.3	1.8	1.6	1.5	2.8	2.3	1.6
CO_2 per GDP	0.8	0.4	0.3	0.3	0.3	0.2	0.3	0.1
European Union								
Population	473	499	514	514	514	521	521	521
% World	9	7.5	7	7	7	6	6	6
GDP	6,881	15,692	18,541	18,541	18,541	23,875	23,875	23,875
% World	28	22	17	17	17	14.5	14.5	14.5
Energy Demand (Mtoe)	1,632	1,749	1,753	1,723	1,690	1,831	1,732	1,665
Energy per Capita	3.5	3.5	3.4	3.4	3.3	3.5	3.3	3.2
CO_2	4,054	3,850	3,612	3,348	3,167	3,498	2,780	1,837
% Share of CO_2	19	12	10	10	10	8	8	8
CO_2 per Capita	8.6	7.7	7	6.5	6.2	6.7	5.3	3.5
CO_2 per GDP	0.6	0.3	0.2	0.2	0.2	0.2	0.1	0.1
United States								
Population	250	305	338	338	338	369	369	369
% World	5	5	4	4	4	4	4	4
GDP	5,801	14,369	18,223	18,223	18,223	24,890	24,890	24,890
% World	23	20.5	17	17	17	15	15	15
Energy Demand (Mtoe)	1,915	2,281	2,313	2,290	2,224	2,366	2,272	2,091
Energy per Capita	7.7	7.5	6.9	6.8	6.6	6.4	6.2	5.7
CO_2	4,869	5,596	5,420	5,307	5,030	5,202	4,442	2,942
% Share of CO_2	23	19	15	16	16	12	12.5	13.5
CO_2 per Capita	20	18	16	16	15	14	12	8
CO_2 per GDP	0.8	0.4	0.3	0.3	0.3	0.2	0.2	0.1

SOURCES: Population projections (excluding EU): World Bank Database, Total population projections 2010–2050. Available at http://go.worldbank.org/H4UN4D5KIo. EU population projections: EUROSTAT. Available at http://epp.eurostat.ec.europa.eu/tgm/table.do?tab=table&init=1&language=en&pcode=tps00002&plugin=1. GDP figures: IMF, *World Economic Outlook Database* (October 2010 edition). *WEO 2010*, pp. 59–62, 64, 68, 618–621, 630–633, 638–641, 670–677. IEA. *CO_2 Emissions from Fuel Combustion* (2010 edition), pp. 11.4, 11.6, 11.34, 11.36, 11.43, 11.45, 11.46, 11.48, 11.55, 11.57. IEA.

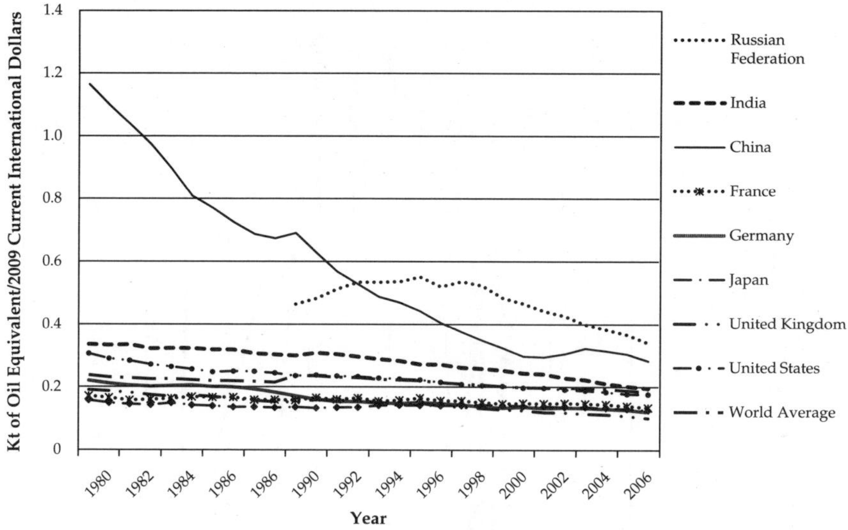

FIGURE 6.3 Total energy use per unit of GDP, various countries, 1980–2006
SOURCE: Created by author from data from World Development Indicators Database, available at http://data.worldbank.org. Accessed November 29, 2010.

depend heavily on it. Coal consumption by China has increased rapidly: in 2006, China consumed more coal than the United States and India combined and more than the rest of the remaining countries of the world. By 2030, China is expected to consume more coal than all the other countries of the world combined.[20] Coal is abundant and cheap in both China and India. Absent any taxes on carbon or any other harmful by-products of its use (like sulfur dioxide and nitrogen oxide), it is the cheapest and therefore the preferred energy source.

Rapidly Rising CO_2 Emissions

While there still remains some debate over the connection between CO_2 emissions and global warming, particularly in the United States, the overwhelming weight of world scientific opinion indicates a strong connection between CO_2 emissions and global annual temperatures. The bulk of scientific opinion holds that to keep global temperatures from rising more than two degrees Celsius from those prevailing

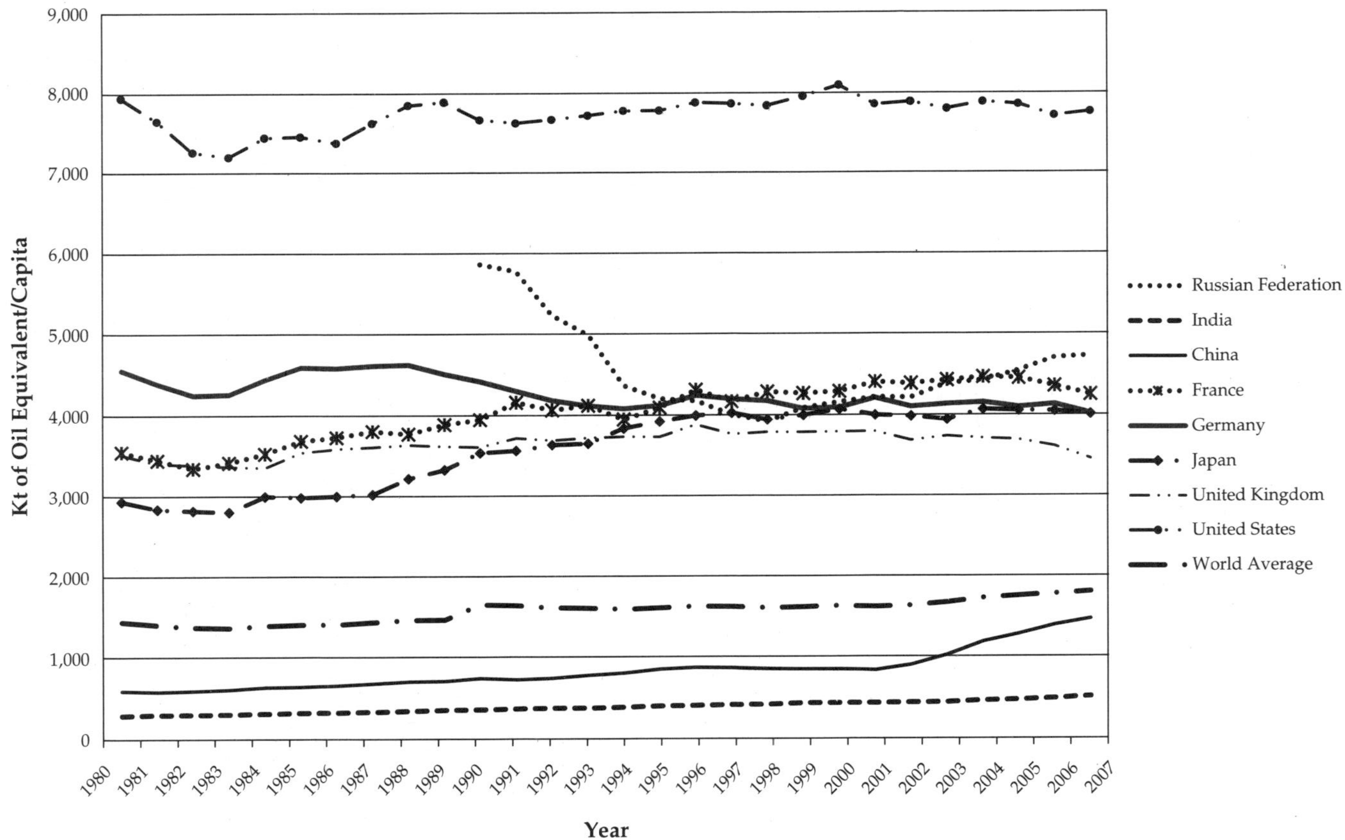

FIGURE 6.4 Total energy use per capita, various countries, 1980–2007

SOURCE: Created by author from data from World Development Indicators Database, available at http://data.worldbank.org. Accessed November 29, 2010.

before the Industrial Revolution, CO_2 concentration needs to be kept below 450 parts per million.[21]

CO_2 emissions per person vary significantly even among countries at the same level of per capita income (Figure 6.5). France, for example, has a much lower level of per capita emissions than the other European countries. Moreover, France and Germany have been significantly reducing their CO_2 emissions over time as a result of using cleaner energy technologies.[22] The United States reduced its energy intensity per capita over time between 1950 and 1980 but has not reduced it much since then.

Although developed countries have been reducing or at least maintaining constant CO_2 emissions per capita over time, China and India have been increasing theirs. This is a normal part of economic development as countries move from agrarian to industrial societies. Nevertheless, the very rapid increase in CO_2 emissions per capita in China is notable. In 2008, China surpassed the United States in absolute emissions. Its emissions per capita had been roughly half the global average in 1990, but by 2009, they were above the average.

Table 6.4, compiled from the International Energy Agency's *World Energy Outlook*, helps put projected energy and CO_2 emissions from China and India in global perspective. The IEA considers three scenarios in its projections. The "current policies" scenario takes into consideration only policies that have been adopted as of mid-2010. The "new policies" scenario assumes cautious implementation of the pledges made by countries under the Copenhagen Accord of December 2009 to reduce greenhouse gas emissions by 2020 and to phase out fossil fuel energy subsidies. The "450 scenario" is the IEA's estimate of what it would take to achieve the objective of limiting the concentration of greenhouse gases in the atmosphere to 450 parts per million of CO_2-equivalent and the global temperature increase to two degrees Celsius.[23]

In the new policies scenario, between 2008 and 2035, 57 percent of the world's total increase in energy demand will come from China and India alone (38 percent from China, 19 percent from India). Because they use a high percentage of carbon-based fuels (coal in particular) and have less energy-efficient technologies than developed countries, they will account for 91 percent of the increase in the world's total CO_2 emissions between 2009 and 2035 (59 percent from China, 32 from India).[24] Another way to look at the challenge is that by 2035 the CO_2 emissions of these two countries alone are projected to be roughly two-thirds of 1990 total world CO_2 emissions. Thus, it is clear that to keep the

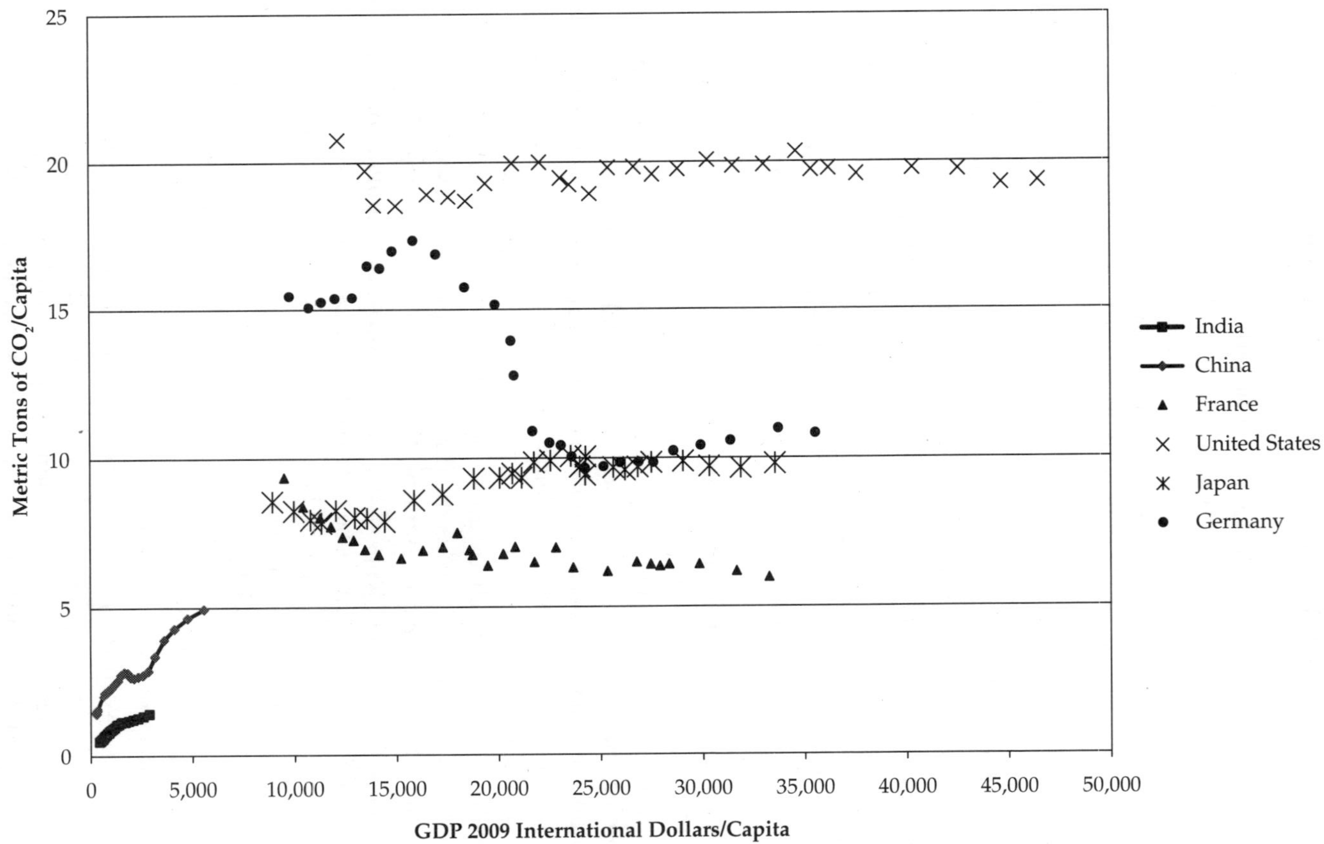

FIGURE 6.5 Time series on CO_2 emissions per capita versus GDP/capita, major energy users, 1980–2007

SOURCE: Created by author from data from World Development Indicators Database, available at http://data.worldbank.org. Accessed November 29, 2010.

temperature increase to only two degrees Celsius, both countries need to be part of a more aggressive global emissions reduction program.

There Is a Stalemate on Action to Deal with Climate Change Because It Is a Zero-Sum Game

China's and India's unwillingness to commit to limits on CO_2 emissions is a deal breaker for the United States, the other main player. If China, the United States, and India, which are, respectively, the first, second, and fifth largest emitters, do not commit to greater reductions, then the efforts to reduce global warming will fail. Even if the other countries were to reduce their emissions to half the 1990 levels, it would not be enough to stop global temperature rises above the two degrees Celsius limit. Under the current business-as-usual scenario, the emissions from the United States, China, and India by 2035 will be more than the world's total emissions in 1990 (Table 6.4).

The difficulties in reaching an agreement involve cost, equity, efficiency, competitiveness concerns, and problems of collective action.

Costs

Studies such as IEA (2009) and McKinsey (2008) argue that as much as 25 percent of the CO_2 reduction required by 2020 can be achieved using existing technology with investments that would pay for themselves from the energy savings. Although some reduction in emissions is cost effective because of the energy savings of adopting the more efficient existing technologies, reducing emissions to below 1990 levels involves increased costs as well as much greater R&D spending to develop new, more efficient technologies.

Estimates of the costs of reducing CO_2 emissions to mitigate climate change range from $140 to $175 billion a year in developing countries by 2030. These have associated financing needs of $265 to $565 billion a year to cover the upfront financing costs. Adaptation costs for developing countries are estimated at $30 to $100 billion a year.[25]

Implementing existing energy-efficient technologies and developing new ones is expensive. Developed countries are hurting from the costs of the 2008–2009 financial and economic crisis. In this financially constrained environment, the United States is unwilling to commit to tighter limits on CO_2 emissions or to transfer the technology and resources demanded by developing countries if China and India will not commit to absolute reductions in emissions.

Equity

Developing countries such as China and India argue that their emissions would not be a problem if the advanced countries had not been emitting CO_2 since the start of the coal-based Industrial Revolution. They object to having to bear the cost of capping their emissions while they are still poor countries. China's per capita income is one-fifteenth that of the United States, and India's is less than one-fortieth. They acknowledge that some of the CO_2 reductions can be achieved more efficiently in their countries than in developed countries, but they are unwilling to undertake the costs involved unless they get technology and resources from the advanced countries to do so.

Efficiency

It makes sense to transfer resources and technology to help developing countries with mitigation efforts because the cost effectiveness of undertaking some of these efforts in developing countries may be much higher than undertaking additional mitigation efforts in developed countries.[26] An example is helping a developing country offset the cost of a more expensive but more efficient and less polluting power plant that is likely to have an operational life of 40 to 50 years rather than retrofitting an old power plant in a developed country that has a much shorter operational life. There is already an UN-sponsored Clean Development Mechanism through which industrial countries can meet part of their Kyoto emission-reduction targets by supporting emission reductions/removal projects in developing countries. However, the funding is too small, and it has some limitations.[27]

At the December 2009 Copenhagen Summit, the advanced countries pledged to transfer up to $100 billion a year to developing countries by 2020 to help them mitigate emissions and adapt to global warming. However, no specifics for how this was to be accomplished were put in place. Which developing countries should benefit from these funds and how to allocate them will be very complicated issues. Here it is useful to differentiate between China and India. China is already above the world average in terms of energy consumption and CO_2 emissions per capita, and projections are for rapid rises unless much more aggressive mitigation actions are taken. On the other hand, India is still at such a low level of per capita income and industrialization that its energy consumption and CO_2 emissions per capita are projected to remain below the global average even through 2035 (Table 6.4). Thus, China is rapidly moving toward the profile of a developed economy on energy use and emissions, whereas India is still much more representative of a low-income developing country.

One proposal that was floated at the 2009 Copenhagen Climate Conference by He Yafei, the chief Chinese negotiator, was that China might not bid for the funds made available to developing countries.[28] This was initially reported by the *Financial Times*, but it was not formally confirmed by China.[29] If China were to follow through on that commitment, it would gain strong support from the developing world and put more pressure on the United States to tackle global warming seriously. The United States would need to follow through on its commitment to help fund the $100 billion a year that are supposed to be made available to help developing countries' mitigation and adaptation efforts.[30]

Competitiveness

Industry in the United States is concerned about the expense of reducing CO_2 emissions. To incur that cost would put U.S. industries at a competitive disadvantage with respect to China and India. Legislation working its way through Congress would put border taxes on imports from countries that have lower emissions standards.[31]

Collective Action

The Obama administration has proposed to lower emissions in the United States by 17 percent of 2005 levels by 2020. That will put U.S. emissions in 2020 just barely below its emissions in 1990. The European Union has committed to lowering its emissions to 20–30 percent below its emissions of 1990. Japan has committed to reducing its emissions to 25 percent below its 1990 level. Both the European Union and Japan have said that they are willing to go lower if there is a global deal that involves significant commitments by the United States and China. The Obama administration's 17 percent reduction proposal still needs to be ratified by the U.S. Congress, which is unwilling to commit to even this modest reduction unless China does more. China has committed to reducing the intensity of its emissions per unit of GDP by 40 to 45 percent of its 2005 levels by 2020.[32] Because of China's rapid growth, even a 45 percent reduction in CO_2 emissions per unit of GDP would still lead to total emissions in 2020 of more than four times its emissions in 1990. India has said that it is not willing to begin to put absolute caps on its emissions until the developed world has reduced its emissions to 40–45 percent below their 1990 levels, but it has committed to reducing its emission intensity by 20 to 25 percent of its 2005 intensity by 2020.[33]

Contrast with Success of Montreal Protocol to Reduce Ozone Emissions

The difficulties in reaching agreement on limiting CO_2 emissions stand in stark contrast to the success of international efforts to control the ozone emissions agreed to as part of the Montreal Protocol. Initially, there was strong resistance to this initiative by the main companies producing chlorofluorocarbons. But as scientific evidence that ozone depletion was being caused by the release of these gases into the atmosphere mounted, there was increasing pressure to act. The treaty was presented in 1987, became effective in 1989, and has been revised seven times, the last in Beijing in 1999. It has been ratified by all countries, and it is generally believed that it will be successful in limiting ozone depletion. Why did the Montreal Protocol work while the Copenhagen Climate Summit failed? There are four key reasons. One is that the nature of the problem was much smaller—substituting a refrigerant whose total sales were probably no more than a few billion dollars. Second, there were only a handful of producers. Third, the main producer, DuPont, had committed to making a change if there was compelling scientific evidence of the problem. Finally, DuPont also produced the substitute for the refrigerant, so it was not as negatively affected by the substitution.[34]

Recently, it has been suggested that the Montreal Protocol could be amended for use as a mechanism to remove hydrofluorocarbons (HFCs). Hydrofluorocarbons were the refrigerants that replaced the aerosols and other chemicals that were creating a hole in the ozone. They have thousands of times the global warming potential of CO_2.[35] Although removing HFCs may buy some time, it would not be enough to deal with the problem of temperature rise. There is also the practical problem that the Montreal Protocol was specifically designed to deal with ozone depletion. Since HFCs do not create a problem for the ozone layer, technically they are not covered under the provisions of the protocol. Therefore, the Montreal Protocol would have to be modified, and it is not clear how feasible this would be.

The Risky Geo-engineering Alternative

Another possible solution is geo-engineering, an umbrella term to cover different human-made procedures ranging from managing solar radiation to greenhouse gas remediation to carbon sequestration. One of the most common geo-engineering proposals is stratospheric aerosol injections into space to provide a sunshade with the potential of cooling the earth.[36] Another is seeding the sea with iron to increase the CO_2 it traps. There are many more.[37] A problem with these approaches is that they will provide only temporary relief. A more serious concern is that nobody knows the long-term effects these "solutions" will have on the earth's biocapacity. Therefore, they are considered risky. However, there is concern that some country may be tempted to use one of these emergency solutions if it begins to suffer too many problems from global warming.[38]

Technological Innovation Is a Way to Break the Climate Change Deadlock, but Not Enough Investments in R&D Are Being Made

Action on climate change is in gridlock because of the very different approaches and positions between the United States on one side and China and India on the other. This gridlock persists to a large extent because the issue has been framed as a zero-sum game: there is a finite amount of CO_2 that can be put into the atmosphere. To keep global temperatures from rising beyond two degrees Celsius, total emissions by 2050 must be 50 percent below the 1990 world total.[39]

Even if the rest of the world went to zero emissions, the business-as-usual projection for the emissions of China and India—assuming they implement the reductions they have pledged as of the middle of 2010—is that by 2035 their annual emissions will be almost two-thirds of the world's 1990 total. Therefore, it is clear that China and India need to reduce their emission intensity much more than they have volunteered so far.

The most productive way to go forward is to change the approach from a zero-sum game to a positive-sum game. What needs to be done to make this change? The obvious answer is to focus on developing better energy technologies.[40] However, not enough is being spent on R&D in this area. According to the International Energy Agency, public spending on clean energy R&D is only around $10 billion a year, whereas they estimate that $50 to $100 billion a year are necessary to achieve the CO_2 reduction targets required.[41] The IEA notes that the stimulus packages adopted to fight the global economic downturn in 2008–2009 increased public budget allocations to low carbon energy development, but these were one-shot deals, not long-term commitments. To achieve a major energy transformation, much larger commitments will be necessary over a sustained period of time.[42] Nothing like this sort of money is being allocated to the task.[43]

Interestingly, a recent study found that in six emerging economies—Brazil, Russia, India, Mexico, China, and South Africa—governments and state-owned enterprises invested more than $13.8 billion PPP in R&D in 2008. This was slightly higher than the total of investments by the governments of members of the International Energy Agency, all of which are members of the OECD. Their total investment in energy innovation was $12.7 billion PPP. This suggests that the governments of the advanced countries should invest more in energy R&D.[44]

Such an expanded R&D effort should consist of two components, both of which call for international collaboration. The first is massive investment in basic knowledge to underpin new energy technology. Investments in basic research will need to come from the public sector. The leaders in R&D are the United States, the European Union, Japan, China, Russia, and India.[45] It would make sense to establish a global energy research consortium led by the United States, China, and India that is open to others. This would be precompetitive research and could be justified as a global public good.

The second component is investment in developing, prototyping, demonstrating, and commercializing specific energy technologies. This is more complicated because there will be difficult issues of intellectual property rights.

Several points are worth noting. The first is that a large part of developing, prototyping, pilot testing, and demonstrating some of the technologies will still need to be financed by public funds. Private companies will not undertake projects on their own if they are too expensive or risky, if they cannot maintain control of the intellectual property developed, or if there is no clear prospect of a charge on CO_2 emissions. One example of where public finance will be necessary is pilot commercial-scale carbon sequestration technologies using different carbon capture technologies as well as mediums of sequestration.[46]

The second point is that various public and private partners can work out arrangements for sharing technology development and prototyping. For example, a country or company can work out an agreement such that by participating in a consortium and contributing to or taking responsibility for one type of approach or technology development, it gets access to the results of the efforts of others, or the participants share in the eventual licensing of the commercial technology that is developed.

There are some prior examples of collaborative programs at the regional, national, and international levels, although none of them would come close to what is required. Perhaps the best-known international public good collaborative R&D program is the Consultative Group on International Agricultural Research (CGIAR). This has been an ongoing program funded by governments, private foundations, and multilateral institutions.[47] Programs at the regional level include many of the EU framework programs on cooperative research. There are more examples of national-level programs. The best known is the Manhattan Project in the United States to develop the nuclear bomb during World War II or the Apollo Program to put a man on the moon. Other well-known programs are the Sematech consortium in the United States to help its semiconductor manufacturers compete with Japan.[48] Japan has had experience with many large-scale national programs. A review of the experiences of these various programs would be very helpful for lessons on how to structure the kind of large-scale program needed to carry out research in CO_2 emission reduction.

Developing a program to support a major energy technology revolution will be even more challenging than the programs just mentioned. Weiss and Bonvillian point out that such a program is more complex because it requires the support of multiple technologies as well as many actors.[49] Although their book focuses on the United States, their analysis provides a useful framework for what needs to be done at the global level. They argue that an appropriate approach should support a wide range of technological efforts; distinguish the types of obstacles these efforts are likely to face in the marketplace; and identify the kinds of incentive, policy, and organizational support they should receive.[50] They then propose three institutional innovations to fill in the gaps. These are a public cross-sectoral research project funding agency for energy "to identify innovation challenges and nurture the breakthrough needs to meet them;[51] a government corporation for financing demonstration, manufacturing, and scale-up; and road-mapping think tanks for technology assessment and policy research."[52] Most of these elements, including some of the proposed institutional arrangements, are relevant for the global technology push on energy technology.

Besides the complex organizational and management issues surrounding the big technology push, there is the problem of funding. Developed countries are cash constrained in the wake of the global economic crisis and do not have much money to put into this fund. In both the United States and the European Union, the funds that will be raised by carbon-cap programs are mostly earmarked to offset costs to consumers and the main energy users or, in some of the EU countries, to go back into the central budget. A very small amount of these funds is being allocated to increase R&D.[53] However, if greater awareness of the importance of the technology push is created, resources could be generated from other sources, such as a tax surcharge on energy, an earmarked contribution from special drawing rights, or some other mechanism.

It is ironic that although there is not enough money for R&D, $312 billion a year is currently spent by governments on subsidies for fossil fuel consumers. Most of this is in developing countries.[54] This money could be put to better use in financing the R&D in alternative energy technologies. The International Energy Agency also estimates that if the subsidies were completely removed, global energy demand would fall by 5 percent, equivalent to one-quarter of current U.S. demand.[55] This would reduce CO_2 emissions by 5.8 percent by 2020, which is a good part of the abatement necessary to meet the reduced emissions by 2020. In addition, they point out that although the subsidies are typically justified in terms of helping the poor, the bulk of them actually go to middle- and upper-income persons.[56] Therefore, reallocating some of the subsidies would provide the double benefit of reducing energy demand and CO_2 emissions as well as helping to finance R&D on alternative technologies.

Successfully dealing with climate change involves not only a big technology push along the lines outlined but also a strong demand pull. Although growing awareness about the problem of global warming may lead to some conservation efforts by consumers and firms, they will not be enough to make a significant change. Real reduction of consumption by consumers and industrial users of energy will require a significant increase in the prices of energy or an explicit tax or price on the carbon content of products. Such a pricing mechanism will trigger more conservation efforts by individual and industrial consumers. It will also stimulate the development of more efficient conventional energy technologies as well as lower-cost alternative energy technologies.

Europe and Japan have already developed some carbon trading mechanisms. Legislation has been proposed but not yet adopted in the United States, and the prospects are not clear.[57] China is said to be considering establishing a carbon trading system, and India seems to be contemplating one. In 2009, the United States established various cooperative energy development projects with China[58] and India. Although the funding for these projects does not seem to be assured, they are a base to build upon. They are, however, too modest to solve the problem.

China also needs to take much more aggressive action on energy efficiency and reduction of CO_2 emissions. China surpassed the United States as the largest user of energy in 2009.[59] It is the world's largest user of coal and is expected to account for most of the world's net increase in the use of coal for energy. Because of the nature of its political system, China has a strong advantage in implementing energy-saving and more environmentally friendly technology. It is already implementing tougher energy-efficiency standards than the United States for automobiles. It is also making large R&D investments to develop more environmentally friendly technologies. It is already the largest producer of photovoltaic cells and wind turbines for power and will account for the largest use of hybrid and electric cars.[60] Continuing to invest in these technologies will bring production down the learning curve and reduce costs. Improvements to clean coal technology and carbon sequestration will have a major impact on CO_2 emission reduction. Moreover, as China improves clean coal technology, it will develop a competitive advantage to export to other countries, and it will help address its own pollution-related health problems. The country that dominates energy-efficient technologies is likely to be the world's next innovation leader.

Given China's and India's very speedy growth and the hundreds of millions of people they are going to be assimilating into cities over the next 20 years, both would stand to gain from steering their future development strategy toward a sustainable path. For example, they could develop more environmentally sustainable urbanization strategies. These should take into account the energy and environmental requirements of different urban configurations, including not just land use but the location of work, living, and leisure activities, and the use of mass transit versus private cars. The European and Japanese models of compact cities with good public infrastructure are more appropriate for China and India than the high reliance on cars for personal transportation and large urban sprawl that are typical of the United States.[61]

There Is Also Increasing Pressure on the Environment from the Growth of Other Developing Countries

The challenge, however, goes beyond what China and India need to do. The United Nations projects that global population will rise to about 9 billion by 2050 and then stabilize.[62] Figure 6.6 shows the regional distribution of world population from 1950 to 2050. The ascent of China and India is indicative of the growing pressures of population increase. The population increase combined with rising incomes and the use of more energy and material inputs as countries get richer will compound pressure on the earth's carrying capacity. Such pressures are

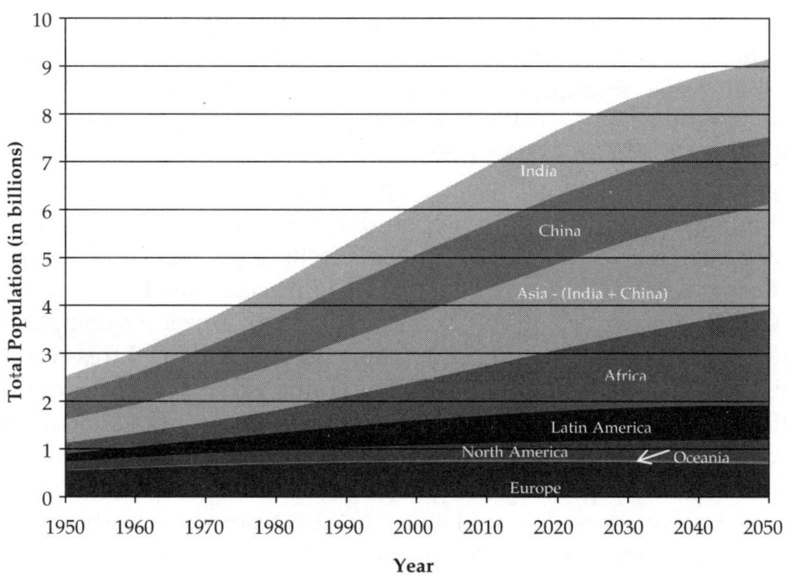

FIGURE 6.6 Increasing share of developing countries/regions in world population, 1950–2050

SOURCE: Created by author with data from UN Population Division databank, available at http://esa.un.org/unpp/index.asp. Accessed November 26, 2010.

NOTE: Population is shaded by country or region.

not independent of how resources are managed, who controls them, or technology and social justice.

Technological improvement will be an important part of the solution to the pressure of population growth on limited environmental resources. Technology can make it possible to find and use more mineral and other resources, to use resources more efficiently (including recycling), and to develop synthetic substitutes.[63] Technology can also improve welfare and increase life spans. Longer lives, however, will also put more pressure on the environment.

Coming up with alternative development models is a tremendous but necessary challenge and opportunity for China, India, and other low-income developing countries. Most still have rural populations that have not yet benefited from the amenities of urban life. The potential is that they can learn from mistakes made by other countries, including China, in their development strategy. One area with tremendous potential is environmentally sustainable urbanization. For example, the urban population in India in 2008 was only 30 percent compared with a weighted average of 75 percent for upper-middle-income countries.[64] India is about to undergo massive urbanization. Projections are that by 2040 between 50 and 60 percent of its population will be urban.[65] If India can handle this demographic shift in a more energy-efficient and sustainable way than others have, it will save itself much cost. This means creating more energy-efficient mass transit systems along the European model, designing more energy-efficient residences and workplaces, and better urban planning. As a relative latecomer to urbanization, India can take advantage of the lessons from other countries to develop more ecofriendly and sustainable cities.

Planning for more sustainable lifestyles is a challenge facing developed and developing countries alike. It will require more money and resources for research, experimentation, and pilot implementation. It will also require a change in mind-set.

CHAPTER 7

Power Shifts and Rising Frictions Have Implications for the Global System and the United States

ACCOMMODATING THE SWIFT ASCENT of China and India will not be easy for economic, environmental, and geopolitical reasons. The first section of this chapter summarizes the changes in the relative importance of these two countries across the seven elements of the framework developed in Chapter 2. These confirm that a major power shift is under way. The next section summarizes the frictions resulting from this power shift. The current global system was designed within a different context 60 years ago. There are now new issues and new major powers. The following section focuses on the risk that tensions may lead to more serious problems, the most obvious being wars over trade, resources, and climate change. There are also risks that the geopolitical frictions could break out into a new type of cold war or even worse. The next section puts the current system into historical perspective and argues that it is already in a process of change. The following section focuses on what this means for the United States as the main architect and major power in the current system. The United States faces some serious challenges and has difficult choices to make. It needs to strengthen its economic fundamentals and work with other powers to meet the challenge of China's swift ascent or face a more rapid decline in the relative welfare of its population. This will involve forceful negotiations with China on many factors that are threatening the existing international system and that need to be addressed by all the major powers.

The Rapid Rise of China and India Is Putting Pressure on the Global Governance System

Table 7.1 summarizes the changes in the relative shares of the United States, the European Union, China, and India in six of the seven elements of the framework developed in Chapter 2.[1] China has already become the largest country in 9 of the 18 indicators in the table: population, merchandise exports, foreign exchange reserves, total energy use, total CO_2 emissions, tertiary students, mobile phone users, Internet users, and military personnel. It is quite telling that by 2007 it had already surpassed the United States and the European Union in cell phone and Internet users, showing how information and telecommunications technologies are diffusing and reflecting the impact of large population size. It is also remarkable that China is ahead of Japan[2] and Germany (the other two major economies besides the United States) in all the remaining indicators except exports of services, where it is likely to pass Japan by 2011 and Germany by 2013. Moreover, at the current differential in growth rates, China probably will be larger than the United States in all the remaining indicators by 2030.

India is lagging far behind China in all of the indicators but population, although it has also shown a very swift increase in cell phone and Internet use. India's relative importance on the global scene has also increased rapidly. Its GDP measured in PPP will surpass Japan's by 2012. If India continues its current growth trends, in fewer than two decades it will have the relative shares that China now has. By 2035, it will consume almost as much energy as the European Union, but its CO_2 emissions will be higher because of its higher proportion of carbon-based fuels and lower energy efficiency (Table 6.4). Consequently, India will also be putting very large pressures on the global system. In addition, it risks possible collision with China in various areas, including trade, the environment, and geopolitics, as will be developed below.

Growing Friction Areas Are Beyond the Current Capabilities of the International System

Globalization is a double-edged sword: the world as a whole has benefited from globalization through specialization and exchange, but interdependence has also increased tensions across countries. The swift

TABLE 7.1 Power shifts: Changing global shares for U.S., EU, China, and India, 1980–2009 (percentage of global total)

	U.S.				EU				CHINA				INDIA			
	1980	1990	2000	2009	1980	1990	2000	2009	1980	1990	2000	2009	1980	1990	2000	2009
Population	5.1	4.7	4.6	4.5	10.0	8.7	7.7	7.2	22.1	21.5	20.8	19.7	15.5	16.1	16.7	17.1
GDP in PPP	22.6	22.8	23.3	19.7	27.3	26.6	24.7	21.2	2.0	3.5	7.0	12.6	2.4	3.0	3.8	5.2
Nominal GDP	25.2	26.3	30.5	24.5	33.2	33.3	26.5	28.1	1.7	1.6	3.7	8.6	1.7	1.4	1.4	2.3
Merchandise Exports[a]	11.4	11.3	12.1	8.5	40.1	43.9	37.1	35.6	0.9	1.8	3.9	9.6	0.4	0.5	0.7	1.3
Service Exports	10.1	16.3	18.4	14.1	54.6	49.7	42.0	44.6	0.0	0.7	2.0	4.4	0.8	0.6	1.1	3.1
FDI Inflows (net)	31.1	22.8	20.0	12.1	42.1	49.6	55.1	41.6	0.0	1.6	2.4	7.0	0.2	0.1	0.2	3.1
FDI Outflows (net)	27.8	12.9	10.5	14.2	35.7	38.5	55.5	30.6	0.0	0.7	0.2	6.9	0.0	0.0	0.1	3.7
Foreign Reserve	25.3	13.6	5.8	4.3	60.4	39.3	17.7	7.5	1.5	2.7	7.7	26.1	1.8	0.4	1.8	3.0
Market Capitalization	N/A	32.5	46.9	31.0	N/A	21.6	24.9	18.4	N/A	0.0	1.8	10.3	N/A	0.4	0.5	2.4
Energy Consumption (08)	25.4	22.4	22.6	18.6	21.2	18.5	17.0	14.3	8.4	10.1	11.2	17.4	2.9	3.7	4.6	5.1
CO_2 Emissions (08)	24.2	21.6	23.2	19.1	22.3	17.9	15.4	13.0	7.5	10.9	13.8	22.4	1.8	3.1	4.8	4.9
Tertiary Students (08)	N/A	23.6	13.4	11.5	N/A	14.2	13.8	10.4	N/A	6.8	7.5	16.8	N/A	8.3	9.5	9.4
R&D Spending (08)	N/A	N/A	29.8	23.7	N/A	N/A	21.0	18.4	N/A	N/A	2.9	8.4	N/A	N/A	1.3	1.9
S&T Articles (07)	39.9	40.3	30.6	27.7	34.6	32.8	34.5	31.6	0.3	1.3	2.9	7.5	3.5	1.9	1.6	2.4
Mobile Telephone Users (07)	47.1	14.8	7.9	6.7	27.6	35.3	17.1	15.6	0.2	11.6	16.4	15.9	0.0	0.5	7.0	8.6
Internet Users (07)	75.8	31.5	16.3	14.5	12.5	25.3	20.9	19.4	0.0	5.7	15.7	18.8	0.0	1.4	3.4	3.3
Military Spending	24.1	32.9	31.7	34.2	20.2	19.4	20.9	14.6	4.8	2.6	5.6	9.5	0.8	2.6	5.1	5.8
Military Personnel	8.5	9.1	5.0	5.6	16.8	14.6	8.9	8.5	19.2	14.6	13.3	10.5	4.6	5.3	8.1	9.4

SOURCE: Created by author from World Bank, Development Indicators database.

NOTE: Parentheses in first column refer to the latest year for which data are available if earlier than 2009.

[a] The trade and foreign investment figures in this table are the sum for each country in the world. The data for the EU are therefore overestimated because it does not net out the trade or direct foreign investment within the EU. Roughly two-thirds of the EU's exports are among its member countries. Exports to countries outside the EU in 2009 were only 17.4% of world exports net of intra-EU trade. Similarly, net imports of the EU from the rest of the world were only 16.3% of world imports net of intra-EU trade. The net GDP of the EU would also be smaller than in the table once trade activity across the countries was netted out.

growth of China and India is creating frictions with the rest of the world in many areas. These tensions can be grouped under three headings: economic, environmental, and geopolitical/security. The trade, technology, and finance issues covered in Chapter 5 are likely to lead to trade confrontations and perhaps even a trade war. The environmental issues covered in Chapter 6 are likely to lead to resource wars as well as a higher risk of climate change. Geopolitical competition could lead to ideological wars reminiscent of the Cold War era. Finally, security frictions could lead to a new type of cold war, cyberwarfare, and military confrontations or, in a worst-case scenario, to hegemonic war.

With an understanding of these tensions, it is important to examine the extent to which the existing international system can help manage them. The operation of the international system depends on the power and prestige of the main states and the rights and rules recognized for the interaction across national borders. The latter can be formal, but many international issues are dealt with informally, especially among the larger powers.

An examination of the rise of China and India indicates that there are three problems with the existing international governance system: an increasing power vacuum in global governance, outdated global governance institutions, and missing institutions or mechanisms for global governance. Regarding the first, the United States is not as hegemonic as it was during the post–World War II era. Coming out of World War II, the United States dominated the world economy, accounting for 27 percent of global GDP in PPP terms.[3] It developed the main institutions of the global governance system—the IMF, the World Bank, and the GATT (now the WTO)—and the dollar became the global reserve currency. It promoted the reconstruction of Europe and Japan, whose economies recovered quickly. By the 1980s, Europe had 24 percent of world GDP, Japan had 8 percent, and the United States had fallen to 22 percent in PPP terms.[4] In addition, from about 1980 to the present, there has been a profound shift of economic power from the United States and Europe to emerging Asia, in particular to China and India (Table 7.1). The area in which the United States still maintains overwhelming power is military capability.

However, as can be seen from the United States' difficulties in Vietnam and more recently in Iraq and Afghanistan, military might alone is not sufficient to guarantee security. Moreover, the unpopularity of the U.S. invasion of Iraq and the flaws in the U.S. financial system that were made evident by the 2008–2009 financial and economic crisis have somewhat sapped its international prestige and economic power. The United States has been living beyond its means and has become the world's biggest debtor. The weakness of the United States is exacerbating some of the problems of the international system, as currently there is no other country or group of countries that can provide the stability the system needs. The European Union is having major currency problems, which are threatening the very composition of the union. Furthermore, China and India, or even all the BRICs together, are still too small and uncoordinated to balance the system.

In his classic book *After Hegemony,* Keohane argues that, in a global system in which there is no longer such a dominant hegemonic power as the United States was after World War II, it is more important to develop effective international institutions, or "international regimes," to facilitate cooperation across self-serving nation-states. For each of the friction areas identified by the rise of China and India, Table 7.2 lists the existing global governance institutions or mechanisms and what is missing or not working for each of them. Although there has been limited progress in some areas, it is clear that there is still a long way to go in developing an appropriate international regime.

The first problem is that these institutions or mechanisms do not cover the issues of an unstable financial system, increased competition for resources (especially energy and water), the risks of disastrous climate change, insufficient support for R&D to deal with global problems (such as climate change, famines, global pandemics, etc.), or the new threat of cybersecurity. The second is that they cannot deal with some of the newer aspects of traditional international issues such as unfair trade regimes, undervalued currencies, balance of payments surpluses, foreign direct investment from developing countries, intellectual property piracy, nuclear proliferation, or increasing global inequality.

The third problem is that the formal institutions established by the strong hand of the United States and its Western European allies in the post–World War II period[5] have governance structures that represent economic power as it was at the end of World War II, not the current distribution of economic power. In addition, institutions based on a one country–one vote system like the UN and the WTO do not adequately represent economic power or population. Moreover, because of the growth in the number of member countries, their governance structures have become unwieldy. It is difficult to reach global consensus given the great diversity of interests of their members. No one has the power to lead, but there is a multiplicity of veto players. This has led to a

TABLE 7.2 Frictions, global governance institutions, and mechanisms

Friction	Institution/Mechanism	Missing Area or Weakness
Trade		
Unfair trade competition (i)	WTO for trade rules and disputes	Doha Trade Rounds have failed; a new round is needed Slow process to examine and adjudicate trade disputes
Exchange rate undervaluation (i)	WTO	Undervalued exchange rate not covered under WTO IMF lacks a mechanism to deal with exchange rate undervaluation
International Finance		
Global financial crisis 2008–2009 (m)	Financial Stability Board	Missing stronger national and international regulation of financial institutions and of global financial systemic risk
Balance of payments surpluses (i)	IMF	IMF was set up to deal with balance of payment deficits, not surpluses, and has no enforcement mechanism for surplus countries
Foreign direct investment (i)		No global institution for regulation of FDI, only bilateral investment treaties
Technology		
Intellectual property piracy (i)	WTO provisions on intellectual property rights	Lack of mechanisms to induce enforcement and appropriate penalties
Insufficient research on global public goods (m)	CGIAR for international agricultural research	No formal mechanisms to induce greater joint development of technologies for global public goods outside agriculture, except for some private efforts.
Environment		
CO_2 emissions (m)	Kyoto Protocol UNFCC	U.S. did not sign because China and India were exempted; cumbersome UN system led to limited accomplishments of the 2009 Copenhagen Climate Summit; need new organization or mechanism to deal with rising CO_2 emissions

(*Continued*)

TABLE 7.2 *(Continued)*

Friction	Institution/Mechanism	Missing Area or Weakness
Energy (m)	International Energy Agency	China and India are not members since agency was created in 1970s to represent main countries on demand for energy side to offset supply side power of OPEC
Water (m)		No global institution with enforcement capability
Competition for other resources (m)		No global institution with enforcement capability
Environmental sustainability (m)		No formal institution for sustainable development strategies.
Geopolitical and Social Issues		
International relations (i)	United Nations General Assembly/G-7, G8, G-20	UN not representative of population and unwieldy, difficult to make decisions; "G" groups unrepresentative
Increasing global inequality (i)	Bilateral foreign aid-DAC/OECD	Development aid is small, no major global redistributive mechanism; China and India not in DAC since not OECD
	World Bank and regional development banks	Limited in their ability to bring about change since they have to work with governments, which are often the problem
International Security		
Military frictions (i)	UN Security Council	No permanent seat for India; no mechanism on terrorism
Nuclear proliferation (i)	Non-proliferation treaty	India has not signed; China supports rogue states such as North Korea and Iran
Terrorism (m)		No mechanism
Cybersecurity (m)		No mechanism
Hegemonic war (m)		Very difficult to contain major powers if opt for war

SOURCE: Created by author.

NOTE: (i) stands for incomplete or not sufficiently effective institution/mechanism to deal with the problem; (m) stands for missing institution.

proliferation of ad hoc groups expanding from the G-6 to G-7, G-8, and most recently, G-20.[6] However, they all suffer from a lack of legitimacy from the perspective of the countries that are excluded.

Risks That Frictions May Lead to Greater Problems

Improving the representation of rising powers such as China and India in global governance institutions and developing more appropriate institutions will help give these countries a greater influence in developing appropriate ways to work out some of these tensions, but this will take time. Incumbent powers are resisting changes in relative power and are dragging their feet on reform because there are no adequate intergovernmental controls to compel them to contribute more to the global commons. Rising powers are too closely examining their narrow short-term interests and not taking on larger global responsibilities. There is a risk that in pursuing their own national goals without heeding the consequences for the rest of the world, they may destabilize the global system. The risks are a trade war, resource wars, climate change, cold wars, cyberwars, conventional wars, and in the worst-case scenario, a hegemonic war (Table 7.3).

Risk of Trade War

The increased technological capability of China and India and the swift expansion of their exports (manufactured products in the case of China and information-enabled services in the case of India) are putting a great deal of restructuring pressure on the global economy. Even before the 2008–2009 economic crisis, there were already worries about the downside of trade, particularly in developed economies as opposed to the main developing countries which were expanding their exports. These have been accelerated by the crisis. The Pew Global Attitudes Project, for example, found that the percentage of respondents saying that trade was a good thing fell from 78 percent in 2002 to 66 percent in 2010 in the United States, from 88 percent to 79 percent in France, and from 78 percent to 71 percent in Mexico. In contrast, in China it increased from 90 percent to 93 percent and in India from 88 percent to 90 percent over the same period.[7]

In advanced countries such as the United States and the countries of the European Union, there is now a broad popular perception that globalization is contributing to stagnating wages, increasing inequality,

TABLE 7.3 Increasing frictions: China and India with respect to the world and to each other

	China and Rest of World	India and Rest of World	Between China and India
Trade War			
Subsumes: • exchange rate • global imbalances	Tension because of China's exchange rate undervaluation and large trade surpluses	Not as likely as China since it has trade deficits	Possible; they compete in many product areas
• FDI from developing countries	Concern about China buying natural resources and technology firms	Like China, although Indian state-owned firms are not as active	Not clear they will have common position on Doha trade rounds
• Intellectual piracy	Extensive complaints about Chinese IP piracy	Fewer complaints about IP piracy than with China	IPR may become more problematic as they compete more in trade
Resource Wars	Possibly over energy and resources, such as over islands in East and South China Seas	Possibly over energy in general and water with neighbors, including China	Yes, especially over water from Himalayan glaciers that feed main rivers in Asia
Climate Change			
Not controlling emissions will lead to global warming	China argues that it's unfair to make it pay for CO_2 since problem was created by earlier emissions of now-developed countries	Same argument as China, plus the fact that it is a smaller emitter and a poorer country	Perhaps, because China is already above global average per capita energy consumption and CO_2 emissions, while India will be below global averages even up to 2035
Risk of geo-engineering attempts with unknown consequences if mitigation efforts fail	China may go for geo-engineering if it begins to experience negative consequences of climate change	India may go for geo-engineering if it begins to suffer costs of climate change	

Geopolitical Competition and Ideological War			
Note: This is also over human rights, nuclear nonproliferation, and form of government	Yes with respect to Western democracies and Japan	Not so likely with Western democracies and Japan because India's democratic government and market-oriented system are more consistent with those countries	Yes because of different ideologies combined with frictions on borders, water, and possibly trade
Security Conflicts			
Cyberwarfare	Many current cyberattacks are traced to China	India potentially has great capability in this area, but there is little evidence that it is active	Possible if frictions between them increase
Military Conflict	Possibly over Taiwan or other neighbors in South China Seas; China's support of N. Korea is also a potential problem	Possibly with Pakistan because of old rivalries and unstable region	Limited to border tensions in short run
Hegemonic War	Perhaps with U.S. in long term	Less likely since India is ideologically closer to existing powers and not considered as big a security threat as much larger China	Hegemonic war between them unlikely until both become dominant powers

SOURCE: Created by author.

rising unemployment, and a falling standard of living. To counter these negative effects, governments are focusing on improving social safety nets and increasing adjustment assistance. However, because of the 2008–2009 economic crisis, most developed countries have poor fiscal conditions and many have had to cut back on adjustment assistance. As a result, they are pushing more strongly internationally for a "level playing field" on labor and environmental standards and market exchange rates.

China and other developing countries are concerned that advanced countries are trying to contain their upsurge by using indirect protectionist barriers, tightening rules on trade subsidies and the use of industrial policy to develop domestic industries. They also complain that developed countries are using safeguards on labor conditions, environmental impact, and product safety to constrain their growth. In sum, developing countries argue the developed countries are barring the use of the policies that they successfully used to promote their own development.[8] However, there is some concern among other developing countries that China's very swift expansion of manufactured exports is also negatively affecting their prospects for export-led growth.[9] Therefore, both developed economies and China (and to a lesser extent India) need to provide more favorable conditions for trading with the least developed economies.

The Eighth Global Trade Monitoring Report released on November 8, 2010,[10] found that the G-20[11] countries have failed to live up to their pledge from the meeting of November 20, 2008, at which world leaders agreed not to resort to protectionist measures. The report found that since November 2008, governments had implemented 692 discriminatory measures that were likely to harm foreign commercial interests. In addition, the discriminatory measures were disproportionally directed against the lower-income countries.[12] Table 7.4 summarizes the number of protectionist actions undertaken since November 2008 by the European Union, the United States, the BRICs (Brazil, Russia, India, and China), and Japan. The table also includes the number of tariff lines, sectors, and trading partners affected. As can be inferred, protectionism has been increasing very fast over the last two years.

The two countries hit hardest with protectionist actions are China, with a total of 337 measures, and the United States, with 260. Although the pace of protectionism pressure has declined somewhat since the June 2010 G-20 Toronto Summit, the focus has changed to criticism of exchange-rate manipulation, especially against China. Leading the

TABLE 7.4 Summary of protectionist trade measures since November 2008 G-20 meeting to October 2010

Country/ Region	Number of Discriminatory Measures (global rank from most to least measures)	Number of Tariff Lines Affected (out of 4-digit product classification)	Number of Sectors Affected (out of 2-digit sector classification)	Number of Trading Partners Affected (out of 229)
EU 27	166	467	57	168
Russia	85	426	36	143
India	47	365	32	145
Brazil	32	240	29	130
China	22	338	28	160
U.S.	15	140	22	124
Japan	12	135	12	112

SOURCE: Created by author from data in Evenett, Simon J., ed. 2010. *Tensions Contained . . . for Now: The 8th GTA Report*. Centre for Economic Policy Research (CEPR). London: CEPR.

charge, the United States tried to get other countries to support it in putting pressure on China to appreciate its currency faster at the October 2010 IMF meetings in Washington, D.C., and also at the G-20 Summit in Korea in November 2010. But it got pushback from other countries, including Germany, Japan, and Brazil (whose currency was appreciating due to large financial inflows from developed countries seeking higher returns in its booming market).[13] In addition, at the November 2010 summit, many countries criticized the United States for its Federal Reserve's decision to buy $600 billion of long-term debt, which was seen as an attempt to depreciate the dollar. Thus, the focus seems to have shifted at least temporarily to currency wars as a way to deal with competitiveness issues. Currency manipulation is a substitute for tariff wars to some extent. As global imbalances continue, unemployment in developed countries remains high, and countries like the United States go into election cycles, it is quite likely that protectionist pressures through tariff and nontariff barriers and other discriminatory trading practices or manipulated currency depreciations will continue to escalate. These could develop into major confrontations that could lead to a reduction of global trade and a loss of overall global welfare.

An additional factor that increases the risk of trade wars is the environmental legislation that has been working its way through the U.S. Congress.[14] Several of the bills in process propose to establish carbon taxes against imports of products from countries whose environmental legislation is not as strong as the United States'. This country-specific discrimination is contrary to WTO principles. Were it to be implemented, it could lead to major trade wars that could undermine the global trading system.[15]

For a sobering example of the dangers of trade wars leading to downward spirals, it is instructive to go back to the interwar years of the twentieth century, which saw the Smoot-Hawley Tariff Act and the trade wars it unleashed. Smoot-Hawley was passed in the United States in June 1930 to counteract overcapacity in the U.S. economy and a weak labor market. The act quadrupled previous tariff rates and imposed an effective tax of 60 percent on more than 3,200 products and materials imported into the United States. The U.S. imports decreased 66 percent and exports decreased 61 percent between 1929 and 1933. It is hard to separate the effects of the increased tariff and nontariff barriers to world trade from the effects of the Great Depression.[16] However, although the tariff was passed after the stock market crash of October 1929, many economic historians argue that the discussions leading up to passage of the act were one of the factors responsible for the crash and that the trade wars that ensued made the recession worse.[17]

Resource Nationalism and Resource Wars

As noted in Chapter 6, both China and India are very natural resource poor on a per capita basis and must therefore import many raw materials and commodities from the rest of the world. In addition, as noted in Chapter 5, both countries are also buying up natural resource companies in Australia, Africa, and Latin America.[18] Their large appetite and strong drive to secure natural resources worry other countries that also need to import natural resources, namely, the United States, the European Union, and Japan.[19] This tension raises the specter of resource wars.[20] In addition, China has already shown a predisposition to use natural resources as a political bargaining tool when it banned the export of rare earths to Japan for part of 2010 when it had a diplomatic dispute over the arrest of the captain of a Chinese fishing boat that collided with two Japanese patrol boats in disputed waters of the East China Sea.[21]

The Middle East is a tinderbox for conflicts over oil. China and India have been investing heavily in various Middle Eastern countries, including Iran. This complicates relations with the United States and the European Union because of Iran's nuclear ambitions. In addition, as seen in Chapter 2, there have already been several wars in the Middle East over oil.

Water scarcity is probably as serious a problem as energy for India and China. This problem will be compounded by climate change, but it is already a major issue in its own right. Both China and India are water poor on a per capita basis, and the problems of water shortages are becoming more serious. In addition, both countries are very dependent on the Himalayan glaciers, which feed 20 major rivers providing water to more than 40 percent of the world's population. These include the Indus, the Brahmaputra, the Ganges, and the Mekong. Because of its water shortages, China has been diverting water from the more water-abundant south to the dry northwest. This large project is running into problems, as the sources in the south have not been able to meet the needs; hence, China is planning to divert water from the Himalayan glaciers. There are also reported plans to build a dam on the Brahmaputra at the point where it enters India. There are no bilateral agreements between China and India covering water flows on their common rivers. Water depletion from the melting of the Himalayan glaciers due to global warming, water diversion, and the building of dams by China raises the risk of water wars between China and India.[22]

China is also building many dams on the rivers that flow into Cambodia, Thailand, and Vietnam. There is a need to develop an appropriate institution to manage water sources and distribution in the area.[23]

Risk of Climate Change

Despite the evidence of the impact of human activity on rising global temperatures, there has been little progress on reducing CO_2 emissions. Copenhagen failed to achieve its expectations. This is the classic problem of collective action and free riders. Although everyone knows that concerted action will be to the benefit of all, many countries are not willing to shoulder the costs if they can get away with free riding on the actions of others. As noted in Chapter 6, to break the deadlock, it will help to turn the situation from a zero-sum to a positive-sum game. One key approach is to create a global initiative to make major energy technology improvements. The United States, China, and India have very strong stakes in developing an effective mechanism to address global warming; they also have considerable technological capability.

The three countries should scale up their current limited cooperation programs to a major global program and invite other countries to join. This will require major resources as well as commitment from all three countries to do much more than what they have pledged so far. If the United States, China, and India can increase their commitments, the European Union, Japan, and the rest of the world are likely to increase their commitments, too.

The most effective way to get real action on climate change, besides a big push on the technology development side, is to develop a global pricing mechanism for CO_2 emissions. The advantage of pricing this negative externality is that it affects both the demand and the supply sides. On the demand side, higher prices will encourage less energy consumption, the use of more energy-efficient and less CO_2-emitting technologies, less energy-intensive urbanization, and lifestyle changes toward conservation.[24] On the supply side, higher prices will encourage the development of more energy-efficient alternative technologies. Without higher prices, there is no real incentive to adopt more environmentally sound practices or encourage the development of better technologies. It should be recalled that the reason the concerns about limits to growth in the 1970s[25] proved unfounded was that rising prices led to more conservation and to the development and deployment of more efficient technologies. Without price signals or strong regulations, there will not be much progress on global warming. Prices are a more efficient way than regulations to equalize the costs and benefits of different actions. Regulations may force more expensive solutions in some regulated sectors than could be obtained by more cost-effective adaptation efforts in other sectors.

In short, there is need for aggressive leadership to break the logjam of the collective action needed to deal with the problem of global warming. The United States and China are the two largest laggards; it is time for them to become leaders. The European Union and Japan have already done the most, and they are willing to do more if the United States and China come on board. India and other developing countries would be likely to join a broader global effort, particularly if funding were available to help them deal with mitigation and adaptation efforts. Russia will be the most challenging to bring into the fold because it has so much to gain from maintaining the status quo, given its vast hydrocarbon reserves and geographic location. However, evidence is piling up that Russia, too, will incur major costs from climate change.[26]

Growing Geopolitical Frictions

Economic competition can spill over into Cold War–style ideological competition.[27] There is a risk that the competition between the United States and China could degenerate into an ideological battle in which China becomes the "new USSR."[28] Several authors, such as Halper and Ramos,[29] have pointed out the growing influence of what they call an alternative "Beijing Consensus" set of economic policies inspired by China's development model in opposition to the "Washington Consensus" promoted by the United States and U.S.-dominated institutions such as the IMF and the World Bank. This alternative system is gaining adherents, particularly among strong states whose leaders find this autocratic system more attractive and easier to deal with than the Western systems which impose conditionality tied to progress toward democracy and respect for human rights. If the world were to fragment into two economic/political systems along these two axes, it is likely that this could feed a new arms race like that which occurred during the Cold War. That arms race led to misallocation of resources toward military buildup. Arguably, the cost of the military escalation of the Cold War led to the eventual collapse of the Soviet Union and to large environmental costs from weapons production and testing in both countries.[30] It also led to large budget deficits and inflation in the United States. The major powers should avoid this and focus instead on challenges such as climate change, water scarcity, cooperation on fighting nuclear proliferation and terrorism, and reducing global inequalities.

China is considered to have very strong capabilities in all aspects of a new kind of war: cyberwarfare.[31] India potentially has this capability as well, but it is not discussed much. Cyberwarfare can include partial warfare, such as hacking attacks to steal military secrets and strategic logistical and tactical information. It can include hacking attacks to steal sophisticated technology from the military, government, private firms, universities, and research institutions. It can involve cyberattacks to disable critical infrastructure such as the electricity grid, the air traffic control system, or the financial sector.[32] It can also be an important element in a broader conventional war because military command and control systems are so dependent on electronic information management and communications.

Cybersecurity is a broader problem than just cyberwarfare.[33] The 2010 WikiLeaks release of hundreds of thousands of U.S. State Department cables shows the damage that can be done to international relations by cybertheft. Cyberattacks are also becoming an increased security concern for commercial enterprises. The cables included indications that the attacks against Google and 30 other large multinationals in China in early 2010 may have been cleared, if not orchestrated, by people at high levels of the Chinese government.

There is also the risk of conventional war. In the medium term, there is likely to be increased tension over water scarcity that could degenerate into some sort of military confrontation between China and India. Additionally, the regional flashpoints of China (Taiwan and support for North Korea) and of India (Pakistan and Kashmir) could escalate into larger wars involving the United States and China.

In the longer term, when the size of the Chinese economy surpasses that of the United States, there is some risk of a major war between the two countries.[34] This scenario may appear farfetched, particularly because China and India have so far sought to play a greater role within the global system rather than challenge it. Realist strategists argue, however, that a country's economic size matters because economic resources give it the latent power to be a security threat to the reigning hegemon and must therefore be contained.[35] More generally, there is a concern that even democratic states often act ruthlessly in pursuing the narrow interests of their leaders, as when U.S. President George W. Bush decided to invade Iraq after September 11, 2001, even though there was no concrete evidence of Iraqi involvement in the attack or that Iraq had weapons of mass destruction. There is a greater worry, then, of what a large authoritarian state pursuing its self-interests may do when it becomes the largest economy and has the power to do or take what it desires—for instance, to discipline or subdue a state that has somehow affronted it economically or politically or to take critical resources that it cannot obtain by trade.

Evolution Within the Existing System or the Rise of a New System?

It can be argued that the world has gone through five major systems over the last 200 years. These are:

- Mercantilism until 1849 (Netherlands, France, Spain, United Kingdom), with United Kingdom as leader
- Liberalism and relatively free trade under United Kingdom rule until World War I

- Breakdown of trade—World War I followed by Great Depression, the 1930s trade wars, and World War II
- The Bretton Woods system—the golden years of trade expansion and world growth 1945–1972
- The post–Bretton Woods system—1972–2008/2009

Using the framework developed in Chapter 2, Table 7.5 summarizes the main characteristics of each system, except for the period between the start of World War I and the end of World War II, when the global system broke down. The last column of the table identifies some of the main characteristics or uncertainties for the emerging system in each of the interdependent areas.

The trade system is under duress because of the large financial imbalances resulting from trade surpluses and deficits. There is a risk that the trade frictions and accusations on currency manipulations could lead to trade wars and the possible splintering of the global trading system into regional blocs. These would most probably be an Asian bloc (China, Hong Kong, Japan, Korea, Singapore, and Taiwan—which together accounted for 24 percent of world exports in 2009), the European Union (which accounted for 37 percent of world exports in 2009), and the North American Free Trade Association (NAFTA; 17 percent of world exports).[36] The countries representing the remaining 21 percent of world exports would probably be aligned with one of these three blocs, with the rest of Asia and most of Africa and Latin America aligned with the China bloc because of the importance of the China market for their commodity exports. The European Union and NAFTA may also consolidate, and India and the remaining developing countries might join them.

The 2008–2009 global financial crisis caused extensive global damage. Although the crisis was contained, the fundamental problems of the financial system that led to it have not been properly addressed. In addition, the role of the U.S. dollar as the world's main reserve currency is being questioned by the rest of the world. It continues to play a major role because there is not yet any viable alternative, particularly with the weakness of the euro in light of the frictions between the weak and strong countries in the euro zone. The renminbi cannot replace the dollar because it is not a convertible currency.

On the technology front, we are seeing the emergence of promising new biotechnology and nanotechnology which would form the underpinnings of a new technoeconomic paradigm. These technologies have

TABLE 7.5 Evolution of the international system over the last 200 years

	Mercantilism Until 1849	Liberalism Until WWI	Bretton Woods Post-WWII	Post–Bretton Woods After 1971	Emerging System Post-2008–2009
Trade	Management of trade to build up reserves of gold and silver	Relatively free trade in industrial goods; developed countries sell them to developing countries, import raw materials	Movement back toward free trade in merchandise goods, but developed countries protect agriculture	Movement toward freer trade including in services due to policy and rise of Internet-enabled trade in services	Continued liberal trading system or move to trade/regional trading blocs?
Finance and Reserve Currency	Limited financial flows	Large financial flows from UK to rest of world	Rapid growth of international finance	Even faster growth of international finance	More regulated international finance?
	Gold and silver as reserve currency	British pound as main reserve currency	U.S. dollar as main reserve currency	U.S. dollar under duress; creation of euro	Alternatives to U.S. dollar as main reserve currency?
Technology	First Industrial Revolution, led by UK	Second Industrial Revolution, led by UK; second and third technology revolutions, led by Germany and U.S., fourth led by U.S. mass production	Fifth (nuclear) technological revolution, led by U.S.	Sixth revolution–information and communications technology, led by U.S.	Seventh revolution, based on green, nano-, and biotech technologies, and new Internet?
			U.S.-dominated world innovation system	Rise of European and Japanese innovation	Rise of Asian innovation system?
			Rapid expansion of electricity		

Environment	Little environmental concern except for population growth	Rapid increase in pollution and CO_2 emissions as result of industrialization of developed world	Continued rapid increase in pollution and CO_2 emissions	Beginning awareness of environmental constraints to growth	Pricing of CO_2 and greater environmental regulations?
International Security	Military force based on land and naval power	Military force based on land and naval power and more sophisticated motorized military equipment, from tanks to ships and airplanes	UN Security Council Cold War (NATO vs. Warsaw Pact) U.S. as global policeman	Cold War peaks, ends in 1991 Increasing U.S. unilateral action Shanghai Cooperation Treaty Concern over nuclear proliferation	Growing military capability of emerging Asia Increasing concerns about cybersecurity, nonstate terrorism, nuclear proliferation?
Global Governance	Multiple wars and treaties		UN	UN, G-7/G-8 U.S. hegemony in decline	G-20; moving to another bipolar system with a stronger China?

SOURCE: Created by author.

yet to realize their full potential; China is investing heavily in them. The development of alternative energy technologies is also urgently needed. Given the importance of energy for virtually all economic activity, it would appear that the country that develops and commercializes new energy technologies will take a dominant global economic position. Right now, China is making the largest investments in green technology and will probably emerge as the global leader. However, the world is not doing enough to mitigate the risk of climate change, and it remains to be seen how this challenge will be addressed. Also, not enough R&D is addressing other global technology needs such as dealing with disease pandemics, diseases of the poor, or food security.

On the security front, the major short-term challenges have become fighting nonstate terrorism, containing nuclear proliferation, and mastering the new risk of cyberwarfare and cybercrime. China is rapidly expanding its traditional military capability as well as becoming much stronger in cyberwarfare and space and satellite technologies. More generally, the global governance system is rapidly moving to a much more complex multipolar system. The country making the largest and fastest gains is China. It is getting greater geopolitical influence with rogue states. However, its influence with the rest of the world is also growing because of the importance of its trade for most of the world, as an attractive market for FDI.

Normally, that there is a new, large competitor should not be a cause for alarm. The United States has always hailed the benefits of competition. More competition leads to more innovation and the development of better goods and services. The United States helped rebuild Europe after World War II through the Marshall Plan to create markets for its products and expand its trade. This worked quite well until it became overextended by the arms race with the USSR and the Vietnam War. It began to consume beyond its means and faced greater competition from Europe and even more from Japan. The rapid rise of Japan in the 1970s and 1980s worried the United States in a very similar way to that of China today. Like the Japanese, the Chinese work very hard, give the world cheaper products, and run up trade surpluses. China is also buying U.S. Treasuries and other financial assets that help support the U.S. economy, which has created a strong symbiotic relationship between the two countries.

The problem is that China has been free riding on the global system by getting all the benefits and not sharing the costs. It has also been tilting the playing field to its advantage at a significant cost to others. This is primarily in trade, through exchange-rate manipulation, controlling access to its dynamic market, and intellectual property piracy. Like the United States, it is also free riding on the environment by not paying for the large volume of CO_2 it is emitting. In addition, it is not contributing enough to other elements of the global system such as basic knowledge and security. Furthermore, from a global perspective, it is clear that China is going to become an even more formidable competitor, as it is investing heavily in higher education and R&D. There is concern about China's appetite for natural resources, its growing military strength, and its expanding geopolitical influence. At the same time, the United States is losing competitiveness, becoming weaker economically, and is less able to provide the global public goods necessary for an integrated global system—namely, free trade, international finance, basic knowledge, security, and global governance—while also failing to support environmental sustainability.

This brings us to the question of whether China's rise will be within the existing system or whether it will lead to the creation of a new system. There are different views on this. Some, such as Steinfeld,[37] argue that there is no need to worry about the rise of China because it is playing by rules established by the current global system, and it is in a process of "self obsolescing authoritarianism" and convergence toward the values of the West. Others, such as Jacques,[38] argue that China will not converge but remain a distinctively different system with its own history, culture, and way of doing things. According to Jacques, for the time being, China is modernizing by adapting to many of the international norms of the West. However, China still maintains many of its special characteristics, including a strong pride in what it considers its superior civilization which others must pay tribute to and a system of government where the state has never had to share power with any other class or group. Given its size, its long-term view, its patience, and its superiority complex, it will oblige the rest of the world to agree to its way of doing things as it becomes the largest and most important economy.

I agree that China is not going to adopt the entire range of Western values and institutions. China will continue to pursue its own narrow self-interests pragmatically and unilaterally rather than take on global responsibilities or adopt universal values of democracy and human rights. China's interests are to continue its rapid growth and to improve the welfare of its own people. To maintain the growth and employment it needs for legitimacy and internal stability, the government will also continue with its aggressive export policy and strong focus on indigenous innovation and development of national champions. Given its relative dearth of natural resources, as a matter of strategic security it will do all it can to acquire them from all around the world. To ensure that they can be transported to China, it will build up its military capability, secure their transport, and fend off any military threat to its well-being. It will also continue to very strongly defend its policy of noninterference in matters of national sovereignty and not tolerate any outside interference in its internal affairs.

Members of the realist school, such as Mearsheimer, would argue that the rise of a more assertive China is dangerous for the world and argue for containment. Scholars of the neoliberal school, such as Nye and Keohane,[39] argue that competition is now more in the economic than in the military arena and that the growing interdependence of the world argues for finding cooperative solutions through institutions and other collaborative arrangements. Constructivists would argue that the world has matured over the last few decades to the extent that war and conquest are now somewhat outmoded means of competition. Constructivists would also argue that the approach depends on how policy makers interpret the motives of the rising state. If they interpret the motives as benign and the state as being ready to abide by the rules, they are likely to opt for a cooperative approach. If they are uncertain of how the rising state may act in the future, they are more likely to opt for containment or confrontation. Thus, the global governance system is in flux, and there is a risk that the tensions in the economic area could spill over into serious confrontations, particularly between the United States and China.

Even Henry Kissinger, who was the architect of the rapprochement between the United States and China in 1972, is worried about U.S.–China relations. *The Economist* quoted him from a September 2010 meeting of the Center for Strategic Studies in Washington, D.C.:[40]

> It is not an issue of integrating a European-style nation-state, but a full-fledged continental power. . . . The DNA of both [America and China] could generate a growing adversarial relationship, much as Germany and Britain drifted from friendship to confrontation. . . . Neither Washington nor Beijing has much practice in co-operative relations with equals. Yet their leaders have no more important task than to implement the truths that neither country will ever be able to dominate the other, and that conflict between them would exhaust their societies and undermine the prospects for world peace.

What Can/Should the United States Do?

The United States can rise to the challenge of China, or it can continue to muddle along, lose influence and competitiveness, and see its standard of living decline over time.[41] Awaking the United States to the challenge involves a strong cultural shift that has various dimensions. The first is understanding that the international environment has become much more demanding. There is insufficient awareness among most Americans of the special situation the United States had coming out of World War II and how rapidly that situation has changed. The United States is facing increasing competition from the rest of the world and in particular from the swift ascent of emerging countries such as China and India. This competition has resulted in the loss of jobs and slower wage growth for the middle and lower classes. Painful economic restructuring is necessary along with retraining programs and adjustment assistance for the groups least able to find new employment opportunities.

The development of China and India also means moving from a short-term to a medium- and long-term strategic vision. This is something China has but the United States and India both lack. Rising to the challenge in the United States will require more leadership and serious attention from politicians to the painful but critical changes that need to be made to strengthen the country's long-term prospects. The short-term orientation of the U.S. political system, like those in most other democratic countries, makes it difficult to deal with long-term challenges. Any politician who proposes raising taxes or cutting spending to deal with the country's growing fiscal deficit is voted out of office. The same is true for anyone who proposes increasing the price of energy or imposing a carbon tax.[42] Therefore, the challenge is a big one and will require a lot of rethinking and sustained effort.[43] The United States has tremendous resilience and can rise to new challenges when it needs to. It has in the past, and it must in the future.[44] It is high time that it rise to the challenges and take action now.

Frictions between the rising and established powers are not new. As noted in Chapter 2, in Gilpin's framework,[45] there are five possible responses to a rising power by the reigning hegemon. They are to buckle down and rebuild its strengths; to retreat from global overextension, which dissipates power; to form alliances with other countries to counterbalance the ascent of the new emerging power; to appease the rising power; or to undertake a preemptive war to abort its expansion.

The United States should use all of the options in the Gilpin framework except the last one.[46] The strategy of military preemption is too costly in resources, human lives, and principles, particularly for a country that has prided itself on equality of opportunity and human rights. It is also too dangerous because of the risk of nuclear war. The fourth strategy, rather than appeasement, which has not worked, should be changed to forceful engagement to develop a workable partnership, as will be developed in Chapter 8.

Strengthen the Economy to Maintain Competitive Strength and Global Leadership

As measured by the global competitiveness indicators covered in Chapter 5, the United States is now very weak on macroeconomic stability, health, institutions, and financial markets.[47] It needs to rebuild its economic fundamentals and invest in education, research, and infrastructure. However, this cannot be done without addressing the United States' large fiscal deficits and ballooning federal debt. The United States cannot continue to live beyond its means. The rest of the world will not continue to finance its trade and fiscal deficits. Rebuilding its economic strength will be the hardest task but also the most critical. The United States is suffering from the characteristics of an aging hegemon. It has become weak because it has become accustomed to being the one to set the rules. Americans feel they have a right to a high standard of living and take for granted their large consumption of energy and resources—more than twice the per capita levels of citizens of other developed countries and several multiples of those of developing countries. The government has to cut wasteful expenditures, raise taxes, and redirect expenditures to more productive long-term investment such as education, R&D, and infrastructure. Politically, this will be very difficult because of the United States' fragmented and short-term-oriented political system, but it must be done. The basic need is to shift the economy from its focus on consumption and imports to saving and exports—essentially the opposite of what China needs to do.

Some of the necessary rebalancing has occurred as a result of the financial and economic crisis of 2008–2009, which forced the private sector to reduce expenditures and increase savings. Net private savings in the United States increased from 3.5 percent of GDP in 2007 to 6.2 percent in 2009. Government savings have gone in the opposite direction because of the cost of the bailouts and reduced tax revenues from the recession. The government deficit (government dissavings) has increased from 1.5 percent of GDP in 2007 to 8.7 percent in 2009.[48] The government fiscal deficit is expected to be 10 percent in 2010 and 2011. Furthermore, Douglas Elmendorf, the director of the U.S. Congressional Budget Office, estimates that core programs and the rapid growth of entitlement programs are expected to exceed tax revenues by 2016, implying that fiscal deficits will increase unless this problem is tackled.[49] The U.S. gross public debt in 2009 was 78.3 percent of GDP. The IMF projects it will increase to 84.1 percent in 2010 and to 94.5 percent by 2015.[50]

The United States has been financing an increasing percentage of its debt abroad. In 2003, official foreign ownership of U.S. government securities was $1.2 trillion. This almost tripled to $3.2 trillion (roughly 22 percent of U.S. GDP) by the end of 2008. Unless the deficits are brought under control, there is a risk that the United States' foreign creditors will start to doubt its fiscal soundness, fearing that the United States might inflate its way out of its debt, since the dollar is the world's reserve currency. Creditors are therefore likely to begin to charge higher interest rates, which would raise the costs of credit to the U.S. government as well as to businesses and consumers.[51] This would slow growth and further damage the fiscal situation as high interest would also increase the cost of servicing the debt and slower growth would reduce tax revenues. The net effect would be a rapid reduction in the standard of living.

Reduce U.S. Military Overextension

The wars in Iraq and Afghanistan have been very costly both financially and in American and foreign lives. The cost of the wars as of 2010 is estimated to be at least $3 trillion.[52] More than 5,800 American soldiers' lives had been lost by the end of November 2010.[53] The number of Iraqi and Afghan lives lost, most of them civilians, is in the hundreds of thousands. In addition, by acting unilaterally against the very ideals of national sovereignty and human values that it espouses, the United States has lost prestige and has arguably created even more terrorists and terrorist activity against U.S. targets abroad and domestically. Its inability to achieve sustainable victory against small groups of insurgents in poor countries is costing the U.S. military loss of face. The United States needs to preserve its military strength to respond to more strategic security needs.

Seek Alliances with Other Countries to Counterbalance China's Rise

This should include the European Union, Japan, and other developed countries as well as developing countries to counterbalance the rising power and influence of China's rise. It will be tricky because the United States does not have the economic or moral credibility it had after emerging victorious from World War II. It has to convince other countries that it will be a better global citizen than it has been. This means addressing some of the problems it has created in the global economic system, as will be detailed in Chapter 8.

Engage with China, Together with the European Union and Other Powers, to Create a Viable Global System

The longer the United States and the European Union wait, the stronger a position China will have in its negotiations with the rest of the world. Engagement will be difficult because China is likely to feel that the existing powers are attempting to constrain its development. The key point, however, is that unless there is pushback from the rest of the world to the way China is tilting trade, technology, and the use of its domestic market to its advantage, China will continue to free ride the global system. Therefore, this pushback is necessary for China to adjust its strategy. As a very pragmatic player, China will respond to this pressure. At the same time, it has some real concerns of its own that it will articulate. These include the lack of fiscal discipline on the U.S. side. It will articulate how that is becoming a risk to the global system, particularly because the United States is so much in debt to the rest of the world and is not getting its financial house in order. There is real concern in China about how to prevent the United States from declining too quickly because it is hard to find which other country or countries (including China) could provide the public good of a stable international system.[54] It will also most likely bring up the issue of the U.S. tendency to be the world's police officer and to unilaterally launch invasions of other countries. Therefore, all these issues need to be put on the table. The goal would be to work out a set of rules that all can live with regardless of who is the biggest or strongest.[55] The system must also take into account the needs of the rest of the world. This must be an honest assessment, and it must be done now. This is the topic of the final chapter of this book.

CHAPTER 8

How Will the World Adjust to the Swift Ascent of China and India?

THE ANALYSIS UP TO THIS POINT raises the important issue of whether the frictions caused by the rapid rise of China and India can be handled in a cooperative way or whether they will increase and lead to strong disruptions. Which way the system goes will depend on the actions of the main powers. The first section of this chapter considers four scenarios: one is the world's current situation; the other three comprise a more desirable scenario and two less desirable ones. The current system is drifting toward an undesirable scenario. The next section discusses some of the issues that must be addressed to move toward the more desirable scenario. The following section considers the implications of the evolving system for the rest of the developing countries, which will be putting pressure on the global system as their populations and incomes also increase. China and India represent 37 percent of the world's population, and the rest of the developing world accounts for another 47 percent.[1] There is a risk that a large part of the developing world will be left behind. The final section concludes that how smoothly the transition is made toward a more sustainable and more equitable global system, one that accommodates the rise of developing countries, will depend on the extent to which the United States, the European Union, and China can act beyond their narrow self-interests for the greater global welfare.

Alternative Scenarios

Although there are three dimensions to the current state of the global system—economic, environmental, and geopolitical—for expository purposes it is useful to represent them on a two-by-two matrix (Figure 8.1). The horizontal axis is the extent to which the global system is integrated. The vertical axis is the extent to which it is environmentally sustainable. There is a scenario for each quadrant. Each of the scenarios includes a brief description of the most plausible situation of the other

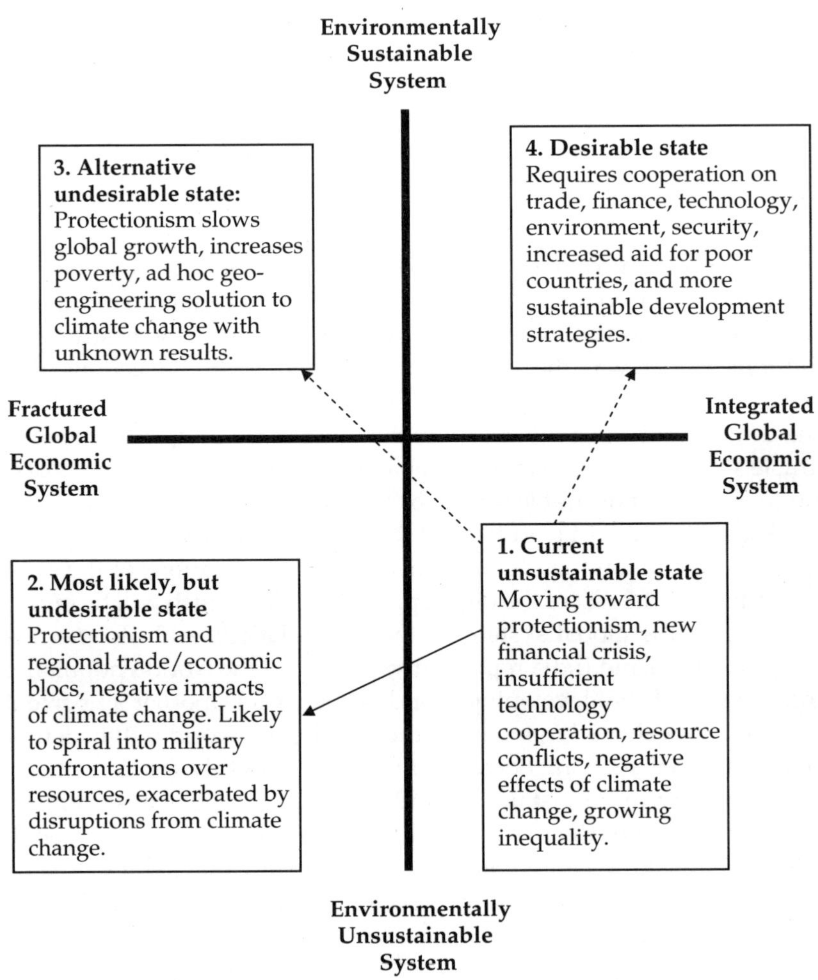

FIGURE 8.1 Current state of the international system and three alternative scenarios

SOURCE: Created by author.

elements of the framework, although there are many possible permutations. The scenarios are only a heuristic device to help sharpen stability and sustainability issues and the uncertainty about the direction of change of the system. Figure 8.1 illustrates the directions in which the system is moving and the alternative scenarios. Table 8.1 describes the different scenarios.

As has been argued throughout this book, we are currently in scenario 1, which is not sustainable because of the strong economic pressure from the rise of China and the strong environmental pressures from the rise of China and India. Unless the major global powers are able to manage these frictions, the world will tend to move down to scenario 2—a very undesirable outcome. A fragmented economic system that does not deal with climate change is unstable. Problems of climate change–induced natural disasters such as rising sea levels, floods, heat waves, droughts, and increased disease are likely to lead to conflict over shrinking habitable areas, access to food, and destabilizing mass migrations. They are also likely to lead to increasing military conflict within and across regions.

Scenario 3 is an alternative but also undesirable scenario. In this hypothetical situation of a fragmented global economic system, it is also assumed that there is no global cooperative agreement to combat climate change. Therefore, the scenario is that a country, such as China or India, that begins to be overwhelmed by the natural disasters associated with climate change may take matters into its own hands and undertake a major geo-engineering action. One example might be launching particles into the stratosphere to provide solar sunshade, as described in Chapter 6. Although this may provide short-term relief, it has many unknown side effects. Some of these could be negative, such as reducing the amount of sunlight needed for agriculture or other sun- and weather-related effects that could cause different sustainability problems.

Scenario 4 is the ideal scenario of global cooperation to create a sustainable and equitable global system. Although it is the most desirable scenario, it is also the most difficult to achieve because it requires developing a stronger overall global governance system and much better cooperative behavior by the main powers than has been achieved so far. Thus, it is more of an idealized than fully realistic scenario but one worth trying to move toward. The next section will discuss some of the issues that need to be addressed to move toward this scenario. The expectation is that there will be sufficient movement in this direction to at least keep the current system from sliding into scenario 2.

TABLE 8.1 Brief description of current state and alternative scenarios

State of the World	Economic (trade, finance, and technology)	Environmental (resources and climate change)	Geopolitical/Security
Scenario 1. Current Unsteady State Unsustainable global economic and environmental system	Increasing frictions on trade, shaky financial system, insufficient funding of R&D to tackle global issues	Risk of resource wars, insufficient action to address climate change	Geopolitical tensions due to growing economic and military power of China
Scenario 2. Most Likely Noncooperative State Increasing divide between U.S./EU system vs. Beijing Consensus	System moving toward regional trade blocs, with little trade across blocs Little international financial flows Increasing technonationalism	Resource wars Climate change not slowed sufficiently to avoid increased climate-related natural disasters leading to large population migrations across borders	Tensions across economic blocs Terrorism and nuclear proliferation increase High probability of spiraling into military confrontations from local to hegemonic
Scenario 3. Alternative Noncooperative State Increasing divide between U.S./EU system vs. Beijing Consensus, but some mitigation of climate change	System with reduced trade across economic blocs Minimal financial flows Technonationalism No funding of global R&D efforts	Resource wars Negative climate change effects lead to geo-engineering solutions with unknown consequences	Tensions across economic blocs Military and cybersecurity clashes
Scenario 4. Idealized Desirable State Cooperative global system able to deal with climate change	Responsible stakeholders on trade Integrated and regulated global financial system Strong public-good technology efforts, respect for intellectual property rights	Global framework for access to resources Transfer of finance and resources from rich to poor countries to deal with CO_2 and development	Cooperation on dealing with nuclear nonproliferation, terrorism, cybersecurity, failed states

SOURCE: Created by author.

An alternative scenario—not included here but relevant to cover a broader range of possible outcomes—is the impact on the world if China were to suffer an economic collapse. The impact, of course, would depend on the specific causes and severity of the collapse. For expository purposes, let's assume an extreme case on the magnitude of the economic collapse of the former USSR, when economic activity fell over 50 percent and the union fragmented into different countries. The positive impact from this would be a dramatic reduction in both emissions and the global pressure on natural resources (including energy). But the negative impact would perhaps be even more dramatic. Besides the likely loss of lives in China from resulting internal struggles, there would be significant negative impacts on the rest of the world. There would be a major disruption in the supply of manufactured products to the world, since China has become so central to the global production supply chains for world manufactures.[2] While the slack might eventually be taken up by other developing countries, this would take time. In addition, products would likely be more expensive because China had a price advantage thanks to its economies of scale and scope in supply. This would be a negative for consumers of the world who have been benefiting so much from the lower prices of manufactured exports from China. For exporters of natural resources and basic commodities, a sharp fall in demand from China would lead to a significant fall in prices. This would likely hit Australian, Latin American, and African exporters of mining and commodity exports and Russian and Middle Eastern exporters of oil and gas. The growth and future prospects of these regions would be very negatively affected as they have become so dependent on exports to China.

On the financial side, the United States would find it more expensive to finance its growing public debt because the Chinese would not continue to make the large purchases of U.S. Treasuries and other U.S. securities. In addition, exporters of machinery, equipment, components, and high-value services from more developed countries would lose that attractive market, and MNCs that had been using China as an export platform or as a major market would also suffer losses.

The reason for considering this alternative of a Chinese economic collapse is to make the point that China is already such a key element in the global economic system that its economic well-being matters to the rest of the world. It is therefore critical to develop a more sustainable system that works for both China and other countries.

Moving Toward a More Sustainable System

To move toward the ideal scenario, it is necessary to honestly assess the impact of the major powers on the global system. Table 8.2 provides a quick initial balance sheet of the positive and negative contributions of the United States and China to the global system. Such an analysis should be extended to include the European Union, India, and Japan and should also take into account what it implies for the rest of the world (see the next section).

Rebalancing Trade

In the short run, the most critical area to be addressed is to defuse the risk of trade wars. A trade war would be detrimental to the parties directly involved and to the rest of the world. The most likely scenario is a trade war between the United States and the European Union on one side and China on the other. If this were to start, it would likely spread around the world. To avoid this negative outcome, the United States, the European Union, and China need to manage their trade frictions carefully.

In this area, China has the most responsibility. It cannot continue to free ride the global system as extensively as it has. Among the major economies of the world, China is the most dependent on trade for imports of natural resources, capital goods, and components and for foreign markets to buy its output. Therefore, it has a very large stake in the stability of the global trading system. Its trade-oriented strategy has paid great dividends in terms of growth, employment, and foreign exchange accumulation. The expansion of trade has been positive for global economic growth, leading to specialization and exchange. Likewise, competition has led to greater innovation and increased productivity. However, China's rapid expansion of exports is exerting too much competitive pressure and causing job disruption in the rest of the world. Such pressure risks a major protectionist pushback from the countries most negatively affected. China's trade surpluses are not just with the United States but also with some countries of the European Union and some developing manufacturing exporters.[3] Protectionism could escalate to a trade war, which would be detrimental for all, particularly China.

China needs to rebalance its economy more toward its domestic market. One of the key steps China could take is to let its exchange rate

TABLE 8.2 Positive and negative contributions to the global system by the U.S. and China

	U.S.	China
Economic Size	+ As largest consumer market, drove global growth until 2008–2009 crisis – Weakened by financial crisis, has to cut back on consumption	+ Now largest growth market in world – Uses its market to get economic and technological advantages from foreign firms
Trade	+ Promoted an open trading system for manufactured products and services – Protected its agricultural sector to detriment of developing-country agricultural exporters	+ Lower-cost manufactured exports benefit global consumers + As major importer, creates windfalls for commodity exporters – Favors domestic market through undervalued currency, industrial policy, and national standards – Strong export growth puts excessive competitive pressure on foreign industries, causing loss of jobs – Free rides on global trading system without contributing much to its stability
Finance	+ Was source of global finance until 1986 + Has been main reserve currency since WWII, providing liquidity for the international system – Became a net borrower in 1986; consumed beyond its means. – Fiscal situation is unsustainable; deficits are 10% of GDP; national debt will rise above 100% of GDP unless it cuts expenditures or increases taxes; creates concern that it will inflate to reduce debt – Did not appropriately regulate its financial system and created major global recession 2008–2009	+ Has become major source of finance for U.S. government debt; however, it may pull back because it is concerned about U.S. fiscal sustainability and soundness of U.S. dollar as global reserve currency; fears U.S. inflation will lead to depreciation of U.S. dollar, which will lower value of dollar-denominated assets it holds – Chinese yuan cannot become reserve currency until China opens its capital account + Has become major foreign direct investor – Other countries worry about China's increased foreign direct investment in commodity and high-tech companies

(Continued)

TABLE 8.2 *(Continued)*

	U.S.	China
Technology	+ Main global innovator over last century – Undertakes less basic research within its overall research effort than it did a generation ago because of cutbacks in government funding for R&D – Is not investing enough in developing green technology	– Appropriates intellectual property developed by other countries – Does not contribute much to basic research + Is investing heavily in developing green technology
Environment	– Is responsible for largest global share of accumulated CO_2 emissions – Has refused to formally commit to CO_2 reduction	– Has become world's largest CO_2 emitter – Has not made sufficient commitments to help the world avoid climate change
Global Security	+ Provided security umbrella vs. USSR – Started unilateral wars in Afghanistan and Iraq, which have created greater terrorism and instability	– Has not contributed much to global security – Does not cooperate enough on containing North Korean or Iranian nuclear programs – Is building up its military capability and making claims to additional territory, which raises security concerns for neighbors and the U.S.
Global Governance	+ Designed the post-WWII global governance system – System is outdated, does not cover new issues, or fully represent new powers	– Has not contributed much to the global governance system; free rides on this global public good, particularly with regard to trade, technology, and security

SOURCE: Created by author.

appreciate, although by itself this is not going to solve the problem. Structural issues also need to be addressed in both surplus countries like China, Germany, and Japan[4] and in deficit countries like the United States and the United Kingdom. It also requires restructuring the Chinese economy away from its excessive dependence on exports toward domestic consumption. This is necessary in any event because of the fall in demand for its imports from the advanced countries in general and the United States in particular. It also makes good sense from the perspective of China's own development priorities.[5] This restructuring will have multiple benefits. One is to defuse the strong protectionist sentiment that has been building up against China. Another is to reduce its enormous demand for natural resources and energy and to reduce its global environmental footprint in general and with respect to CO_2. Part of China's very large demand for natural resource imports, including energy, is that it is exporting so many energy- and resource-intensive products to the rest of the world.

One of the reasons the Chinese save at such a high rate is their need to protect themselves against future costs of unemployment and medical insurance. China therefore needs to strengthen its social safety net and invest more in health. Another aspect of the high savings is that public enterprises retain earnings instead of distributing them to their stockholders. Forcing greater distribution of dividends could increase disposable income for the population.[6]

China's development to date has been very capital-, resource-, and energy-intensive. The share of its industrial sector in GDP is high for a country with its per capita income. In addition, as noted in Chapter 3, the amount of capital necessary to create additional growth has been rising because of inefficiencies in China's financial system and the capital-intensive nature of its growth. On the other hand, the size of China's service sector is lower than would be expected given its per capita income. China can achieve less capital-, energy-, and environmentally intensive growth if it focuses on developing its service sector. Service-sector growth will also provide more employment than capital-intensive industrial growth.[7] Service growth depends largely on an educated populace. China is investing heavily in the education of its people, so it should be in a good position to expand this sector.

The Chinese government is fully aware of the importance of such restructuring and has started to take steps in this direction. Although it has made some investments in expanding unemployment insurance and the pension system, it is still investing extensively in export-oriented industries. It should do more to achieve this restructuring, as it will take some time to come to fruition.

The United States needs to do essentially the opposite of China: increase savings and exports and decrease fiscal deficits and imports. This is easy to prescribe but hard to do. Increasing exports depends on both the competitiveness of U.S. industry and the dollar exchange rate. The exchange rate has proven less easy to manipulate than would be expected. From 2001 to mid-2008, the real U.S. exchange rate depreciated about 20 percent, and between 2005 and mid-2008, it even depreciated relative to the renminbi. This is what most economists would have expected given the large U.S. trade deficit. This helped make its exports more competitive. However, with the 2008–2009 economic crisis and the flight of world capital to the security of the dollar, the dollar appreciated again through mid-2009, hurting U.S. exporters. It began to depreciate again in the second half of 2009. However, the Greek and Irish crises in 2010 led to a loss of confidence in the euro and a renewed appreciation of the dollar. Even the increased intervention of the U.S. Federal Reserve Bank to inject more money into the U.S. economy by buying long-term debt, starting in November 2010, has not had a significant effect on U.S. exchange rates because money keeps flowing into the United States due to the weakness of the euro. Although there may be some depreciation of the dollar in the future, the key element to increasing exports will be to improve productivity, which requires innovation.

The medium-term goal should be to develop more effective global mechanisms to prohibit and monitor unfair trade-related rules such as exchange-rate manipulation and subsidies. But it will also be necessary to develop mechanisms to give countries more policy space to adjust to the pressures of globalization. This is because of the difficulties of integrating the needs of countries at different levels of development and capability as well as tensions between what may be appropriate to the nation-state as a whole and what its citizens perceive as fair to them.

One economist, Dani Rodrik,[8] makes the argument that globalization must be saved from the globalizers. Writing before the 2008 global crisis, he argues that more important than trade liberalization (which has reached diminishing returns unless liberalization in international labor movements is added in efforts such as the Doha Round) is to save the global system from a collapse toward protectionism and bilateralism. He points out that liberalization leads to strong welfare gains in a country only when there is deep economic integration, such as within a large nation-state like the United States, where national labor and capital markets can reallocate factors to their most efficient use and the state can in theory deal with necessary redistributive policies. There is also a conflict between the benefits to each nation-state in the aggregate and to interest groups within it, who are hurt or benefit in different ways by greater liberalization. Unless there are appropriate redistribution and adjustment mechanisms, this creates tension between the state and its citizens in democratic states where those citizens are more vocal in their opposition to the costs of trade liberalization. Some of these challenges are being played out in the European Union, where there are great tensions and high transactions costs in integrating policies across different nation-states.

Avoiding Resource Wars

This will require developing guidelines for fair competition as well as avoiding overly nationalistic reactions to purchases of resources and the companies that control them. Developing a commonly agreed upon set of principles for foreign investments could contribute to reducing China's concerns about access to natural resources as well as reducing its need to deal with rogue states. Targeted negotiation across different areas of concern is another way to avoid an unwanted and harmful outcome. A relevant example was the announcement on April 12, 2010, that China has agreed to join the United States and other countries in discussing sanctions against Iran over its nuclear problem, thanks to assurances from the United States that China's energy supply will remain secure.[9]

Obviously, avoiding resource wars is more complex than rules of foreign investment. Mutually satisfactory arrangements for access to critical natural resources such as water and energy will also be necessary to avoid escalating tensions. One example of this is developing sound principles for sharing access to water rights when water crosses national boundaries. This could help prevent the brewing Himalayan glaciers problem from escalating into water wars between China and India.

Improving Supervision of International Finance

Another key area to address is the problems of the financial system. The United States has the primary responsibility here because it was the source of the 2008–2009 global financial crisis that spread to the rest of the world. This crisis was the worst since the Great Depression and has had a devastating effect on the world economy. The GDP of virtually all developed countries fell, as did the growth of almost all developing economies. Just in the United States, between mid-2007 and the end of 2008, households lost $13 trillion, almost 20 percent of their net worth.[10] Unemployment increased by tens of millions of workers to 207 million workers globally in 2009.[11] The number of people below the international poverty line (U.S. $1.25 PPP per day) increased by more than 60 million.[12]

The fiscal and monetary stimulus programs carried out by the major developed countries and China helped contain the crisis from becoming as severe as the Great Depression. While the system has somewhat stabilized for now, the United States and other developed countries have yet to do enough to assure a sound global financial system. Most developed country governments have had to bail out their financial systems at great taxpayer expense and considerable hardship to ordinary citizens in terms of lost jobs and personal wealth. The global financial system has become more consolidated as a result of the crisis. The problems of systemic risks and moral hazards are still built into the system, and another international financial crisis is likely to occur.

The United States will need to undertake major reforms of its financial system, the poor regulation and excesses of which led to the 2008–2009 financial and economic crisis. More effective international regulations on bank and nonbank financial institutions must be put in place if a similar collapse is to be avoided in the future. A Financial Stability Board was set up after the November 2009 London G-20 summit to monitor and make recommendations on the global financial system.[13] It has made some recommendations, several of which have been accepted in principle by subsequent meetings of the G-20.[14] However, there has not been enough action on these, and what has been put in place is still not adequate. The increased interdependence of global financial systems, as well as their interdependence with the jobs and wealth of people around the world, calls for better global monitoring of systemic financial risk and stronger measures to avoid moral hazard and systemic failures. In addition, international financial speculation, which often bets against a country's currency and can destabilize economies, must also be better regulated. Major reform will be a difficult task not only because the issues are complex but also because the powerful financial industry will resist it. Because the financial system is global, the redesign of its architecture and regulatory systems needs to be worked out among the major countries. This will take time and strong political will to achieve.

China and India were only indirectly affected by the financial crisis through the collapse of demand for their exports. However, their growth was slowed and their economies lost millions of export jobs. In China alone, an estimated 20 million lost their jobs because of the contraction in global demand. The crisis also increased the interdependence between the United States and China, as China used its surpluses to buy many financial and other firms in the United States.

Developing countries are understandably concerned about the international financial system and want greater regulation and accountability. China and India should be more involved in the development of the regulation and supervision of global finance, not just the G-7. They also want greater controls and safeguards before they are willing to open up their international capital accounts. A longer-term goal for China is moving toward freer international capital flows. This is likely to take time, but it will happen eventually. Down the road, it will help make the Chinese renminbi one of the world's main reserve currencies.

Addressing Concerns About Foreign Direct Investment

There is also concern that China and other surplus countries will use their large reserves to invest in foreign companies for strategic purposes. In the past, there have been attempts to develop a code of conduct for investment. All of them failed because of strong opposition from various developed and developing countries. Now that some developed countries are on the defensive regarding FDI from developing countries, it may be appropriate to revisit this issue. Developing countries such as China and India, which are facing nationalistic reactions to their own foreign investments, are probably interested in setting up more transparent and monitorable procedures with appropriate grievance mechanisms. Developed countries like the United States, European Union countries, and Japan may also be ready to revisit this issue, as they are concerned about China's investments that may give it access to high technology or control of strategic assets. There is also some concern that China may be less open to FDI than it has been in the past.

One possibility would be to develop a commonly agreed upon set of criteria to determine whether a foreign investment constitutes a national security threat. Theodore Moran has proposed a useful methodology for use by the U.S. Committee on Foreign Investment, which makes this determination in the U.S. Congress. The framework distinguishes three categories of potential threats. The first is denial of goods or services by a foreign-controlled supplier. The criteria are whether the industry is so tightly concentrated and substitutes are so limited that foreign investment would pose a threat.[15] The second is the leakage of technology or expertise to a foreign-controlled entity. The criteria are whether the technology is available from others and what difference the acquisition of the technology makes to the new home government. The first can be subjected to the same industry concentration test as mentioned above; the second would require more specialized, sometimes classified knowledge, so it would be more difficult to implement. However, it may not be necessary if the project fails the first criterion: that the technology is easily available. The third category is foreign acquisitions as a channel for infiltration, surveillance, or sabotage.[16] This requires careful examination by competent authorities. However, most purchases are likely to fall into the first two categories and to pose no threat. These rules of thumb are a good start; it would be worthwhile to pursue some global agreement on a set of rules to be adopted across all countries.

Avoiding Climate Catastrophe

The major longer-term area to deal with is the environment, in particular, the risk of climate change. However, concrete actions need to start now. The United States is responsible for the largest cumulative share of CO_2 emissions (19 percent vs. 13 for the European Union, 9 for China, and only 3 for India)[17] and has shown the least disposition among the major developed countries to address this problem. It comes from the concern that if it were to adopt controls, its firms would lose competitiveness to China and India, which were exempted by the Kyoto Protocol. However, if China and India are to be brought on board, the United States will need to make stronger commitments and take more action. China and India also must take stronger action because, if they do not lower their emissions significantly, CO_2 emissions will not be reduced enough to avert the risk of global climate change, even if the rest of the world cuts its emissions to half the levels of 1990.

It is essential that more progress be made. Much greater investment in a large technology push is the key way to turn the zero-sum game of fixed emissions into a positive-sum game. This requires much greater resources than are currently being allocated. Here there are also opportunities for more public international collaborative precompetitive research and development efforts. But better mechanisms for commercialization and deployment of the new alternative energy technologies will also be necessary to make an impact. This will require better mechanisms to deal with the IPR issues of new commercial technology as well as international finance and technology.

The European Union and Japan have been more willing than the United States to recognize their environmental debt to developing countries. The European Union already has roughly half the level of CO_2 emission per unit of GDP or per person than the United States and has committed to adopting even lower levels if the United States, China, and India follow suit. In the absence of stronger commitments from the outliers, and given the competitive pressures they are already facing, forces within the European Union could reasonably argue that they are hurting their competitiveness by maintaining higher standards. European Union countries therefore are likely to start tougher negotiations with respect to the United States and China.

The United States will also have to do much more to reduce CO_2 emissions than the 17 percent reduction from 2007 levels proposed by President Obama at the December 2009 Copenhagen Climate Summit. The problems of collective action have already been noted. Bold new initiatives are needed to break the current stalemate. Global warming skeptics and well-financed lobbies in Congress will make this difficult. It will be important to raise awareness of what is at stake.

There are many measures that can be taken to reduce CO_2 emissions. The most effective is a tax on carbon-based fuels or CO_2 emissions. This would have multiple benefits. The tax could help reduce governments' budget deficits. Higher prices on carbon-based fuels would create incentives to lower their use and find alternative energies. These measures would also stimulate research and development on more environmentally friendly technologies. Furthermore, the countries that develop more energy-efficient and environmentally friendly technologies will have an important competitive edge.

Fostering Technology Development and Addressing Problems of Intellectual Property

As developed throughout the book, technological innovation plays a critical role in growth and welfare and in the rise of nations. Technology can be used for war or to advance human welfare. It is a key element in the solution to many of the world's problems. In the last three decades, there have been an increasing codification of science and the advent of information-processing technologies that have accelerated the process of technological development and innovation.

The United States has been the main creator of knowledge over the last 100 years. Now that much more knowledge is being created abroad, the United States will need to devote more effort to importing this knowledge. It will also need to invest more in its own innovation to stay ahead of the competition. There are many technological opportunities in nano- and biotechnology. The United States will have to invest more in these areas and participate more actively in global knowledge exchanges. It will also need to put more effort into the dissemination and use of knowledge. Stimulating more innovation will require more scientists and engineers as well as creative people.[18] This has implications for the focus of higher education. More attention will also need to be given to supporting the transition from new basic knowledge to applied knowledge and further dissemination throughout the economy.[19]

China has become the world's second largest spender on R&D. However, its R&D effort, like that of Japan, is focused mostly on development, application, and deployment. It has been relying mainly on acquiring global knowledge through formal and informal means, including extensive pirating. Now that it is spending so much on R&D, it needs to contribute more to the advancement of basic knowledge instead of free riding so much on global knowledge. It also must do more to respect intellectual property rights.

India faces many of the challenges common to other developing countries. Because it has greater innovation capability than any other developing economy except China, it has developed many innovations that are relevant for other developing countries. These include more than 60,000 grassroots innovations developed by farmers and others: small improvements in everyday activities from fetching water to irrigation, farming, basic food processing, and basic health and medicines.[20] They also include many innovations that use modern technology to deliver goods and services to poor people when basic infrastructure and services are limited, such as cheap, no-frills computers, basic cell phones, Tata's $2,500 car, GE's mini-CT scan, small water-purification devices, Internet banking, and computer-driven pictographic literacy programs available in many different languages. India has tremendous potential to continue to develop these bottom-of-the-pyramid[21] innovations and export them to other countries.[22] India has also been developing cutting-edge technology in many fields, including software, Internet applications, pharmaceuticals, nuclear energy, and aerospace.

China and India have been very good at rapid technological catch-up, and now they are beginning to innovate on their own. Although much has been acquired through formal means such as imports of capital goods and components, FDI, technology licensing, and foreign education and training, much has also been acquired through copying and piracy. Given the speed with which both countries are catching up, the issue of intellectual property (IP) piracy is becoming one of the top concerns of developed countries.[23] In the short run, it will be necessary to develop stronger enforcement of IPR in China and India and to increase penalties for violations. Both countries, but especially China, have a strong incentive to improve intellectual property regimes, as they now have considerable technological capability. China has in fact moved aggressively to strengthen its laws, enforcement capability, and penalties. However, it is still too attractive for individual firms to steal intellectual property, whether foreign or domestic. Only a credible history of enforcement and higher penalties will make it clear that the government is serious about IPR protection, and this is likely to take some time.

In the medium term, it will be important to develop better systems of IPR protection. This has at least two components. One is to address the needs of developing countries. Developed countries borrowed and stole technology from more advanced countries, so they know the importance of making use of available technology. Therefore, it is appropriate to cut poor countries some slack in the appropriation of existing knowledge. There has already been some movement to give the least developed countries some flexibility in adopting less strict IPR rules in health-related and medical technologies. This should be extended to other areas that are critical to basic needs.

The second component is the recognition that IPR regimes have become too strict in general. Even in advanced countries, there is concern that the balance may have shifted too far toward privatization of knowledge.[24] This has led to the development of a strong open-innovation movement among firms,[25] which emphasizes that innovation has become globalized and takes place beyond the walls of any one organization. Firms need to work in more collaborative ways with customers, suppliers, competitors, and universities to improve the development, production, and distribution of goods and services. This open-innovation model is particularly strong in the area of software.

Even large firms that had emphasized proprietary knowledge have become involved in the open-innovation movement. IBM, for example, has developed the Eclipse platform to work with competitors, research institutes, suppliers, and customers to develop new core infrastructures to deliver open-source software that individual companies can then customize for specific applications.[26] The balance between traditional strict IPR and more open innovation approaches needs to be thought through for different fields and technologies.[27]

On the institutional side, the World Trade Organization has not been very effective in protecting intellectual property rights because most of its focus has been on whether countries have the appropriate laws in place. These laws may not be sufficiently enforced, and if they are, the penalties are often small. In addition, the extension of the WTO's mandate to intellectual property protection has been controversial, particularly in the area of health. The protection of high prices for pharmaceuticals when the lives of millions of people are at stake has been a key controversy. On the other hand, there is no formal institution to encourage research on global needs such as environmental sustainability and health.[28]

At the same time that more protection needs to be given to IPR, much more needs to be done to develop international R&D on critical global issues of public good such as water, energy, and health. Water shortages loom as large as energy shortages, with the risk of water wars between China and India. Therefore, concerted international cooperation on improving existing technologies and developing new ones to deal with water, energy efficiency, and CO_2 emissions is paramount. For water, critical areas include water management, less water-intensive crops and irrigation systems, drought-resistant seeds, and desalination technologies. For energy and global warming, critical areas include alternative energy technologies that are cost competitive with carbon-based energy,[29] technologies to increase energy efficiency, clean-coal technologies, carbon capture and sequestration technologies, and radical new technologies.[30] The impact of climate change on developing countries is made worse by sanitation and shelter inadequacies.

It is also important to develop global R&D on problems of tropical diseases, such as malaria, as well as other infectious diseases such as avian and swine flu that can easily become global pandemics, as we have already seen. For highly infectious diseases that can easily become pandemics, R&D could include rapid assessment techniques as well as technologies to quickly develop appropriate vaccines for new strains and deploy them as needed.

Much more could also be done to develop innovations to address the needs of the poor. Such innovations in products, processes, or technologies include low-cost, no-frills phones and computers, medical diagnostic and testing equipment, and technologies to provide safe drinking water and increase the agricultural productivity or nutritional value of traditional crops. This is an area in which India has been making some headway not just by collecting and disseminating indigenous innovation but also by harnessing modern technology to address the problems of the poor. One example is the use of weather satellite systems to identify sources of water for poor rural communities. Another is the development of a portable CT scan device that can be put on the back of a bicycle and taken to rural health centers.[31] Such efforts need to be encouraged and expanded.

China, the United States, and India need to do more to address common problems of global concern, such as energy efficiency, clean coal and carbon sequestration, adaptation to climate change, water management, and control of global disease pandemics. There is scope for much greater collaboration with other global players on basic and precompetitive research. If these three countries manage to increase cooperation on global R&D needs, the European Union and other countries are likely to jump on board.

Strengthening Global Security

A longer-term issue is the role of China, India, and other rising countries in global governance and security. The United States will not continue to be as dominant in military power and will need to adjust to its lower global profile and new fiscal constraints. The European Union will have to step up to do more, particularly with respect to its own defense.

China should play a more active role in international security issues. Principal among this is a stronger stance against proliferation of nuclear weapons, including a stronger willingness to support sanctions against countries such as Iran and North Korea. Its concern about securing access to oil is understandable, however. As noted earlier, it would be in everyone's interest to assure China's access to natural resource supplies without its resorting to rogue states.

The broader security issues are very difficult. The West needs to remember that its record for preventing wars is very poor. The two world wars of the last century started out as wars among Western countries. Thus, setting up a better global security system to try to prevent major wars is a long-term challenge that goes beyond which countries sit on the UN Security Council. It will require greater appreciation of the mutual benefits of working together to address global threats such as the proliferation of weapons of mass destruction, nonstate terrorism, cyberattacks, and climate change. It will also require developing greater understanding of the legitimate goals and needs of other countries, particularly in the context of limited resources.

Improving Global Governance

There are many challenges to improving global governance. As noted in Chapter 7, the existing institutions are not adequate to the challenges of the current much more demanding, fast-paced, and more interdependent global system. It is also not just that there are new rising state powers such as China and India and a larger number of nation-states which makes reaching consensus more difficult but also that there are new challenges such as climate change, cybersecurity, terrorists with access to weapons of mass destruction, and fast-spreading global pandemics. There is also the continuation of old challenges such as severe global financial crises, trade wars, resource wars, conventional wars, increasing global inequality, failing states, and a greater risk of destabilizing mass migrations as large populations flee areas of war, famine, drought, floods, and rising sea levels. This will require the improvement of existing global governance institutions as well as the development of new institutions and mechanisms to address them, all of which is going to be a long-term process.

Within all this, it will be important to work out larger roles for China and India. As rising powers with a strong stake in the global system, they will need to contribute much more to the stability of the evolving system and help to address and deal with these challenges across the board.

China would also advance its own and global interests if it took a stronger stance on humanitarian, governance, and corruption issues in the countries with which it interacts. China's policy of nonintervention in the internal affairs of other countries has prevented it from taking these issues into account in its trade relations and foreign aid with other developing countries. The carrot of Chinese trade, investment, and aid could be positive incentives for countries to improve their human rights and governance. China would also increase its soft power and reduce tensions with the rest of the world over its continued interaction with rogue states such as Iran, Somalia, Myanmar, and others. It will need to balance the advantage of preferential access that it has in interacting with states shunned by the rest of the world against disapproval and possible recrimination by the United States, European Union, Japan, and other countries that have put sanctions on companies that trade with these rogue states.

Implications for Other Developing Countries Vary

Other developing countries are positively or negatively affected by the rise of China and India depending on their natural resource endowments, level of development, and economic and industrial structure. Natural resource exporters are likely to do well in the short run but will face challenges in the medium and longer run. Exporters of manufactured products or information-enabled services will find increasing competition from the growing strength of China and India and will need to develop strategies to improve their own competitiveness, including strategic alliances with China and India or other key powers. All need to worry about the problems that will come with climate change. They will need to lobby the big players more actively to provide them greater financial and technical assistance to mitigate the cost of CO_2 abatement measures, to help them deal with adaptation to climate change, and generally, to take action that is in the global interest. And they would be wise to put more effort into adaptation strategies given the slow progress that has been made on mitigation efforts to date.

Poverty and instability in the rest of the world are critical areas that need to be addressed by global governance systems. Many parts of the developing world are at risk of being left behind. In 1980, the world's richest country was 200 times wealthier than the poorest in per capita income; in 2008, it was 600 times wealthier.[32] While China and India have had strong growth and hundreds of millions of their citizens have been brought out of poverty, many other developing economies have not shared much in the global growth. This raises two concerns.

One is the extent to which China's and India's success may be preempting development opportunities for other countries. It is hard to compete with China in labor-intensive manufactured exports because its advantage is not only in low wages (lower than in many African countries) but also in economies of scale in purchasing, production, and distribution. India also has a major first-mover advantage in the export of information-enabled services. Although wages for Indian ICT workers have been rising rapidly because of skill-supply constraints, there are efforts underway to increase the provision of higher education to train more people to work in the ICT sector.[33]

The second concern is that effective participation in today's competitive and fast-paced global system may be beyond the capability of most developing countries. Many do not have the skills, infrastructure (physical or informational), education, business experience, effective governance institutions, or technological capability to take advantage of globalization. Thus, it is becoming increasingly difficult for many developing countries to create viable development strategies. Those with natural resources are getting temporary rent windfalls from the demand from China and to a lesser extent India. They need strategies to channel those windfalls into investments in human capital, institutions, and infrastructure for sustainable development to avoid a "natural resource curse."

In 1981, the number of people living below U.S. $2 PPP per capita was 2,542 million, roughly 56 percent of the world's population. In 2005 (the latest year for which data are available), the number was almost identical at 2,564 million, or roughly 40 percent of the world's population. Thus, while there has been a dramatic fall in the percentage of the population living below the poverty line, the absolute number has increased, particularly as a result of the 2008–2009 global economic crisis. The absolute number of poor in China fell by almost 500 million to 470 million during this period; in India, it increased by about 200 million to 830 million. The number of poor in the rest of the world increased from 960 million to 1,260 million.[34]

Rising powers and incumbents both share an interest in seeing that the countries at risk of falling behind hold together and take positive development steps. One reason is the problems that arise in failed states; another is the benefit of growing global markets for exports. It is necessary to increase international aid to help the countries that are being left behind reap some of the benefits of globalization and global growth. However, at the international level, there are no effective systems for global redistribution to support or compensate groups left behind by competition and economic restructuring. In nation-states, redistribution can be achieved by progressive taxation and expenditures on public goods such as education, health, security, and targeted poverty and redistribution policies. At the global level, greater trade liberalization is wiping out industries and the income opportunities in many weaker economies.

Foreign aid, which totals less than 0.35 percent of global gross national income,[35] is very limited in the face of the needs. More must be done at the international level to help poorer developing countries compete effectively and benefit from globalization. This also involves loosening for them the ever-tightening trade and IPR rules promoted by the WTO and the proliferation of bilateral trade treaties. China and India need to take this into account in their own trade and foreign-aid policies. To a large extent, they have been two of the strongest beneficiaries of the more open global trading system, and it is now their turn to help less developed countries.

The Doha Trade Rounds, which started in 2001 and were supposed to conclude by 2008, failed to achieve an agreement on reducing agricultural subsidies and opening developed-country agricultural markets more to imports from developing countries. The main controversy was originally over opening agricultural markets in developed countries in exchange for further liberalization of manufacturing and services in developing countries. The strong agricultural lobbies in the developed countries prevented them from conceding much on agriculture. Ironically, the talks broke down when India also took a defensive policy on agricultural safeguards out of concern for and political pressure from its farmers, who feared imports from other countries. China backed India, which led to the breakdown of the talks.[36]

China can take a stronger role helping the Doha Trade Round liberalize trade in agriculture, goods, and services. It could also expand trade preferences for imports from the least developed economies.[37] China can also play a larger role in foreign aid. While China's foreign aid has been increasing over the last decade, it has been too narrowly focused on investment in physical infrastructure that facilitates its access to extra resources from developing countries. This follows the pre–World War II practice of the old colonial powers in Africa and elsewhere. China even takes its own workers to the developing countries it operates in to build the roads and railroads needed to get commodity exports out, denying employment opportunities to the countries it is claiming to help.

From a narrow economic perspective, China can argue that it manages its own aid and brings its own workers for infrastructure projects to bypass problems of government corruption and incompetence while getting its projects completed on time. However, to increase the development impact and to project greater soft power, China needs to broaden the focus of its aid to develop more domestic capability. As noted, inequality is increasing across countries. In the absence of a global government that can tax and redistribute, countries with the means to do more, like China, need to assume their fair share of the burden. This means allocating more to projects for education and health and building domestic institutions that can help countries help themselves. It also means sharing its development experience more broadly.[38]

Conclusion: The Main Powers Need to Take Stronger Actions to Ensure a More Sustainable and Equitable Global System

The focus of this book has been on China and India, but the global issues it raises are larger. These two countries represent the "rise of the rest."[39] The issue is not just how many people the earth can support; it is also reducing the gap in standards of living and welfare and providing basic rights such as security and freedom. These relate to the values and performance of different national systems, to what is considered fair, and to the rules of the global system for peaceful interaction across states.

This book has reviewed the daunting issues that must be tackled by the main countries and regions of the world. These need immediate attention, even if some of them will take a long time to be resolved. There are also many opportunities for collective action by the main countries, including ensuring a fair global trading system, better regulation of international finance, breaking the deadlock on climate change, finding more sustainable development strategies, addressing the problems of growing global inequality, and guaranteeing security—in particular, nuclear nonproliferation and control of terrorism.

China, the United States, the European Union, and India can play key roles in supporting these global public-good efforts, and through their example, they can and must help bring other countries into the initiatives. Several suggestions have been made over the course of this book. Inaction on the issues of trade, finance, energy, and environment could lead to major problems in world stability, sustainability, and welfare, which could be much worse an outcome for most players than the costs of compromising on autonomy to ensure stability.

How policy makers and the public in different countries approach these issues matters. The extent to which they consider only their national interests versus a broader global perspective, including the needs of the rising number of people in developing countries, will affect the decisions they make and how well the global system will work. National political systems are not very adept at addressing international issues, particularly if they require painful domestic adjustments.

There are many reasons it is so difficult to get action on many of these issues. One is the lack of a coherent understanding of the interdependencies and the seriousness of the issues. A second is the difference between national and global interests. A third is a mismatch between the short-term perspective of decision making and the longer time frame of the issues. A fourth is the difficulty for democratic political systems to make economically painful decisions and the tendency to put off decisions that do not affect the immediate future. The main powers need to undertake more action on their own to help maintain global economic stability and sustainability while working to create more appropriate multilateral institutions.

It is necessary to promote greater awareness among all—governments, businesses, organizations, and individuals—of what is at stake, who stands to benefit, and who stands to lose from current frictions and downward spirals. There is a need to understand the interdependence among the issues, to be willing to make trade-offs across different areas, to identify and take action to address the most immediate challenges, and to start working on medium- and longer-term solutions.

This book has provided a framework of analysis to better understand these interdependent issues and the actions involved in solving them. The main message is that the global system is not sustainable as currently configured. It is drifting toward greater tensions and confrontations across countries as well as broader sustainability risks because of environmental constraints. Much more concerted effort needs to be put into managing these risks and moving the system toward more sustainable outcomes. That will not be easy. Much is at stake for all parties directly involved as well as for the rest of the world. The United States and China, in particular, must recognize that they need to work together to ensure the emergence of a workable system. As the two biggest powers, how they interact between themselves and with others will affect how well the system works. They would do well to develop a system that works regardless of which country ends up the biggest player. It should also be emphasized that many of the critical issues such as not dealing with climate change or pandemics or famines or terrorists or rogue states with access to weapons of mass destruction create global problems no matter which country is the hegemon. It is hoped that this book will contribute in a meaningful way to thinking about these issues now before frictions lead to more adversarial relationships which will make it more difficult to cooperate to ensure global stability and sustainability.

Notes

Chapter 1

1. At market exchange rates, they increased their share of global GDP from 3 percent in 1980 to 11 percent in 2009. See Table 7.1 in Chapter 7.

2. There has been an explosion of books on each of these countries as well as a few on both. For some of the more recent, see Bardhan (2010), Bergsten et al. (2008), Eichengreen et al. (2010), Jacques (2009), Kynge (2007), Meredith (2007), Nilekani (2009), Panagariya (2008), Steinfeld (2010), and Winters and Yusuf (2007).

3. International Energy Agency (2010c).

Chapter 2

1. See Toynbee (1946), Kennedy (1989), Gilpin (1981), Keohane (1984), Keohane and Nye (2001), and Nye (2007).

2. Economist Jacob Viner (1948) nicely captured these two objectives in his seminal essay "Power vs. Plenty as Objectives of Foreign Policy in the Seventeenth and Eighteenth Centuries."

3. The founder of the realism school, Kenneth Waltz, argued that five criteria determine great powers: population and territory, resource endowment, economic capability, political stability and competence, and military strength. By all these criteria, China and India are already great powers, although they are relatively poor in natural resources per capita and do not have as well-equipped militaries as the United States, United Kingdom, France, or Russia, even though both have nuclear capability.

4. Meirsheimer (2001), pp. 9, 15.

5. Nye (2007).

6. Nye (2007).

7. Hegemonic stability theory was coined by Keohane (1980) but was initially developed by Kindleberger (1973). Kindleberger, a key adviser for the Marshall Plan, espoused a public goods view of hegemonic power. This holds that the strongest economy has three functions: maintaining a relatively open market for imports, providing contracyclical long-term lending, and supplying short-term financing in the event of a crisis (Cohen, 2008, p. 72). However, while the Cold War was still raging, Webb and Krasner (1989) proposed an alternative "security" version where "hegemony might be exercised coercively rather than benevolently, seeking to benefit the leader even at the expense of the others" (Cohen, 2008, p. 72).

8. Keohane (1984), for example, wrote *After Hegemony* in 1984, worrying about what kind of system could provide global stability if there was no hegemon. Kennedy (1987) wrote *The Rise and Fall of Great Powers* in 1987 very much in the belief that the United States had become overextended and was going to be weakened by military competition with the USSR and economic competition with quickly developing Japan. As it turned out, these rising powers went into decline or stagnated after 1991, while the United States enjoyed a growth spurt in the last decade of the twentieth century. The capitalist system espoused by the United States appeared to emerge triumphant. Note, however, that the 2008–2009 financial and economic crisis suggests that the United States is in decline again. The lesson is that prediction is a hazardous endeavor, although some of the central tendencies may prove to be valid.

9. Gilpin (1993 paperback edition), p. 26.

10. Gilpin (1993 paperback edition), p. 34.

11. The point about the advantages of backwardness for economic catch-up was originally made by Gerschenkron (1962) and further developed by Abramovitz (1986).

12. In Gilpin's formulation, there are two versions of this: one is to move to positions of greater strength, and the other is to retrench. However, the distinction is not very clear, so they have been subsumed into one.

13. Gilpin does not elaborate on this, but it is implicit in the way he dismisses the others that he believes this option is almost inevitable.

14. Examples of hegemonic wars that led to the establishment of new global systems are the Thirty Years' War (1618–1648) in Europe, the Napoleonic Wars (1803–1815), and World War II; see Gilpin (1981).

15. Friedman concludes: "What is needed for an era of peace and prosperity with China, as with others, is a joining together to build international economic institutions that will provide for the information age what the Bretton Woods system did for the age of mass production and mass consumption, that is, make it easier for governments to deliver the goods to their people so that militaristic and nativistic demagogues do not meet with a popular response to their hate-filled appeals that blame the foreign. If Washington cannot help lead the world in that better direction, if reformers do not continue to win the power struggle in China, then

its rise to power could indeed lead to disasters similar to those associated with the rise of Germany in the first half of the twentieth century" (p. 243).

16. The increase in trade as a share of global GDP is the result of technological change which has reduced transportation and communication costs, as well as a significant reduction in quota restrictions and average tariffs on world trade.

17. Advances in information technology and connectivity through the Internet have also increased the threat of cybersecurity for personal and commercial transactions as well as increased possibilities for cyberwarfare.

18. Data from the International Monetary Fund.

19. United Nations Conference on Trade and Development, *World Investment Report*, various years.

20. Jaruzelski and Dehoff (2008).

21. United Nations Conference on Trade and Development, various years.

22. See Bernstein (2008) for an enlightening analysis of trade over time, which shows the intricate relationship between military power and trade. The terms of trade are sometimes the result of military power of one country over another, and sometimes trade is a substitute for the need for military conquest to obtain resources or goods.

23. See World Trade Organization (1998), "Fiftieth Anniversary of the Multilateral Trading System—Press Brief." http://www.wto.org/english/thewto_e/minist_e/min96_e/chrono.htm. Retrieved July 3, 2009.

24. Because India had been one of the original members of the GATT, it got automatic membership into the WTO upon its creation. However, it maintained restrictive trade policies and even today is a much more closed economy than China.

25. Beattie and Frances (2008), "Doha Trade Talks Collapse," *Financial Times* (July 29). http://www.ft.com/cms/s/0/0638a320–5d8a-11dd-8129–000077b07658.html?nclick_check=1. Retrieved July 3, 2009.

26. Negotiations resumed in November 2009 and continued into 2010 but with no progress before this book went to press.

27. The benefits of free trade are being reconsidered in developed countries as they experience strong competition leading to unemployment and pressures to restructure. Some theoretical work such as Krugman (1986), Gomory and Baumol (2000), and Samuelson (2004) also argues that under certain conditions free trade may not be optimal for a country.

28. Finance is very important for economic growth. The main role of the financial system is to intermediate between savers, who want to earn a return on their money, and investors, who need money to build or expand businesses.

29. See Reinhart and Rogoff (2009) for an excellent history of financial crises over the last 800 years.

30. Three key points from the Great Depression are relevant in terms of global interdependence and the 2008–2009 great contraction. The first is that these disruptions in the U.S. financial market spread throughout the world. The second is that following the passage of the Smoot-Hawley tariffs in 1930, the retaliatory action by other countries led to strong protectionism, which resulted in the collapse of trade that also postponed the recovery. The third is that as a result of all these interactions and negative feedback loops, it took a long time get out of the Great Depression (until World War II for the United States).

31. Unlike the 2008–2009 crisis, this credit boom was mostly in the United States. The spread of mortgage-backed securities and credit default swaps preceding the current crisis spread rapidly in advanced country markets as part of the greater internationalization and interdependence of the financial system.

32. There is general agreement that one of the main causes of the Depression of 1929 was the tightening of the money supply in 1928, which was aimed at reducing stock market speculation. In addition, the international gold exchange standard then prevailing led to a tightening of domestic credit in countries such as Germany and the United Kingdom, which had gold outflows to the United States. In 2008–2009, the U.S. monetary supply was expanded by over 15 percent.

33. An important difference, however, is that in the Depression of 1929, the United States, Germany, and the United Kingdom were already experiencing falling prices and low or zero inflation before the crisis, whereas prior to the 2008–2009 crisis, most countries were experiencing above-average inflation. The latter cushioned the deflationary pressures that exacerbated the 1929 crisis, as general price declines made the real value of loans higher and compounded the problems of repayments.

34. China was also not affected by the Asian financial crisis of 1997, which was caused by lack of investor confidence in East Asia after the 1995 Mexican financial crisis. China did not devalue, which helped Asian economies recover more quickly. Devaluing would have made the exports of other Asian countries less competitive, creating more difficulty for them to reduce their negative trade balances.

35. The first major technological innovation was the development of agriculture in 9000 B.C. Other important innovations were the development of the plow and irrigation between 4000 B.C. and 5000 B.C., which facilitated some small growth of world population. The development of metallurgy and writing date from around 3000 B.C. The development of mathematics dates from about 2000 B.C. World population continued to increase very slowly. Life expectancy during the Greek and Roman Empires averaged about 20 years, which was not much higher than in the preceding few millennia. See Fogel (1999) for more details.

36. At the broadest level, average per capita income is a good summary measure of the effective application of knowledge to the production of

goods and services, although with comparisons across countries it is necessary to be mindful of cases where profits from the sale of natural resources such as oil bias per capita income upward.

37. See Maddison (2001) for a millennial historical overview.

38. Perez (2002), p. 8.

39. See Smil (2003) for a development of this argument.

40. These dates are just indicative, as the revolutions overlap, and all the technologies still coexist, as some of the earlier ones are still in use in developing countries which have not caught up.

41. See Organisation for Economic Co-operation and Development (2008).

42. This argument was first made by Gerschenkron (1962) and then by Abramovitz (1986).

43. McNeill's comprehensive coverage of the interaction between human activity in the twentieth century and the environment is sobering. Without being unduly alarmist, he makes it clear that if we do not make significant changes in the way we interact with the environment—particularly in terms of energy use and water—we will face traumatic consequences.

44. However, it could be argued that the first modern writer to raise the issue of environmental limits to growth was Thomas Malthus in his 1798 classic *An Essay on the Principle of Population.*

45. See Meadows (1973).

46. The effects of the oil crisis were significant. First, there was a large transfer of wealth to the oil-rich members of the cartel, which gave them the opportunity to grow. It also created a need to recycle these "petrodollars," many of which were deposited in banks, which then had a strong incentive to lend to developing countries, which led to overindebtedness during the 1970s. Second, it created a serious balance-of-payments crisis for the United States and many developing countries, which led to crisis in 1981. Third, it led to a change in consumer preference from gas guzzlers to more efficient smaller cars. This provided the Japanese, with their more energy-efficient cars, with an excellent opportunity to enter the U.S. auto market.

47. Many developing economies overborrowed in U.S. dollars after the first oil shock to help foot their oil-import bills and because interest rates were low. When the second oil crisis hit in 1979, many countries could not service their foreign loans. In addition, after the initial oil price rise in 1979 and 1980, there was an oil glut and collapse of oil and commodity prices. This led to sovereign default, currency crisis, high real interest rates, and high inflation in 1981. The crisis hit developing countries in Latin America, Africa, and Asia.

48. International Monetary Fund, *WEO* (April 2009), pp. 110–117.

49. McNeill (2000); World Bank, *WDR* (2010).

50. The proximate explanation for Hitler's rise to power was Germany's reaction against the high costs of reparation payments for World War I.

Other not mutually exclusive explanations included the Great Depression, hyperinflation, and virulent anti-Semitism.

51. This also includes the USSR–Afghan War of 1979–1987, which proved very expensive for the USSR and also serves as a cautionary tale for the current U.S. war in Afghanistan.

52. In addition, the United States and the USSR sought to limit the costly buildup of nuclear weapons through the Strategic Arms Limitation Agreements (SALT I) in 1972. However, President Reagan heated up the Cold War again with the launch of the Strategic Defense Initiative (Star Wars) program to develop an antiballistic missile shield. This renewed a military buildup on both sides. Combined with Reagan's tax cuts, this led to a weakening of the U.S. fiscal balance and the need for additional foreign borrowing. On the Russian side, the expense of the military buildup, combined with poor industrial productivity, contributed to the end of the Cold War and the breakup of the USSR in 1991.

53. See Altman (2009a and 2009b) for a development of this argument.

54. The rough divisions that follow are made by Gilpin (1981) and Nye (2007).

55. The Congress of Vienna was convened in 1814 and lasted more than a year. It is a good example of an international agreement to mediate global conflicts and could be considered a precursor to the League of Nations and the United Nations.

56. The League of Nations was founded in 1919 as part of the provisions of the Versailles Treaty. It eventually reached 58 members in 1934. Its objective was to prevent wars, promote disarmament, and support human rights. It did not have a standing army with which to enforce its decisions.

57. For more details and analysis on the League of Nations, including its shortcomings, see Henig (1973).

58. Nominal figure taken from Cohen (2008).

59. Each country has one vote in the General Assembly. A two-thirds majority is required to pass resolutions. In 2010, there were 192 member states.

60. This was Taiwan, not mainland China. China eventually replaced Taiwan in 1971.

61. This is based on the painstaking life work of the late Angus Maddison (2001 and 2003). For convenience, I will use the terms China, India, Italy, Germany, and the United States to refer to those geographic areas before any such political entities existed. I use United Kingdom (strictly speaking, created in 1922) to mean Great Britain.

62. Among other criticisms, Maddison's series are based on purchasing power parity conversions that were revised significantly in December 2007. The new PPP benchmarks, based on a comparison of a basket of 1,000 goods and adjusted for differences in urban and rural prices, indicated that the old series overestimated the size of China's and India's GDP by

40 percent. However, the general trends are still indicative of the relative changes in economic size.

63. Rome also would have been shown as a large power for much of the first few centuries.

64. The dominance of China and India for the first 18 centuries is a historical fact that is usually missed in typically Eurocentric and Western analyses of great power politics.

65. See Lieber (2007).

66. Mowery and Rosenberg (1989).

67. For a good account of Japan's strategy of rapid technological catch-up with the West, see Odagiri and Goto (1996).

68. For a good study of the rise of Japan, see Vogel (1979).

69. Table 2.3 is based on shares of global GDP in current purchasing power parity and uses the new PPP series adjusted in December 2007. Therefore, they are not directly comparable to the series used in Figure 2.1. However, they show the same trends as do the older series. It is particularly noteworthy that, even after these significant adjustments, China and India are among the top four economies. By 2009, the ranking of countries in terms of economic size in PPP terms is: United States ($14.3 trillion), China ($8.7), Japan ($4.3), and India ($3.5). If the changes are tracked in nominal dollars instead of PPP adjusted dollars, the share of global GDP of advanced countries in 1980 was 70 percent and that of emerging and developing economies 30 percent—roughly the same split as in 2009. However, this masks significant changes, including the relative decline of the former USSR and the rise of China and India.

70. Developing Asia is East Asia minus Japan, South Korea, Hong Kong, Taiwan, and Singapore.

71. Another group that increased very rapidly was the four newly industrialized Asian economies (NIAEs): Hong Kong, Singapore, South Korea, and Taiwan. These have also been called "The Gang of Four" and in the 1990s were held up as paragons of rapid development, so much so that over the last 30 years they moved from being considered developing economies to developed countries. Their share of world GDP more than doubled from 1.7 percent in 1980 to 3.6 percent in 2000 but has not increased much since then.

72. See Alesina and Giavazzi (2008).

73. After its financial and exchange crisis of 1998, Russia followed a strong growth path based on its vast natural resources and petroleum-based exports. In dollar terms, its economy increased ninefold between 1999 and 2008. Its vast energy reserves (it is the main energy supplier of the European Union), military capability, and strong leadership under Vladimir Putin have once again made it a power to be reckoned with on the world stage, albeit one with its own agenda and a different perspective on natural resource scarcity and global warming, as will be developed in

Chapter 6. However, Russia was hit hard by the 2008–2009 economic crisis, which led to a sharp fall in petroleum and natural gas prices. Russia's GDP fell by 9 percent from 2008 to 2009

74. See Yergin (1991), Chapter 13.

75. Kupchan (2010).

76. See Gilpin (1981) for an excellent framework for analyzing power shifts and the contrasts between rising and declining powers. This framework will be used in Chapter 7.

Chapter 3

1. In 2007, China's merchandise exports surpassed those of the United States, and in 2009, they surpassed Germany's.

2. The importance of large labor forces and large markets will be taken up in Chapter 5.

3. For a multivolume work on scientific and technological inventions in China, see Needham (1954).

4. Collis (1946).

5. In the First Sino–Japanese War (1894–1895), the weak Qing dynasty had to cede Taiwan to Japan and recognize the independence of Korea, which was eventually annexed by Japan.

6. For more on China's and India's ambitious science and technology plans, see Chapter 4.

7. There are many studies on the contribution of capital, labor, and technical change in explaining growth in China and India. They get different results depending on the specific forms of the equations used and the extent to which they adjust for the quality of the inputs (such as capacity utilization, education and skills of the labor force, land, etc.). I have chosen Bosworth and Collins because they use the same methodology for both countries and also include an analysis of other high-performing East Asian economies, as the comparison with them is also instructive. Bosworth and Collins use a formulation in which output is a function of capital, labor, education, and total factor productivity. Their equation is $Y = AK^{a}(LH)^{1-a}$, which is a Cobb-Douglas production function with constant factor shares which are assumed to be equal in both countries. In their equation, Y, K, A, and a are measures of output, physical capital services, total factor productivity (technical change that augments the productivity of all factors), and capital share, respectively. L is labor, which they adjust for years of education, labeled H (for human capital, assuming a constant 7 percent rate of return for each year of additional education). They assume that the capital share (a) is equal in both countries, although they allow for the role of land in agriculture. They assume a capital share of 0.4 in both countries because of the difficulty of imputed income shares in economies such as India and China, where there are a large number of self-employed persons

in agriculture. (Agricultural employment in 2004 still absorbed 47 percent of labor in China and 57 percent in India.)

8. The break was made at 1993 because there was a change in the Indian series at that date. It also helps differentiate the performance of the period before the 1991 crisis and the subsequent opening up of the economy.

9. This is a typical procedure of dividing both sides of the equation from footnote 7 by labor to give output in terms of output per worker on the left side and the contribution of the different factors on the right side.

10. In developed economies, population growth is much slower, so labor force growth is much lower. For instance, in the period 1990–2008, labor force growth averaged 0.7 percent for high-income economies compared with 1.4 percent for developing economies (and 0.9 percent and 1.6 percent for China and India, respectively).

11. Average rates of growth of investment in high-income countries averaged 3.3 percent from 1990 to 2000 and 2.3 percent from 2000 to 2008 (averages weighted by GDP). Average rates of growth of investment in developing countries averaged 3.0 percent for the first period and 9.7 percent for the second period (because of the large weight of China and India in the weighted averages).

12. From 1990 to 2000, the average rate of growth of investment in China was 11.7 percent, and from 2000 to 2008, it was 12.1 percent. The corresponding rates for India were 6.9 percent and 15.0 percent (World Bank, *WDI*, 2010, pp. 258–260).

13. The results depend on the particular form of equation used, the weights given to the contribution of capital and labor in the equation, and the extent to which other factors such as education (which in effect also embodies knowledge and thereby reduces the size of the residual TFP) are included explicitly as inputs in the equation. There has been much analysis of TFP growth in China and India, which shows worrying results.

14. As noted in Chapter 2, many economists, including Gerschenkron (1962) and Abramovitz (1986), have pointed out the advantages for growth of lagging behind the technological frontier. However, it is clear that this is a potential that most developing countries have not been able to realize. Achieving high growth requires effective government, macrostability, high rates of saving and investment, and effective development strategies. For a good analysis of the characteristics of the handful of developing countries that have managed to grow more than 7 percent for 25 years or more, see Commission on Growth and Development (2008).

15. Not surprisingly, the rate of TFP in the other East Asian economies slowed in the last period, although this is partly due to the negative impact of the East Asian crisis of 1997.

16. The Chinese investment rate has been one of the highest in the world, averaging 43 percent from 2003 to 2007. Thanks to its very high savings rate, the cost of capital in China has been extremely low for a very long period. A low cost of capital is a critical variable to induce greater investment.

However, the bulk of the investment is directed to state enterprises, and the capital output ratio has been rising in China. The real cost of capital in India has been more in line with the real interest rate in developed economies. However, the banking system in India is also more developed and more efficient than China's. Thus, India has gotten more bang for its buck, but China has invested more bucks.

17. The ratio of investment to GDP, which used to average around 20 percent in India in the 1980s and 1990s, increased to 33 percent between 2003 and 2007 and to 40 percent in 2008.

18. Interestingly, output per worker was higher in services in India than in industry, but the opposite was true in China. See Bosworth and Collins (2008), p. 58.

19. Bosworth and Collins (2008), p. 59, disaggregate the contribution to overall growth in output per worker in each country between the growth rate of output in each sector and the effects due to the reallocation of labor to the higher-productivity sectors. In India for the first period, contributions are roughly equal from the growth of each sector and the reallocation effect. For the second period, the contribution of services growth tripled while that of factor reallocation doubled. In China, the contribution from the growth of the industrial sector accounted for more than a third of total growth in the first period and more than half during the second period. The contribution from reallocation in China was nearly 50 percent higher during the first period compared with India but was similar in the second period. See Table 3.4 for the changing structure of output and employment in the two countries.

20. For an insight into the Tiananmen incident with interesting historical footage, see the PBS documentary, "The Tank Man," available at http://www.pbs.org/wgbh/pages/frontline/tankman/view/.

21. The Janata Dal Party led the government from 1989 until 1991, when the Congress Party won power again. Congress Party Prime Minister Narasimha Rao appointed Manmohan Singh as finance minister. Singh was instrumental in implementing the 1991 reforms liberalizing trade and the economy. The BJP Party won power in 1996. BJP Prime Minister Vajpayee ran the government until 2004 (except from June 1996 to March 1998 when the government was run by the Janata Dal Party).

22. The Congress Party won the 2009 elections and Prime Minister Singh served a second term.

23. A good example of the difficulty of implementing reform, even when the Congress Party had a large majority, was land redistribution. Prime Minister Nehru attempted agrarian reform from 1948 to 1962, but this was not effectively implemented at the state level because state governments were controlled by the landholding classes, which had no interest in diluting their power. By contrast, the authoritarian central government was successful in implementing land reform. For more details, see Sharma (2008).

24. For an excellent account of China's move toward the market, see Naughton (2007), who divides the market transition into two phases.

25. Naughton (2007).

26. For an excellent account of India's economic liberalization, see Panagariya (2005). He argues that in the first decade the Indian economy was quite liberal but that over time there was increased government control, particularly during Indira Gandhi's rule. Rajiv started "liberalization by stealth" in the mid-1980s. However, the big liberalization push came after the 1991 crisis.

27. Particularly notable are China's greater long-term macrostability, very low interest rates, very high investment rate, and high degree of trade integration. These have facilitated its rapid assimilation and use of global knowledge. That said, India has been relatively stable in recent years. In the past five years, its investment rates have exceeded 30 percent, which, along with its expanded openness to imports and global knowledge, explains a large part of its recent rapid growth.

28. See Naughton (2007).

29. World Bank, *WDI* (2010 and 1999).

30. See Panagariya (2005).

31. World Bank, *WDI* (2010 and 1999).

32. The private IT sector has risen to the challenge by working with engineering schools to improve the curriculum and quality of their graduates in a bid to increase the supply of qualified graduates and reduce the skilled labor shortage. However, the Indian education sector is constrained by poor average quality at all levels. Very deficient basic education creates problems further up the education ladder. See Dahlman (2010).

33. The Indian labor force is about 400 million, but only 11 percent work in the organized sector (roughly equivalent to the formal sector, consisting of firms employing 10 workers or more and paying regular wages). However, roughly two-thirds of workers in the formal sector work for federal, state, or local government, so formal private-sector employment is roughly just 3.5 percent of total employment.

34. See NASSCOM (2008).

35. Other obstacles include the difficulty of acquiring land because of restrictions on land use, small ownership plots, and difficulty for small firms to get credit and grow from small to large.

36. Poverty rates are based on international poverty lines denominated in purchasing power parity (PPP) dollars. In India, there is a lively debate on how to define poverty and a great deal of manipulation of data, as certain benefits accrue to those who fall below a certain level.

37. Bosworth and Maertens (2010).

38. World Bank, *WDI* (2010), p. 115.

39. Dillon (2010).

40. Organisation for Economic Co-operation and Development (2010).

41. Farrel et al. (2005).

42. See Dahlman (2010) for an analysis of the challenges and opportunities in India's tertiary education system.

43. See Dahlman, Zeng, and Wang (2007) for more on lifelong learning as an element to enhance competitiveness.

44. The U.S. market represents 60 percent of Indian IT-enabled services (NASSCOM, 2009).

45. See A. T. Kearney (2007) for a detailed benchmarking of different countries.

46. Even by 2009, the IT-enabled service industry in India did not employ much more than 0.5 percent of the labor force.

47. Accessing foreign technical information in print, and now through the Internet, are also important sources, but it is difficult to get systematic quantitative data on this.

48. See Rhee, Ross-Larson, and Purcell (1984) for an early analysis of the technical information transferred by foreign buyers as part of their sourcing strategies in developing countries.

49. See Dutz (2008).

50. International Finance Corporation, Cost of Doing Business 2010 Website: http://www.doingbusiness.org/CustomQuery/Default.aspx?excel=false, accessed March 13, 2011. It ranks 183 countries surveyed.

51. Motorola, for example, was required to develop an extensive training program for the management of the 1,000 largest state-owned enterprises (Dahlman, Zeng, and Wang, 2007).

52. Gill and Kharas (2007).

53. Qiqing (2009), p. 5. In the context of the debate on global financial imbalances (see Chapter 5), it should also be noted that firms with foreign capital have increased their share of China's foreign trade imbalance from just over 30 percent in the early 2000s to more than 60 percent by 2008.

54. See, for example, Huang and Khanna (2005), who argue that China is too dependent on FDI compared to India and that such dependence has held back the development of domestic entrepreneurship.

55. For an excellent analysis of the impact of FDI in China, including how it has plugged China into global production chains, see Yusuf and Nabeshima (2010a), especially Chapter 3.

56. United Nations Conference on Trade and Development (2008), pp. 285 and 286.

57. However, technology-licensing payments have been rising rapidly in India. Payments in 2008 were 66 percent higher than in 2007, while the increase in China was only 26 percent.

58. United Nations Educational, Scientific and Cultural Organization (2010). This is despite the fact that domestic enrollment rates in China are nearly twice those in India.

59. See Kuznetsov (2009) for an analysis of the Indian case.

60. Goertzel (2008).
61. Cha and Nakashima (2010).
62. *Daily Mail* (2010).
63. Freedom House (2010) scores countries on a scale of 1 to 7 on two indicators—civil liberties and political representation. The scores reported in the table are the average of the two rankings. Because in the original scale a score of 1 was the highest and 7 the lowest, the negative of the value was taken so that the higher on the graph, the better the score.
64. The Heritage Foundation scores countries on 10 indicators of economic freedom: business freedom, trade freedom, fiscal freedom, government spending, monetary freedom, investment freedom, financial freedom, property rights, freedom from corruption, and labor freedom. Thus, it is a broad-based index that also captures many dimensions of economic freedom. Data are available only from 1996. Data on economic freedom for 1975 to 1995 were estimated by the author by comparing the market regime before that time to current rankings of countries with regimes similar to those of China and India at earlier times. Therefore, this is a rough approximation that should be interpreted with caution.

Chapter 4

1. In the simple neoclassical production function, $Q = f(K, L)$, where Q is output, K is capital, and L is labor. In the slightly more sophisticated formulation, $Q = f(K, L, HC, \text{and } T)$, where HC is an adjustment for education and T is technology, which is assumed to be a function of research and development (R&D). This chapter focuses on L, HC, and R&D.
2. For a summary analysis, see Altman (2009).
3. For example, the investments of one of China's largest commercial banks, the Bank of China, in asset-backed securities supported by U.S. subprime mortgages were just 3.5 percent of its investment securities portfolio in March 2008, and by the end of September 2008, the bank had reduced those holdings to 1.4 percent. Its holdings of debt securities related to Fannie Mae and Freddie Mac were higher, but these were safer, since the U.S. government placed them in conservatorship and extended government backing. See Morrison (2009a), p. 3.
4. Morrison (2009a), p. 3.
5. President Hu Jintao announced in early 2009 that China would maintain a growth rate of 8 percent in 2009. Virtually all international forecasters derided that statement, pointing out that China would be very adversely affected by the fall in import demand from developed countries. However, President Hu was right.
6. A measure of inequality ranging from 0 (no inequality) to 100 (maximum inequality).

7. Ravallion and Chaudhuri (2007).
8. World Bank, *WDI* (2010), p. 94.
9. See Dahlman, Zeng, and Wang (2007).
10. World Bank, *WDI* (1998), p. 69.
11. World Bank, *WDI* (2010), p. 95.
12. World Bank, *WDI* (2010), p. 88.
13. Kanbur (2009), p. 33.
14. Hu Jintao, October 15, 2007, cited in Bergsten et al. (2008), p. 5, quoted in Xingua News Agency.
15. For a concise analysis of corruption in China, see Chapter 4 in Bergsten et al. (2008). For an analysis of corruption and politics in India, see Jalan (2005), a former governor of the Reserve Bank of India.
16. This useful distinction is made in Naughton (2007), Chapter 20.
17. World Bank, *WDI* (2010).
18. Air pollution measured as particulate matter concentration per cubic meter; World Bank, *WDI* (2010), pp. 202–204.
19. World Bank, *WDI* (2010), pp. 206–208.
20. Some estimate that in China air pollution is responsible for an extra 100,000 deaths a year. See, for example, Naughton (2007), p. 488.
21. See Table 3.16, column on particulate emission damage, in World Bank, *WDI* (2010), pp. 212–214.
22. See Naughton (2007) for more details.
23. Bergsten et al. (2006), p. 40.
24. A few years back, it seemed there might be a protectionist backlash from countries losing service jobs to India through information technology. This has subsided somewhat but is likely to become another hot election issue in the run-up to the 2012 U.S. elections.
25. India, in contrast, is ranked 16th in the world.
26. Official Chinese data report that the total fertility rate in 2000 was only 1.22, but this is considered too low by many analysts, and there is also evidence that the one-child policy has not been enforced as strongly. There is no doubt that the fertility rate is below the replacement level. See Naughton (2007), p. 166.
27. Economic development leads to a drop in the fertility rate as women get more education and participate more in the formal work force.
28. The dependency ratio is the sum of the population below 15 years of age and the population above 65 years as a share of the working-age population (ages 15–64). Thus, it is a rough proxy for the share of the population that the working-age population needs to support. China's working-age population was 72 percent in 2008, one of the highest in the world (compared with an average of 58 percent for low-income and 66 percent for middle- and high-income countries).
29. Raising the retirement age is a measure most countries, including advanced ones, will need to take to deal with public finance solvency problems, as life expectancies have increased many years beyond what they were when pension systems were originally designed.

30. See Du and Wei (2010), who argue that this unbalanced gender ratio may explain up to half the higher-than-average Chinese savings rate.

31. See World Bank Governance Indicators. Available at http://info.worldbank.org/governance/wgi/index.asp.

32. Interestingly, this ranking also appears to have worsened for the United States.

33. Goldman (2007) argues that the Chinese have been moving from their roles as comrades, which was prevalent during the Mao period, to being citizens demanding more voice and accountability.

34. There was strong public reaction in the United States against Google's compliance with this policy. In January 2010, after suffering a massive hacking attack that went after e-mail addresses of dissidents as well as piracy of its source code, Google threatened to leave China and stopped blocking sites for the government. The U.S. government escalated this issue in discussions with the Chinese government.

35. Interestingly, the political stability index for the United States fell significantly between 2000 and 2003, probably due largely to the contested presidential election of 2000, but it had recovered to some extent by 2008.

36. See Shambaugh (2008) for a detailed and insightful analysis of China's Communist Party.

37. See, for example, Tang (2005).

38. The Three Represents are "advanced social productive forces," "the progressive force of China's advanced culture," and "the interests of the majority." Businessmen and capitalists were added into the advanced social productive forces.

39. Tsai (2007), for example, argues that Chinese entrepreneurs lack class identity because they do not have shared values or interests. Therefore, they seek to resolve problems through informal channels rather than confrontation.

40. Pei (2006).

41. See, for example, Chang (2001), who argued on the eve of China's entry into the WTO in 2001 that the country was about to collapse, and Yang (2007), who argues that China will face internal strife that will slow its growth.

42. In China, the percentage of positive responses had increased continuously from 48 percent in 2002. In India, it had increased from 7 percent in 2002 to a peak of 53 percent in 2009 before falling to 45 percent in 2010. In the United States, it fell from 41 percent in 2002 to a low of 23 percent in 2008 before increasing slightly to 30 percent in 2010. This question was separate from a question on the future of the economy, where the percentage of positive answers in China was even higher. See Pew Research Center (2010). For other surveys showing high approval ratings for the Chinese government and a different Chinese conception of democracy, see Shi (2008) and Tang (2005).

43. See, for example, Shambaugh (2008), who argues for the resilience of the Communist Party. See also Chapter 3, "Democratization or Disorder," in Bergsten et al. (2006), and Chapter 2, "China Debates Its Future," in

Bergsten et al. (2008). Finally, see Shi (2008), who analyzes the results of an independent survey in China (part of a multi-Asian country study) which shows that 84 percent of the respondents already considered the Chinese regime to be partly democratic and expected it to remain so or improve.

44. O'Neill and Poddar (2008).

45. Kohli and Sood (2010).

46. Bardhan (1998).

47. Luce (2007), p. 117.

48. A prominent political scientist, Pratap Bhanu Mehta (2003), has written a book titled *The Burden of Democracy,* in which he explores the challenges of implementing democracy in a country with a largely illiterate and unpropertied population, a lack of accountability, and persistent inequality. A former governor of the Reserve Bank of India, Bimal Jalan (2005), has also written a book on governance, which includes such provocative chapter titles as "The Supply and Demand of Corruption." Both writers, however, are optimistic about India's future.

49. Fareed Zakaria (2003) has made the provocative claim that while democracy has been flourishing in India, liberty has not. He further argues that it is more effective to promote constitutional liberty than democracy in developing countries. His claim is that democracy alone, without the underpinning of liberty as defined by access to education, accountability, and institutional checks on power, can lead to an illiberal democracy.

50. World Bank, *WDI* (2010).

51. Bardhan (2010) develops this argument further.

52. China's roads are second only to the United States in terms of miles, and 71 percent are paved versus only 65 percent in the United States. China's turnpike road system is now larger and more modern than the United States'. In addition, China is developing extensive high-speed train links between Beijing and its other major cities.

53. The Indian rail system is heavily politicized and plays a large patronage role as a major employer. This prevents it from responding rationally to the demand for improving freight services, among other things.

54. Comparative data taken from World Bank, *WDI* (2009), pp. 302–308, and mostly for 2005–2007.

55. This measure includes the number of documents, number of days, and time and cost required to import and export a container of freight; see International Finance Corporation (2010).

56. There have been many terrorist attacks in Mumbai. The main ones include 13 bombs in March 1993 that killed more than 250 people, two bombs in August 2002 that killed more than 40 people, and seven bombs in July 2006 that killed more than 200 people. This last is said to also have been linked to the Lashkar-e-Taiba terrorist group.

57. *Washington Post* (January 8, 2009).

58. China Daily.com, "India, China Reopen Silk Road Pass," July 6, 2006. Available at http://www.chinadaily.com.cn/china/2006-07/06/content_634734.htm, accessed January 10, 2010.

59. For more on the continuing tensions between the two countries, see Sharma (2009), Chapter 5.

60. "Rising Maoist Insurgency in India," *Global Politician* (May 13, 2007). Available at http://globalpolitician.com/22790-india, accessed May 7, 2010.

61. Yardley (2010).

62. Many analysts are pessimistic about the continued rapid growth of China and India. A good, more-pessimistic analysis can be found in Bardhan (2010). See also Eichengreen, Gupta, and Kumar (2010), for another view on the development strategies and prospects for China and India.

63. The World Economic Forum is a nongovernmental organization (NGO) based in Geneva that conducts annual meetings among world business and political leaders. It also publishes various annual reports, one of which is a detailed assessment of the competitiveness of countries. This assessment now covers more than 200 structural and qualitative indicators for 133 countries.

64. Rankings for 2004 are from World Economic Forum (2004), p. 6, and for 2010 from World Economic Forum (2010), p. 15.

65. This nomenclature is currently in use by the International Monetary Fund to refer to the countries that used to be known as the "Gang of Four." These countries are held up as paragons of rapid development; it is useful to include them as a reference point given their high performance and recent transition to developed-country status.

66. Technological readiness consists of nine indicators: availability of latest technologies, firm-level technology absorption, FDI, technology transfer, and five indicators relative to information and telecommunications technology (laws, mobile phone users, Internet users, personal computer users, and broadband Internet subscribers). China and India are ranked low in these indicators because they are normalized by population or economic size, which is not always the most appropriate measure.

67. United Nations Educational, Scientific and Cultural Organization (2010), pp. 162–170.

68. For information on the methodology as well as the rankings over time, see http://www.arwu.org/index.jsp. The total for China given in the 2010 rankings includes universities in Taiwan. Only 22 of the 34 listed appear to be in mainland China.

69. See Dahlman (2010).

70. These include the Indian Institutes of Technology, Institutes of Management, and Institutes of Information Management.

71. Dahlman, Zeng, and Wang (2007).

72. Organization for Economic Co-operation and Development (2007), Figure 6.3.

73. National Science Board (2010), p. O-9.

74. Many of the degrees granted in China and India are not full four-year degrees but two- or three-year technical degrees. The teams sought to standardize the data, and Table 6.5 represents their results. See Wadhwa, Gereffi, Rising, and Ong (2007).

75. Wadhwa, Gereffi, Rising, and Ong (2007).

76. National Science Board (2010), p. O-7.

77. National Science Board (2010), p. O-7.

78. United Nations Educational, Scientific and Cultural Organization (2010), pp. 174, 177, 179. The United States is the largest host country, receiving 624,000 tertiary students from all over the world, followed by the United Kingdom (342,000), France (243,000), Australia (213,000), Germany (189,000), and Japan (126,000). Foreign students represent a large percentage of the student populations in Australia (20.6 percent) and the United Kingdom (14.7 percent) and are an important source of income for their educational systems. For more details, see UNESCO.

79. Wadhwa (2009).

80. For an excellent, more detailed analysis of China's emerging competitive technological edge based on higher education, see Simon and Cao (2009).

81. See Simon and Cao (2009), pp. 344–346 in particular.

82. Patents in the United States rather than patents in their home countries were chosen to standardize for the patent regime because these vary widely across countries. The United States was chosen because it is the largest market.

83. McDonald (2010).

84. The electric car in India is the Revo.

85. This assumes that it is made public in, say, a scientific or technical journal or in a patent application. However, insufficient education to understand the article or intellectual property rights restrictions may limit its actual use.

86. Cao, Suttmeir, and Simon (2006).

87. Typically, 70 to 80 percent of R&D in developing countries is carried out by the government and only 20 to 30 percent by private firms. In developed countries, the ratio between public and private R&D is the inverse.

88. See Dutz (2007) for an analysis of R&D in India that takes into account R&D by foreign MNCs.

89. In India, the additional R&D investments by MNCs, added to increased investments by the domestic private sector, have raised total R&D spending from a 20-year average of 0.80 percent of GDP to 1.1 percent in 2005. This has been concentrated mainly in pharmaceuticals, ICT, electronics, and auto parts; see Dutz (2007).

90. Organization for Economic Co-operation and Development (2007), p. 166.

91. Jaruzelski and Dehoff (2008).

92. This is an estimate in nominal dollars put together by Booz Allen Hamilton using its survey results plus data from the OECD, the IMF, and the World Bank. The estimate is consistent with the author's estimate of world R&D expenditures of $1.1 trillion PPP for 2007.

93. Jaruzelski and Dehoff (2008).

94. Jaruzelski and Dehoff (2008), pp. 52–53.

95. "A patent is an exclusive right granted by law . . . to [an] inventor . . . generally for 20 years. . . . In return for the exclusive rights, the applicant is obliged to disclose the invention to the public in a manner that enables others, skilled in the art, to replicate the invention." Thus, there is a compromise between encouraging invention through property rights and the social-welfare objective of disseminating that knowledge to others. A utility model is an exclusive right granted by some countries for a shorter time (usually 7 to 10 years). The requirements are less stringent than for patents, but they also cannot be renewed. The United States does not grant utility models, but China, Korea, Germany, Russia, and many other countries do. China received the largest number of utility model filings in 2007 (181,374), followed by Korea (21,084), Germany (18,083), Japan (10,315), and Russia (10,075). "A trademark is a distinctive sign that identifies certain goods or services produced or provided by a specific individual or enterprise and gives the holder exclusive rights to use that sign." Unlike patents and utility models, trademarks can be renewed. "An industrial design is the ornamental or aesthetic aspect of an article. The design may consist of three-dimensional features such as the shape or surface of an article, or of two-dimensional features, such as patterns, lines, or color. . . . The term of protection is usually five years with the possibility of renewal up to, in most cases, 15 years. Industrial designs can be registered by filing an application at the relevant national or regional IP office(s), or by filing an international application though the Hague System for International Registration of Industrial Designs." All quotes are from World Intellectual Property Organization (2009).

96. The European Patent Office allows an applicant to apply for coverage in all European Community countries. This creates a possible downward bias in the number of patents registered by individual country members of the European Community, but this bias is not enough to change the relative ranking of China.

97. These are the 7 technology areas (of a total of 35) in which the share of foreign-oriented world patents in China was greater than China's overall share in foreign-oriented patents ("revealed comparative advantage"), from highest to lowest degree of specialization. This concept is analogous to the index of revealed comparative advantage used in trade. The technology areas in which China is relatively less specialized, from lowest to highest are: transport; engines, pumps, turbines; textile and paper machines; macromolecular chemistry, polymers; mechanical elements; other special machines; surface technology, coating; and basic material chemistry; World Intellectual Property Organization (2009), Annex A, p. 80.

98. World Intellectual Property Organization (2009), Annex 8, p. 81.

99. Organization for Economic Co-operation and Development (2008).

100. World Intellectual Property Organization (2010), p. 52.

101. World Intellectual Property Organization (2010), p. 54.

102. World Intellectual Property Organization (2010), p. 65.
103. World Intellectual Property Organization (2010), p. 80.
104. World Intellectual Property Organization (2010), p. 102.
105. The empirical study was based on an analysis of firm-level data from 1995 to 2001. See Hu and Jefferson (2009).
106. See Preeg (2008) and Preeg (2005).
107. See Kohli and Sood (2010) for an excellent analysis of India's future prospects to 2039.
108. See Blinder (2006) for development of this point.

Chapter 5

1. For an earlier assessment of some of the positive and negative impacts, see Winters and Yusuf (2007).
2. Based on breakdown of service exports from UNCTAD trade statistics.
3. It was also caused by speculation in commodity prices.
4. It is also affecting other Southeast Asian developing economies. See Yusuf and Nabeshima (2009 and 2010a).
5. For an analysis of the ways expanded Chinese trade affects other developing countries in Latin America and Asia, see Gallagher and Porzecanski (2010), Lederman, Olarreaga, and Perry (2007), and Lall and Weiss (2003). The work of Goldstein, Pinaud, Reisen, and Chen (2006) concentrates specifically on Africa.
6. See Yusuf and Nabeshima (2010a) for a good analysis of the development of the dynamic intra-Asian production networks.
7. This is not counting SITC 9, which is a residual collection of commodities not elsewhere classified.
8. These are at the SITC two-digit level, which gives a total of 66 product categories.
9. A country has a "revealed comparative advantage" in a product if its share of exports of that product throughout the world is greater than the share of its total merchandise exports to total world merchandise goods.
10. The product and region where India had the largest market share (nearly 10 percent) were food, beverages, and tobacco in developing Asia. It had the greatest growth in oils and lubricants in other developing economies (a nearly 3,500 percent increase) and Asian developing economies (640 percent). In developed Asia, the largest growth was in other manufactures not elsewhere classified (520 percent). In developed countries, it was machinery and transport equipment (395 percent). But in both these markets, India's share in those categories was below 0.5 percent of the respective region's imports.
11. At a more disaggregated level, there have been some changes; see Figure 5.4.

12. The technology intensity of products is determined based on input of the R&D content, including components as determined by input–output matrices. See Organisation for Economic Co-operation and Development (2007) for a definition of technology intensity.

13. Chandra et al. (2009).

14. Yusuf and Nabeshima (2010a), pp. 96–99.

15. See National Science Board (2010), Figure 0-28, for share of value added by the main countries. China includes Hong Kong.

16. For a comparative analysis of the hardware and software sector in China and India, see Gregory, Nollen, and Tenev (2009).

17. However, Honda has a majority-owned joint venture in Guangzhou solely for the export of cars.

18. Tang (2009).

19. For a good exposition on modular production in the electronics industry, see Sturgeon (2002).

20. The use of unbundling for these trends is attributed to Richard Baldwin (2006).

21. The decline in communication costs and the ability to coordinate activities across national boundaries and to integrate suppliers to production and distribution also contribute to the first type of unbundling.

22. Calculation in International Monetary Fund (2007). The total labor forces of China (776 million), India (335 million), and the former Soviet Union (219 million) accounted for 44 percent of the total global labor force of 3,028 million in 2005. However, not all the labor forces are involved in exports. The IMF calculation weighted countries by their degree of export orientation and took into account the change of that export-oriented labor force over time.

23. This point was originally made by Freeman (2006), who argued that the global labor force had doubled with the entry of export-oriented countries.

24. There is much debate on the number of jobs that might actually be outsourced, and Blinder's estimates tend to be at the high end. The key point is that as ICT advances and more tasks can be digitized, many more jobs may be at risk. For an excellent discussion of these issues, see Bhagwati and Blinder (2009).

25. Blinder (2006).

26. In economic theory, this is the prediction of the Stopler Samuelson factor price equalization theorem, which shows that wages between a high-income and low-income economy will be equalized through trade.

27. See International Labor Office (2010).

28. India has a lower labor force participation rate than China, so its economically active population is a lower proportion of its total population.

29. Dutz (2007).

30. World Bank (2009).

31. From International Monetary Fund, *WEO* (2010) database, accessed December 18, 2010.

32. International Monetary Fund, *WEO* (2010) database.

33. The United Kingdom and countries in southern Europe have also been running deficits, but the biggest deficit country by far has been the United States.

34. International Monetary Fund, *WEO* (2010), p. 202.

35. As of the end of 2009, India's foreign exchange reserves were $266 billion.

36. The federal debt held by the public has exploded from less than 40 percent of GDP between 2000 and 2006 to more than 60 percent in 2009. It is projected to increase to about 70 percent by 2019 under the baseline scenario and to about 85 percent under a proposed extension of tax cuts and indexing of the alternative minimum tax. Foreign holdings of the debt have also jumped from around 30 percent between 2000 and 2004 to about 50 percent by the end of 2009. Official foreign holdings have doubled from around 15 percent in 2000 to about 35 percent by the end of 2009. See Elmendorf (2009).

37. U.S.–China Economic and Security Review Commission (2010b), pp. 30, 33, 34.

38. The McKinsey Global Institute estimates that foreign government holding of U.S. Treasuries lowers the interest rate that the U.S. government would have to pay by about $90 billion. Cited in U.S.–China Economic and Security Commission (2010), p. 35.

39. See a summary of some of the debates in Morrison (2009a and 2009b).

40. Some foreign observers have even joked that China's foreign exchange reserves are being managed as a reverse hedge fund (China invests in very safe securities with no upside potential), which is a very poor use of capital given China's many domestic investment needs.

41. In May 2007, a Chinese government agency that was subsequently absorbed by the CIC invested $3 billion in the U.S. private equity firm the Blackstone Group. The stake in the Blackstone Group was also subsequently increased.

42. See Martin (2008).

43. See Martin (2008) for further details.

44. These included the dollar, the yen, the euro, and some others.

45. *Money Week* (2010).

46. In 1987, the Louvre Accord was a meeting of the G-7 (minus Italy) to halt the decline of the dollar brought about by the Plaza Accord.

47. To counter the recession that resulted from the appreciation of the yen, the Japanese government adopted expansionary monetary policies. These led to the real estate bubble that contributed to the 1991 Japanese financial crisis. This expansionary policy was similar to the United States' after the dot-com bubble burst in 2001, which was one of the main contributing factors to the housing bubble that led to the 2008–2009 crisis.

48. The *Basic National Income Identity* is useful as a framework for analyzing current account imbalances. According to this formula, net private saving (the excess of private saving *S* over investment *I*) plus government

saving (the excess of taxes *T* over government spending *G*) must equal the current account surplus (the excess of exports *X* over imports *M*):

$$(S - I) + (T - G) = (X - M)$$

(Net Private Saving) (Government Saving) (Current Account)

For there to be a current account surplus, $(X - M) > 0$, the sum of net private saving and government saving must be a positive number, that is: $(S - I) + (T - G) > 0$. Note that either net private saving or government saving may be negative as long as the other is positive enough to offset it. In the United States, net private saving and government saving are both negative, and thus, there are current account deficits. Having fewer exports than imports is consistent with what is generally believed to be an overvalued dollar. In China, large private savings (over 50 percent of GDP) exceed investments (over 40 percent of GDP), so there is large net private saving that easily compensates for negative government saving, which is relatively low. In recent years, China has maintained a current account surplus of about 10 percent of GDP.

49. There were actually two competing proposals. The British proposal, put forth by Keynes, was to create a world central bank that could create new reserves as necessary. The U.S. proposal was to create a pool of national currencies and gold subscribed to by different countries to manage trade deficits without the need to resort to devaluations. The U.S. proposal won because of the overwhelming strength of the United States and the dependence of the allies on it for reconstruction loans following World War II. The International Monetary Fund was set up as an international organization to maintain exchange-rate rules and manage international balance of payments but not as a world central bank.

50. This problem is known as the Tiffin Dilemma, after the Belgian economist who first noted it in 1960.

51. This was done without consultation with other countries or the IMF, even though consulting the IMF was required by its rules for such a significant change.

52. Euros are roughly 25 percent of global reserves and have been increasing. The other two main reserve currencies are the Japanese yen and the British pound, with a combined share of around 9 percent (International Monetary Fund, *Currency Composition of Official Foreign Exchange Reserves*, various years).

53. These are the estimates of the U.S. Federal Reserve Bank of New York. See http://www.newyorkfed.org/aboutthefed/fedpoint/fed01.html, accessed May 12, 2010.

54. U.S.–China Economic and Security Review Commission (2010b).

55. For a *Wall Street Journal* report, see Batson (2009).

56. This is somewhat similar to the idea that had been proposed by Keynes to create a world central bank that could issue its own global currency—the bancor.

57. See Bergsten (2009) for a good discussion of the issues of the dollar as a reserve currency and why the SDR proposal is limited.

58. U.S. Bureau of Economic Analysis, International Investment Position, Year End Positions 1976–2009. Available at http://www.bea.gov/international/, accessed November 14, 2010. At the end of 2008, the net U.S. international investment position was –$2.7 trillion, including net foreign direct investment position as well as securities and official reserves. Foreign official assets in the United States were $4.4 trillion. Total foreign assets in the United States were $22.1 trillion, or roughly 50 percent higher than total U.S. GDP.

59. United Nations Conference on Trade and Development, *WIR* (2010), pp. 167 and 170.

60. *Washington Post*, "GM Sales in China Surge 67 percent" (January 5, 2010).

61. See Tang (2009), pp. 9, 19.

62. This was a distortion that most economists argued should have been corrected earlier.

63. U.S.–China Business Council (2009).

64. United Nations Conference on Trade and Development (2010), p. 170.

65. United Nations Conference on Trade and Development (2010). Calculated from pp. 170 and 171.

66. See Davies (2010) for more details on outward foreign investments from China, including a list of some of the main mergers and acquisitions and new investments.

67. Based on a survey by a team from Fudan University and Vale Columbia Center on Sustainable Development, cited in Davies (2010).

68. Moran (2010) has done a careful analysis of China's acquisition of natural resources. He concludes that so far most of these acquisitions and special loans to natural resource companies have not created special advantages for Chinese companies in terms of captive suppliers or advantageous pricing but have instead helped to expand and diversify supply. However, he does note the problems created by Chinese investments in rogue regimes, which help them continue to operate outside the international norms against human rights violations, environmental degradation, and support for terrorism.

69. See Davies (2010) for a more extensive list, including mergers and acquisitions.

70. Davies (2010).

71. See Haier Web page, http://www.haier.com/abouthaier/haierworldwide/introduction.asp, accessed December 17, 2010.

72. A Chinese company made a bid to purchase Hummer, but the Chinese government blocked the purchase, presumably because the Hummer was so energy inefficient.

73. China Ministry of Commerce (2009).

74. United Nations Conference on Trade and Development, *WIR* (2010), p. 170.

75. See Satyanand and Raghavendran (2010) for a good summary of Indian outward FDI, including the main mergers and acquisitions as well as new investments.

76. See Satyanand and Raghavendran (2010) for a more detailed list, including mergers and acquisitions.

77. United Nations Conference on Trade and Development, *WRI* (2010).

78. See http://www.niit.com.

79. All four of these acquisitions occurred in 2008.

80. See Clarke (2010) for a discussion of cybersecurity concerns.

81. There is already some literature drawing this parallel and giving advice to Chinese investors on how to avoid raising alarm. See, for example, Milhaupt (2008).

82. India was given until 2005 to extend patent protection to pharmaceutical products. Before that, it only granted patent protection to pharmaceutical processes.

83. World Economic Forum (2004), p. 525, and World Economic Forum (2010), p. 367.

84. China is the top country of 12 on the watch list, and the report devotes three pages to it. The second country, Russia, gets just two-thirds of a page. The others, including India, have only a paragraph. Brazil and Mexico are among the 33 countries on the regular watch list. In 2009, Taiwan and Korea were taken off the list.

85. Office of the United States Trade Representative (2009 and 2010).

86. In 2007, the Office of the United States Trade Representative brought a case to the WTO over deficiencies in China's legal regime for protecting and enforcing copyrights and trademarks on a wide range of products. In March 2009, the WTO Dispute Settlement Body (DSB) ruled in favor of the United States on two of the three claims. The first was that China's denial of copyright protection to works that did not meet its content review standards was not permissible under WTO rules. The second was that China's custom rules could not allow selling seized counterfeit goods. On the third claim—that the criminal threshold for counterfeit goods was too high—the DSB, while accepting the U.S. interpretation of the standards, ruled that it needed more evidence to uphold the claim. Office of the United States Trade Representative (2009), p. 9.

87. Office of the United States Trade Representative (2009), p. 14.

88. In late 2007, the United States also brought a case regarding market access for foreign publications, movies, music, and video, which the United States won; Office of the United States Trade Representative (2010).

89. Office of the United States Trade Representative (2009), pp. 17–18.

90. Office of the United States Trade Representative (2009), pp. 15 and 18.

91. http://www.huawei.com/cn/about/AboutIndex.do.

92. *Washington Post*, "Google Threatens to Leave China" (January 13, 2010), p. 1.

93. Dickie (2010).

94. Anderlini (2010a).

95. European Union Chamber of Commerce in China (2010).

96. Anderlini (2010b).

97. U.S.–China Business Council (2010).

98. See McGregor (2010).

99. McGregor (2010), p. 5.

100. For a good analysis of this case, see Suttmeier, Yao, and Tan (2006), which includes an analysis of six cases involving friction over standards.

101. Suttmeier (2005).

102. Suttmeier suggests that the international community can do much to encourage international collaboration on developing standards that are more accommodating to non-Chinese interests than were the initial standards.

103. The Economists' Index of Democracy is based on five subindices: electoral process and pluralism, functioning of government, political participation, political culture, and civil liberties; Economist Intelligence Unit (2008).

104. See, for example, Ramos (2004) and Halper (2010).

105. See, for example, Altman (2009).

106. Data for ranking countries range from 0 (least market oriented) to 100 (most market oriented). The overall index is based on 10 subindices: business freedom, trade freedom, fiscal freedom, government spending, monetary freedom, investment freedom, financial freedom, property rights, freedom from corruption, and labor freedom.

107. Heritage Foundation (2010).

108. See also Yao (2010), who argues that China is being challenged by the end of the Beijing Consensus, particularly insofar as the government may not be able to continue to guarantee its citizens sustained high economic growth in exchange for reduced political freedom.

109. See Shambaugh (2008) and Bergsten et al. (2008).

110. The Chinese population reacted very strongly to comments about China's repression in Tibet in the run-up to hosting the 2010 Olympic Games. It also periodically reacts very strongly against Japan and Japanese business when there are tensions with Japan. The Chinese government has had to calm these strong outbursts of populist nationalism.

111. Pew Research Center (2010).

112. See Chapter 6 for an analysis of the impact on resources, energy, and CO_2 emissions.

113. To put this in perspective and keeping it in terms of nominal dollars instead of PPP dollars, the growth of the Chinese and Indian economies was $338 and $68 billion, respectively, in 2009. Their growth in 2010 is expected to be $423 and $110 billion, respectively, and $460 and $115 billion, respectively, in 2011. This compares with a drop of $350 billion in the United States in 2009 and expected growth of $441 billion in 2010 and $381 billion in 2011. Growth estimates based on 2008 nominal GNI figures from World Bank, *WDI* (2010 and 2009), and 2010 growth rates from International Monetary Fund, *WEO* (April 2010).

114. See the chart on contribution to global growth in International Monetary Fund, *WEO* (April 2010), p. 4.

115. See Bradsher, *New York Times* (December 14, 2010).

116. See Bradsher, *New York Times* (December 23, 2010).

117. Even for large MNCs from the larger U.S. market, foreign markets have become larger. For example, the transnationality index (average share of foreign sales, assets, and employment) in 2008 was 97 percent for Wal-Mart, 88 percent for Conoco Phillips, 84 percent for GM, 82 percent for Kraft Foods, 76 percent for Johnson and Johnson, 75 percent for General Electric, 72 percent for Pfizer, 71 percent for Ford, 69 percent for United Technologies, 58 percent for Hewlett Packard, 55 percent for Procter and Gamble, and 50 percent for IBM; see United Nations Conference on Trade and Development, *World Investment Report* (2010), Annex Table 26.

Chapter 6

1. Soil, water, and air pollution are also important environmental problems that, in addition to creating serious problems in China and India, become international issues as the effects cross national boundaries. For some analysis of the problem of these other environmental issues, see Smil (2004) and Naughton (2007).

2. International Energy Agency (2010c).

3. International Energy Agency (2010c).

4. Smil (2004), pp. 165–168.

5. Smil (2004), p. 57.

6. The average for high-income countries is 43 percent; World Bank (2010b), p. 172.

7. For much of Indian agriculture, the cost of water is essentially the cost of pumping it out of wells, and the electricity rate for farmers is also subsidized.

8. Lerner (2010).

9. China and India also have a significant problem of relatively low access to improved water sources for human consumption for rural populations, although the situation is worse in Brazil in spite of its abundant water resources.

10. Surprisingly, its imports of petroleum and petroleum products were 7.8 percent of the world's total, which was just below China's share in world imports (8.1 percent).

11. The top five in which India had the largest world share were gold (20 percent), fertilizers (13 percent), vegetables oils and fat (9 percent), nonmetallic minerals (9 percent), and coal and coke briquettes (7 percent).

12. China also exports both of these energy-intensive products.

13. World Bank (2010a), p. 7.

14. The ecological footprint has been developed by the Global Footprint Network; see Ewing et al. (2010). It "measures the amount of biologically productive land and water area required to produce all the resources an individual, population, or activity consumes and to absorb the wastes they generate, given prevailing technology and resource management practices." Biocapacity is "the amount of productive area that is available to generate these resources and to absorb the waste" (p. 8). Although there are many methodological issues with this analysis (including that roughly half the footprint is CO_2 emissions and questionable assumptions about the calculation of the earth's ability to absorb it), it is one of the few methodologies that tries to measure environmental resource availability versus use for all countries of the world.

15. Ewing et al. (2010), p. 18.

16. Ewing et al. (2010), p. 18.

17. Europe in this table is all of Europe minus Russia, which is shown separately.

18. The two major countries with significant surpluses are Brazil (net surplus of 10 percent of world's biocacapity) and Russia (net surplus of 2 percent).

19. This caught analysts by surprise. Most estimates had assumed a continued reduction in energy intensity, so estimates of energy consumption by 2010 were considerably below actual consumption.

20. U.S. Department of Energy (2009).

21. United Nations Intergovernmental Panel on Climate Change (2007).

22. France's share of electricity produced by nuclear power is very high. Nuclear and alternative energy account for 46 percent of total energy use (World Bank 2010b).

23. International Energy Agency (2010c), pp. 59–62.

24. Projections from International Energy Agency (2010c) using the new policies scenario.

25. World Bank (2010c), p. 259.

26. For a good development of this argument, see World Bank (2010c).

27. For more details on the efficiency argument and the debate between equity and efficiency, see World Bank (2010c).

28. See Houser (2010), Houser et al. (2010), and Lewis (2010) for more details on the legislation and its provision for border taxes on carbon.

29. Harvey (2009).

30. Morgan (2010) estimates that as of May 2010 less than $23 billion of the $30 billion that are supposed to be mobilized by developed countries over the next two years have been pledged. Moreover, most of that is not additional money but funds already part of aid programs. In the United States, nobody knows where the money that Secretary of State Clinton pledged the United States would help to raise as part of the $100 billion a year by 2020 is going to come from.

31. See Houser et al. (2010).

32. Morgan (2010).

33. Morgan (2010).

34. Based on communication with Professor Charles Weiss.

35. Broder (2010).

36. See, for example, Lenton and Vaughan (2009), who argue that only stratospheric aerosol injections have the potential to cool the earth back to preindustrial levels.

37. The American Enterprise Institute for Public Policy Research has launched a project to study proposals to counter global climate change through geo-engineering. See Research Areas on the AEI-Geoengineering Web site, http://www.aei.org/yra/100009?parent=1.

38. China is often mentioned, as it has already successfully used aerosols seeded in the atmosphere to create precipitation to alleviate droughts. See, for example, Pollowitz (2009).

39. *Science Daily* (2009).

40. Birdsall and Subramanian (2009) essentially make this point and propose a focus on access to energy services by the developing world. They project that if developing countries are to have the same access to energy services that developed countries had at comparable levels of per capita income, a massive revolution in energy technology will be needed to lower emissions to 50 percent of 1990 levels.

41. International Energy Agency (2010a). They identify nine specific low-carbon energy areas: advanced vehicles (including electric and hybrid), bioenergy, carbon capture and sequestration, energy-efficient buildings, higher efficiency coal, nuclear fission, smart grids, solar energy, and wind energy.

42. Ruttan (2006), based on a study of various fundamental technological transformations, found that it took massive investments and sustained R&D effort over many years to make fundamental technological transformations.

43. World Bank (2010c), p. 292, citing data from the International Energy Agency, points out that public R&D spending for energy has actually fallen by half in absolute terms since 1980 and from 11 percent of government R&D budgets in 1985 to less than 4 percent in 2007. Private spending on energy R&D is estimated at $40 to $60 billion a year, more than two to three times public spending.

44. See Kempener, Anadon, and Condor (2010).

45. As noted before, Russia does not have much of an incentive to participate in this effort because it has the least to lose from climate change. It stands to suffer from a reduction of demand for petroleum and natural gas if there is faster development of alternative noncarbon-based fuels.

46. Some proposals are to store the carbon in salt mines, others under the ocean floor. There is still some uncertainty about which is the best option, and it will also depend on the geography of different countries. Storage in the ocean happens naturally but lowers pH levels and endangers coral reefs and other elements of the ecosystem.

47. The CGIAR was originally launched by the Ford, Rockefeller, and Kellogg Foundations in 1968 to support international agricultural research to improve crop yields in developing countries; Baum (1986). In 1971, the World Bank, FAO, UNDP, and other donors cosponsored and enlarged the funding. CGIAR grew from 13 international research institutes in 1983 to 15 research institutes supported by 64 donors. It is credited with having developed and launched the green revolution that allowed many developing countries to increase agricultural output to feed themselves. All this technology was in the public domain at the time.

48. Sematech was a partnership between the U.S. government and 14 semiconductor manufacturers launched in 1988. Over its first five years, it received $500 million from the U.S. Defense Advanced Research Projects Agency (DARPA). It eventually became a consortium of international semiconductor companies without U.S. government funding.

49. As Weiss and Bonvillian (2009) note, the Manhattan and Apollo programs had much narrower technology objectives and were run by just one agency with a clear mission. The energy revolution proposed requires multiple technologies and many public and private actors.

50. Weiss and Bonvillian propose six generic types of technologies based on their level of development and the kinds of problems their market launch is expected to face: (1) experimental technologies that are still at a very early stage and will require long-term research (such as hydrogen fuel cells for transport); (2) potentially disruptive technologies in niche markets (such as solar or LED lighting); (3) component technologies that will face competition at launch but that are acceptable to recipient industries (such as wind turbines, batteries for plug-in hybrids, geothermal power); (4) component technologies with inherent cost disadvantages facing political and/or nonmarket opposition (biofuel, carbon capture and sequestration, nuclear power); (5) incremental innovations for conservation and end-use efficiency (more efficient engines and furnaces, improved building technologies); and (6) manufacturing production scale-up and generic process improvements, which applies to all of the preceding to go beyond prototyping and design to commercial-scale manufacturing and could include necessary new infrastructure (such as for plug-in vehicles).

51. A DARPA-type organization focusing on energy called E-ARPA was set up in 2007 in the Department of Energy as part of the America COMPETES Act, but it had no funding. It received $400 million in initial funding from the 2009 U.S. stimulus package and is funding research.

52. Weiss and Bonvillian (2009), p. x.

53. See Weiss and Bonvillian (2009) for the European Union and Houser (2010) and Houser et al. (2010) for an analysis of the proposed legislation in the U.S. Congress and Senate.

54. Iran, Saudi Arabia, Russia, India, and China provided the largest subsidies in absolute terms, equivalent to 56 percent of the total. India and

China accounted for only 6.7 and 6.0 percent of the total, respectively. See International Energy Agency (2010c), p. 580.

55. International Energy Agency (2010c).

56. International Energy Agency (2010c), Chapter 19, pp. 569–591.

57. Houser (2010) did a preliminary analysis of the U.S. legislation proposed by Senators Kerry and Lieberman. That legislation includes an emissions trading system that would be a start, but it caps carbon prices at too low a level.

58. For a history of U.S.–China relations and agreements on climate change, see Lewis (2010).

59. International Energy Agency (2010c).

60. International Energy Agency (2010b).

61. China is piloting the concept of ecocities as a more sustainable way to deal with its large urbanization needs.

62. Others, such as Pearce (2010), project that the world's population will peak earlier at around 8 billion, predicting a faster demographic transition to lower fertility in developing countries.

63. Technology will play a role to the extent that environmental resources such as water and negative environmental externalities such as CO_2 emissions are properly priced. If not, there will not be an incentive to conserve them or to develop more efficient technologies. Appropriate regulations must also be put into place to enforce control of emissions in some critical industries.

64. World Bank (2010), pp. 194 and 196.

65. Kohli and Sood (2010).

Chapter 7

1. For size, the indicators are population and GDP in PPP and in nominal terms; for trade, they are merchandise and service exports; for finance, they are FDI inflows and outflows, foreign exchange reserves, and total market capitalization; for innovation capability, they are tertiary students, R&D spending, and scientific and technical (S and T) publications; and for military, they are military spending and personnel. All are presented as a share of the world's total.

2. China surpassed Japan in nominal GDP in the middle of 2010.

3. Maddison (2001), p. 263. Western Europe's share in 1950 was 26 percent.

4. Maddison (2001), p. 263. The declines in the share of the United States and of Western Europe were offset by an increasing share of Japan during this period.

5. These include the IMF, the World Bank, the GATT (which became the WTO), and the UN.

6. There are also other groups such as the G-30, the G-77, the nonaligned movement, etc.

7. See http://pewglobal.org/database/?indicator=16&survey=12&response=Good percent20thing&mode=table, accessed November 30, 2010.

8. For a good articulation of this view, see Chang (2002).

9. See, for example, Gallagher and Porzecanski (2010).

10. The report is produced by Global Trade Alert, an independent NGO coordinated by the London-based Center for Economic Policy Research. See Everett (2010) for a detailed compilation in the Eighth GTA Report.

11. See Table 7.5 for measures and impacts for the European Union, China, India, the United States, and other key developing countries.

12. The regions/countries with the greatest number of discriminatory measures by rank order were the European Union, the Russian Federation, Argentina, India, Germany, Brazil, the United Kingdom, Spain, Indonesia, and Italy.

13. German exports have been helped by the depreciation of the euro against the dollar as a result of the Greek crisis at the beginning of 2010 and the Irish crisis toward the end of 2010. The Japanese central bank started intervening in the foreign exchange market in 2010 to stem the appreciation of the yen.

14. The House passed some of this legislation in 2010 but not the Senate. Work on climate change legislation was stopped when the Republicans gained the majority in the U.S. Congress in the November 2010 elections. However, it is likely that whenever they resume, there will be some sort of provision for border taxes on carbon.

15. See Hufbauer, Charnovitz, and Kim (2009) for a detailed analysis of the proposed U.S. legislation and its potentially disastrous impact on global trade.

16. A study by Madsen (2001), based on export and import equations for 17 countries, concluded that international trade contracted by 33 percent between 1929 and 1933. It estimated that 14 percent of this was due to the fall of GNP in each country, 8 percent to increased tariff rates, 5 percent to deflation-induced tariff increases, and 6 percent to increased nontariff barriers.

17. After the act passed the House of Representatives in May 1929, many countries moved to boycott U.S. products and increase their tariffs on U.S. goods. By September 1929, President Hoover had received protest notes from 23 countries (*The Economist*, 2008). In May 1930, Canada, the United States' largest trading partner, passed retaliatory tariffs on 16 products that accounted for 30 percent of U.S. exports to Canada.

18. Based on an examination of 16 major natural resource acquisitions by China, however, Moran (2009) found that in 13 of them, China's purchases expanded supply to the world rather than tied up supply to itself. Nevertheless, he notes that there are also other related issues, including that many of these investments are in rogue states, and concludes that the issue requires further analysis.

19. See, for example, Emirates Center for Energy Research (2009).

20. See, for example, Klare (2002), who argues that resource wars are the new landscape for global conflict. Paskal (2010) argues that, in addition to anticipating resource wars, countries need to prepare for the natural disasters that will come with climate change, which even advanced developed countries are woefully unprepared for.

21. Contrary to its general resource scarcity, China has abundant deposits of rare earths which are critical inputs into many high-technology products, including electronics, hybrid cars, windmills, etc. China has been the source of over 95 percent of world supply because it became the lowest-cost producer. See Bradsher, *New York Times,* September 22 and November 11, 2010.

22. See Kurup (2010). *The Times of India.* For a more general treatment of the risks of conflict over water, see Wolf (2007).

23. Smil (2003).

24. In the United States, for example, when gasoline prices passed $4.00 a gallon in 2008, there was an appreciable drop in gasoline consumption. People began to reduce the number of miles they drove, sought public transportation and ride-sharing options, and considered the distance from work in making decisions on where to rent or buy housing.

25. Meadows, Meadows, and Randers (2004).

26. In negotiating new commitments, it will be important to start with the current baseline rather than 1990 levels. Russia, for example, is currently consuming less energy and emitting less CO_2 than in 1990 because of the sharp economic downturn and the sectoral shift away from heavy industry that followed the collapse of the USSR. It is now, however, the third largest emitter of CO_2 and needs to be brought into agreements on reducing global warming.

27. For example, Milligan-Whyte and Min (2009) argue that China and the United States' political, social, legal, and business cultures are not converging and that the two countries are on a lose-lose collision course.

28. Unlike the USSR during the Cold War, China has not been aggressively trying to export or otherwise impose its political or economic model on other countries.

29. Halper (2010); Ramos (2004). See also Bremmer (2010), who focuses on the spread of state capitalism among the emerging developing countries, including China, Brazil, and Russia.

30. See McNeill (2001).

31. The U.S. Joint Forces Command report (2010) says the following about cyberwarfare: "With very little investment, and cloaked in a veil of anonymity, our adversaries will inevitably attempt to harm our national interests. Cyberspace will become a main front in both irregular and traditional conflicts. Enemies in cyberspace will include both states and non-states and will range from the unsophisticated amateur to highly trained professional hackers. Through cyberspace, enemies will target industry, academia, government, as well as the military in the air, land, maritime, and space domains. In

much the same way that airpower transformed the battlefield of World War II, cyberspace has fractured the physical barriers that shield a nation from attacks on its commerce and communication. Indeed, adversaries have already taken advantage of computer networks and the power of information technology not only to plan and execute savage acts of terrorism, but also to influence directly the perceptions and will of the U.S. Government and the American population." U.S. Joint Forces Command (2010), p. 36.

32. These attacks can include logic bombs and other disruptive elements set in electronic devices and information networks. See Clarke (2010).

33. Glantz and Markoff (2010).

34. See, for example, Friedman (1997), who worried toward the end of the 1990s that the rise of China created threats similar to the rise of Germany in the early part of the twentieth century.

35. For example, the well-known realist theorist John Mearsheimer concludes in his classic book, *The Tragedy of Great Power Politics* (2001): "A wealthy China would not be a status quo power but an aggressive state determined to achieve regional hegemony. This is not because a rich China would have wicked motives, but because the best way for any state to maximize its prospects for survival is to be the hegemon in its region of the world. Although it is certainly in China's interest to be the hegemon in Northeast Asia, it is clearly not in America's interest to have that happen" (p. 402).

36. Data on share of world exports from the different blocs were computed based on UNCTAD Comtrade data for 2009.

37. Steinfeld (2010).

38. Jacques (2009).

39. Keohane and Nye (2000).

40. *The Economist* (December 4, 2010), p. 5.

41. Nye (2010) makes the important point that the United States is not in absolute decline and that in relative terms it will likely remain more powerful than other states for several decades. He also emphasizes that the United States will need to make more effective use of alliances and networks in a more complex interdependent world.

42. One plausible approach is to lower the income tax in proportion to the carbon tax.

43. The United States complains that it faces an unlevel playing field because countries like China have lower labor costs; subsidize the cost of land, energy, and capital; and have lower production costs because companies there do not have to abide by strict safety and environmental regulations. While there may be some truth to these claims, it is not clear that U.S. labor could compete in many areas with China—which is catching up rapidly in education and skills—even if the playing field were level.

44. This is argued forcefully by Robert Lieber (2010) based on his review of U.S. history.

45. Gilpin (1981).

46. While not using this framework, Economy (2010) also argues that China has become a major global player and that the United States must

work with other countries, stress core values that underpin the international system, and assert its own ideals and strategic priorities when engaging with China.

47. See the rankings in Table 5.1.

48. Bureau of Economic Analysis, Table 5.1, updated April 30, 2010, and available at http://www.bea.gov/national/nipaweb/TableView.asp?SelectedTable=137&ViewSeries=NO&Java=no&Request3Place=N&3Place=N&FromView=YES&Freq=Year&FirstYear=2005&LastYear=2010&3Place=N&Update=Update&JavaBox=no#Mid, accessed May 5, 2010.

49. Core expenses are defense and net interest on the national debt. Entitlement programs are Medicare, Medicaid, and Social Security. See Elmendorf (2009).

50. International Monetary Fund, *WEO* (April 2010), p. 169.

51. Altman and Haas (2010) forcefully develop this point, arguing that either the United States takes serious action to deal with its exploding public debt, or it will be forced to do so more painfully by the international financial markets.

52. This is a conservative estimate. Bilmes and Stiglitz (2008) estimated in early 2008 that the Iraq War alone was likely to cost $3 trillion, consisting of about $1.5 trillion of direct military and equipment costs and another $1.5 trillion in death benefits, disabilities, and medical and other veterans' costs. Belasco (2010) of the U.S. Congressional Research Service estimated that including the appropriation requests for fiscal year 2011, direct war-related funding for Iraq and Afghanistan was nearly $1.3 trillion. She also stated that the U.S. Congressional Budget Office projection in January 2010 is that from 2001 to 2020 the cost of the two wars could rise to $1.6 to $1.9 trillion depending on the speed of the future drawdown of U.S. forces. Therefore, taking into account the additional costs of death benefits, disabilities, and medical costs, the wars are likely to cost at least $1 billion more than the earlier estimate by Bilmes and Stiglitz for just the Iraq War.

53. See the *Washington Post* database of war casualties at http://projects.washingtonpost.com/fallen/, accessed December 3, 2010.

54. Leonard (2008), p. 116.

55. Ikenberry (2008) essentially made this argument in 2005 before it was clear that China would be such a global challenge. It is even more relevant now that China is much bigger and is much more assertive as a result of its success in dealing with the global financial and economic crisis of 2008–2009.

Chapter 8

1. Calculated based on data from World Bank, *WDI* (2010), for populations living below U.S. $2 PPP a day by country for 2005 and world population for 2005.

2. For an excellent analysis of how integrated and critical China is for the international production system as part of globalization, see Steinfeld (2010).

3. See, for example, Gallagher and Porzecanksi (2010) on the negative impact on industry in Latin America.

4. Germany and Japan have been running large trade surpluses with the United States for many decades, which is surprising. As part of a new global trading system, they would also have to reduce their exports and focus more on domestic consumption.

5. As noted by Premier Wen Jiabao at the end of the annual meeting of the Chinese Congress in March 2007, "China's economic growth is unsteady, unbalanced, uncoordinated, and unsustainable" (cited in Bergsten et al. 2008, p. 105). "Imbalance" refers to China's excessive dependence on exports; "unsustainable" refers to the extensive environmental impact of its growth.

6. See Roach (2010) for more details.

7. Yusuf and Nabeshima (2010b).

8. Rodrik (2007).

9. Sanger and Landler, *New York Times* (April 12, 2010).

10. Two-thirds of this was the drop in value of financial assets; one-third was the drop in home values. See Altman (2009a).

11. International Labor Office (2010), p. xiv.

12. Fardoust et al. (2011).

13. The Financial Stability Board built on the Financial Stability Forum, which had been set up by the G-7 in 1999 to provide advice on improving the global financial system. The Financial Stability Board expanded membership to the G-20 countries.

14. See the Financial Stability Board's Web site at http://www.financialstabilityboard.org/ for more information on their recommendations.

15. A good example of this is Chinese Legend's purchase of IBM's personal computer division, which led to the creation of Lenovo. This was allowed because there are many alternative suppliers of both products and technology.

16. A good example analyzed by Moran is the attempted purchase by a Dubai-controlled company of six U.S. port facilities. In this case, there was legitimate concern that a vital piece of U.S. infrastructure should not be owned by a foreign person, "public or private." See Moran (2009).

17. International Energy Agency (2010c).

18. See Florida (2008).

19. In response to the increased international competition, the United States passed the America COMPETES Act in 2007. However, the influential National Academy of Sciences is still concerned that the United States is falling behind. In a 2010 follow-up to a 2005 report warning that the United States was facing a "Gathering Storm," it reported that the storm was becoming a category 5 hurricane. See National Academy of Sciences (2010).

20. Over 60,000 have been cataloged by the Honey Bee Network; see Society for Research and Initiatives for Sustainable Technologies and Institutions (2010).

21. Prahalad (2005) in 2002 coined the term "bottom of the pyramid" to highlight the profit that companies could exploit by developing products appropriate for the needs of the millions of poor people in the world. Examples include shampoo in small daily-use packets, prepaid cell phones, and so forth. See also Prahalad and Mashelkar (2010).

22. See *The Economist,* April 17, 2010, special issue on innovation in emerging markets.

23. For example, it is one of the three key issues raised by the U.S.–China Business Council in its annual briefing to Congress on relations with China (U.S.–China Business Council, 2009). In addition, China and India are on the priority watch list of IPR violators in the USTR reports; see Office of the United States Trade Representative (2010).

24. See, for example, Cohen, Nelson, and Walsh (2000).

25. See Chesbrough (2003) for development of the concept of open innovation.

26. In 2007, IBM's Eclipse platform included 800 people in more than 160 companies working on more than 70 projects.

27. Open innovation does not necessarily preclude patenting. A company participating in an open-innovation network can make its proprietary technology available for the use of the network or even the public at large.

28. An exception in health is the Gates Foundation, which is supporting major health research on the problems of developing countries. It is not a formal institution but an NGO.

29. Major breakthrough technologies that underpin long-term technological revolutions usually require sustained long-term effort. Many have been developed by U.S. defense research. For a fascinating look at this, see Ruttan (2006).

30. For an excellent perspective on what it takes to have a major energy technology revolution, see Weiss and Bonvillian (2009). For a more general perspective on why the government needs to be involved in a major technological revolution, see Ruttan (2006), who argues that fundamentally changing the underlying technological base requires massive R&D investment over a long period of time and that only the military is able to undertake such long-term commitments.

31. For more examples of innovation in developing economies, including but going beyond pro-poor innovation, see the special survey in *The Economist*, April 17, 2010.

32. In 1980, the poorest country was Bhutan with a per capita income of $80, followed by Chad with $120 and Bangladesh with $140. The richest was Switzerland with a per capita income of $16,440. Switzerland per capita income was 205 times that of Bhutan. In 2008, the poorest countries

were Burundi (per capita income of $140) and the Democratic Republic of Congo ($150). The richest country was Norway ($87,340). The per capita income of Norway was 623 times that of Burundi and 582 times that of the Democratic Republic of Congo. These comparisons are in nominal dollars, which means that in real terms the poorest countries in 2008 are actually poorer than the poorest countries in 1980. Data for 1980 are from World Bank, *World Development Report* (1982); for 2008, they are from World Bank, *World Development Report* (2010).

33. Dahlman (2010).

34. Calculated from World Bank, *WDI* (2010), Table 2.8, p. 92.

35. In 2008, net official development assistance, which includes loans and grants from Development Assistance Committee members, multilateral organizations, and non-DAC donors (excluding China, as no official data are available), was estimated to be $128.6 billion, or roughly 0.30 percent of GDP of high-income countries (World Bank, *WDI*, 2010, p. 408). Including estimates of net grants by NGOs of $23.7 billion (World Bank, *WDI*, 2010, p. 402) adds another 0.05 percent, raising total official development assistance and NGO grant aid to 0.35 percent of global GDP of high-income countries. Note that this includes loans. The developed countries with the highest net disbursement of official development assistance in 2008 were Sweden (0.98 percent of GNI), Luxembourg (0.97 percent), and Norway (0.88 percent). Those with the lowest were the United States and Japan, with only 0.19 percent each (World Bank, *WDI*, 2010, p. 402).

36. In 2009, it was decided to put the Doha talks back on the agenda, and negotiations are ongoing. Little headway has been made given the sharp collapse of world trade in 2009 and the strong global protectionist measures. Although trade has recovered, prospects for the future are still unclear. In the meantime, the number of bilateral and regional trade arrangements has proliferated rapidly. From a global point of view, these are inferior to multilateral trade agreements, and they tend to include much more detailed provisions that generally favor the stronger partners in the negotiations. However, many developing countries enter into them as a second-best solution to uncertainty about advances in multilateral negotiations.

37. China has a program of tariff preferences for African countries that covers 95 percent of its tariff lines. However, as in the case of the United States (which has also agreed to give preferences to 97 percent of its tariff line), the imports that are excluded are those that would be most beneficial for the exports of the least developed economies. See Bouet and Debucquet (2010).

38. See Brautigam (2009) for a detailed analysis of China's evolving aid strategies in Africa. Brautigam is more positive than most in Western development circles about the potential of Chinese aid in Africa. Also see Kurlantzick (2007) for a more general treatment of how China is extending its soft power globally through its trade, investment, culture, and diplomatic

and aid activities. Kurlantzick aptly points out that some of China's main values—noninterference, respect for other countries' internal affairs, and economic gradualism directed by the state—have the strongest appeal to other authoritarian states.

39. This phrase was coined by Amsden (2001).

References

Abramovitz, Moses. 1986. Catching up, forging ahead, and falling behind. *Journal of Economic History* 46 (20): 285–406.

Alesina, Alberto, and Francesco Giavazzi. 2008. *The future of Europe: Reform or decline*. Cambridge, Mass.: MIT Press.

Altman, Roger. 2009a. The great crash, 2008. *Foreign Affairs* 88 (1): 2–14.

———. 2009b. Globalization in retreat. *Foreign Affairs* 88 (4): 2–4.

Altman, Roger, and Richard Haas. 2010. American power and profligacy. *Foreign Affairs* 89 (6): 24–25.

Amsden, Alice. 2001. *The rise of the rest: Challenges to the West from late industrializing economies*. New York: Oxford University Press.

Anderlini, Jamil. 2010a. High-speed China changes rail landscape. *Financial Times* (March 16). http://www.ft.com/cms/s/0/a04d14cc-310b-11df-b057-00144feabdc0.html.

———. 2010b. German industrialists attack China. *Financial Times* (July 18).

Annual Ranking of World Universities Web site. http://www.arwu.org/index.jsp. Accessed December 7, 2010.

Baldwin, Richard. 2006. *Globalization: The great unbundling(s)*. Paper presented at Globalization Challenges to Europe and Finland, organized by the Secretariat of the Economic Council, Prime Minister's Office, Helsinki, Finland.

Bardhan, Pranab. 1998. *The political economy of development in India* (2nd ed). New Delhi: Oxford University Press.

———. 2010. *Awakening giants: Feet of clay*. Princeton, N.J.: Princeton University Press.

Batson, Andrew. 2009. China takes aim at dollar. *Wall Street Journal* (March 24). http://online.wsj.com/article/SB123780272456212885.html. Accessed September 20, 2010.

Baum, Warren C. 1986. *Partners against hunger: The Consultative Group on International Agricultural Research*. Washington, D.C.: World Bank.

Beattie, Alan, and William Frances. 2008. Doha trade talks collapse. *Financial Times* (July 29). http://www.ft.com/cms/s/0/0638a320-5d8a-11dd-8129-000077b07658.html?nclick_check=1. Accessed July 3, 2009.

Belasco, Amy. 2010. *The cost of Iraq, Afghanistan, and other global war on terror operations since 9/11.* Washington, D.C.: Congressional Research Service. RL33110. http://www.fas.org/sgp/crs/natsec/RL33110.pdf. Accessed November 6, 2010.

Bergsten, C. Fred. 2009. The dollar and the deficits: How Washington can prevent the next crisis. *Foreign Affairs* 88 (6): 20–38.

Bergsten, C. Fred, Gil Bates, Nicholas R. Lardy, and Derek J. Mitchell. 2006. *China the balance sheet: What the world needs to know about the emerging superpower.* Washington, D.C.: Peterson Institute for International Economics.

———. 2008. *China's rise: Challenges and opportunities.* Washington, D.C.: Peterson Institute for International Economics.

Bernstein, William J. 2008. *A splendid exchange: How trade shaped the world.* New York: Atlantic Press.

Bhagwati, Jagdish, and Alan Blinder. 2009. *Offshoring of American jobs: What response from U.S. economic policy?* Cambridge, Mass.: MIT Press.

Bilmes, Linda J., and Joseph E. Stiglitz. 2008. The Iraq war will cost U.S. 3 trillion, and much more. *Washington Post* (March 9).

Birdsall, Nancy, and Arvind Subramanian. 2009. *Energy needs and efficiency, not emissions: Reframing the climate change narrative.* Working paper 187. Washington, D.C.: Center for Global Development.

Blinder, Alan. 2006. Offshoring: The next industrial revolution? *Foreign Affairs* 85 (2): 113–128.

Bosworth, Barry, and Susan M. Collins. 2008. Accounting for growth: Comparing China and India. *Journal of Economic Perspectives* 22 (1): 45–66.

Bosworth, Barry, and Annemie Maertens. 2010. The role of the service sector in economic growth and employment generation in South Asia. In *The service revolution in South Asia*, Ejaz Ghani, ed. New Delhi: Oxford University Press.

Bouet, Antoine, and David Laborde Debucquet. 2010. Eight years of Doha trade talks: Where do we stand? http://www.mendeley.com/research/eight-years-of-doha-trade-talks-where-do-we-stand/. Accessed September 25, 2010.

Bradsher, Keith. 2010. China is said to be restricting rare earth exports. *New York Times* (September 23).

———. 2010. Rare earths stand is asked of G-20. *New York Times* (November 5).

———. 2010. To conquer wind power, China writes the rules. *New York Times* (December 14).

———. 2010. Sitting out the China trade battles. *New York Times* (December 23).

Brautigam, Deborah. 2009. *The dragon's gift: The real story of China in Africa.* Oxford: Oxford University Press.

Bremmer, Ian. 2010. *The end of the free market: Who wins the wars between states and corporations?* New York: Portfolio, Penguin Books.

Broder, John M. 2010. A novel tactic in climate change gains some traction. *New York Times* (November 8).

Bureau of Economic Analysis. National Economic Accounts. National Income and Product Accounts, Table 5.1: Saving and Investment by Sector. http://www.bea.gov/national/nipaweb/TableView.asp?SelectedTable=137&ViewSeries=NO&Java=no&Request3Place=N&3Place=N&FromView=YES&Freq=Year&FirstYear=2005&LastYear=2010&3Place=N&Update=Update&JavaBox=no#Mid. Accessed May 5, 2010.

Cao, Cong, Richard P. Suttmeier, and Denis Fred Simon. 2006. China's 15-year science and technology plan. *Physics Today* (December): 38–43.

Cha, Ariana Enjung, and Ellen Nakashima. 2010. Google China cyber-attack part of vast espionage campaign, experts say. *Washington Post* (January 14).

Chandra, V., I. Osorio-Rodarte, and C. A. Primo Braga. 2009. Korea and the BICs (Brazil, India, and China): Catching up experiences. In *Innovation and growth: Chasing a moving frontier.* Vandana Chandra, Denise Erocal, Pier Carlo Padoan, and Carlos A. Primo Braga, eds., pp. 25–66. Paris: Organisation for Economic Co-operation and Development.

Chang, Gordon. 2001. *The coming collapse of China.* New York: Random House.

Chang, Ha-Joon. 2002. *Kicking away the ladder: Development strategy in historical perspective.* London: Anthem Press.

Chesbrough, Henry. 2003. *Open innovation: The new imperative for creating and profiting from technology.* Boston: Harvard Business School Press.

China Daily.com. 2006. India, China reopen Silk Road Pass (July 6). http://www.chinadaily.com.cn/china/2006-07/06/content_634734.htm. Accessed January 10, 2010.

China Ministry of Commerce, National Bureau of Statistics, and Stage Administration of Foreign Exchange. 2009. *2008 statistical bulletin of Chinese outward foreign direct investment.* Beijing: China Ministry of Commerce, National Bureau of Statistics, and Stage Administration of Foreign Exchange.

Clarke, Richard. 2010. *Cyber war: The next threat to national security and what to do about it.* New York: Ecco.

Cohen, Benjamin. 2008. *International political economy: An intellectual history.* Princeton, N.J.: Princeton University Press.

Cohen, Wesley, Richard Nelson, and John P. Walsh. 2000. *Protecting their intellectual assets: Appropriability conditions and why U.S. manufacturing firms patent (or not).* Working paper 7572. Cambridge: National Bureau of Economic Research.

Collis, Maurice. 1946. *Foreign mud: Being an account of the opium imbroglio at Canton in the 1830's and the Anglo–Chinese War that followed.* London: Faber and Faber.

Commission on Growth and Development. 2008. *The growth report: Strategies for sustainable growth and inclusive development.* Washington, D.C.: World Bank.

Dahlman, Carl. 2010. Education and growth in services. In *The service revolution in South Asia*, Ejaz Ghani, ed. New Delhi: Oxford University Press.

Dahlman, Carl, Douglas Zhihua Zeng, and Shuilin Wang. 2007. *Enhancing China's competitiveness through lifelong learning.* Washington, D.C.: World Bank.

Daily Mail. 2010. Chinese government "ordered cyber attacks" on Google, WikiLeaks cables reveal (December 5).

Davies, Ken. 2010. *Outward FDI from China and its policy context.* New York: Vale Columbia Center on Sustainable International Investment. Columbia FDI Profiles (October).

Dickie, Mure. 2010. Japan Inc. shoots itself in foot on bullet train. *Financial Times* (July 8). http://www.ft.com/cms/s/0/60da2222-8ab5-11df-8e17-00144feab49a.html.

Dillon, Sam. 2010. Top test scores from Shanghai stun educators. *New York Times* (December 7).

Du, Qingyuan, and Shan-Jin Wei. 2010. *A sexually unbalanced model of current account imbalances.* Working paper 16000. Cambridge: National Bureau of Economic Research (May).

Dutz, Mark, ed. 2007. *Unleashing India's innovation: Toward sustainable and inclusive growth.* Washington, D.C.: World Bank.

———, ed. 2008. *Unleashing India's innovation potential.* Washington, D.C.: World Bank.

The Economist. 2008. The battle of Smoot-Hawley (December 18).

———. 2010. The dangers of a rising China (December 4).

———. 2010. A special report on innovation in emerging markets (April 17). http://www.economist.com/node/15879405. Accessed April 20, 2010.

Economist Intelligence Unit. 2008. *Index of democracy.* http://graphics.eiu.com/PDF/Democracy%20Index%202008.pdf. Accessed September 30, 2010.

Economy, Elizabeth. 2010. The game changer. *Foreign Affairs* 89 (6): 142–152.

Eichengreen, Barry, Poonan Gupta, and Rajiv Kumar, eds. 2010. *Emerging giants: China and India in the world economy.* Oxford: Oxford University Press.

Elmendorf, Douglas W. 2009. *The economic and budget outlook.* Paper presented at the American Association for Budget and Program Analysis. http://www.cbo.gov/ftpdocs/107xx/doc10748/11-24-09AABPA-Presentation.pdf. Accessed January 5, 2010.

Emirates Center for Energy Research. 2009. *China, India, and the United States: Competition for energy resources.* Abu Dhabi: Emirates Center for Strategic Studies.

European Union Chamber of Commerce in China. 2010. *European business in China position paper 20102011.* http://www.europeanchamber.com.cn/view/media/publications. Accessed December 18, 2010.

Everett, Simon J., ed. 2010. *Tensions contained . . . for now: The 8th GTA Report.* Centre for Economic Policy Research (CEPR). London: CEPR. http://www.globaltradealert.org/sites/default/files/GTA8_0.pdf.

Ewing, B., D. Moore, S. Goldfinger, A. Oursler, A. Reed, and M. Wakernagel. 2010. *The ecological footprint atlas 2010.* Oakland, Cal.: Global Footprint Network.

Fardoust, Shahrokh, Kim Youngbeom, and Claudia Paz-Sepulveda, eds. 2011. *Post crisis growth and development.* Washington, D.C.: World Bank.

Farrel, Diana, Martha A. Laiboissiere, and Jaeson Rosenfeld. 2005. Seizing the emerging global labor market. *McKinsey Quarterly* 3: 93–103.

Florida, Richard. 2008. *Who's your city? How the creative economy is making the decision of where you live the most important in your life.* New York: Basic Books.

Fogel, Robert. 1999. Catching up with the economy. *American Economic Review* 89 (1): 1–21.

Freedom House. 2010. *Freedom in the world comparative and historical data.* http://www.freedomhouse.org/template.cfm?page=439. Accessed November 5, 2010.

Freeman, Richard. 2006. *Labor market imbalances: Shortages, or surpluses, or fish stories?* Paper presented at Boston Federal Reserve Economics Conference: Global Imbalance—As Giants Evolve. Chatham, Mass.

Friedman, Edward. 1997. The challenge of a rising China: Another Germany? In *Eagle adrift: American policy at the end of the century,* Robert J. Lieber, ed. New York: Longman.

Fukuyama, Francis. 1992. *The end of history and the last man.* New York: Free Press.

Gallagher, Kevin, and Roberto Porzecanski. 2010. *Dragon in the room: China and the future of Latin American industrialization.* Palo Alto, Cal.: Stanford University Press.

Gerschenkron, Alexander. 1962. *Economic backwardness in historical perspective, a book of essays.* Cambridge, Mass.: Belknap Press of Harvard University Press.

Gill, Indermitt, and Homi Kharas. 2007. *An East Asian renaissance: Ideas for economic growth.* Washington, D.C.: World Bank.

Gilpin, Robert. 1981. *War and change in world politics.* Cambridge: Cambridge University Press.

Glantz, James, and John Markoff. 2010. Vast hacking by a China fearful of the web. *New York Times* (December 4).

Global Politician. 2007. *Rising Maoist insurgency in India* (May 13). http://globalpolitician.com/22790-india. Accessed May 7, 2010.

Goertzel, Mercedes. 2008. *Insider threat in the SDLC*. Booz Allen Hamilton. Software Assurance Forum (October 16). PowerPoint presentation. https://buildsecurityin.us-cert.gov/swa/downloads/Tutorial_Goertzel_Insider_Threat.pdf. Accessed December 17, 2010.

Goldman, Merle. 2007. *From comrade to citizen: The struggle of political rights in China*. Cambridge, Mass.: Harvard University Press.

Goldstein, A., N. Pinaud, H. Reisen, and Xiaobao Chen. 2006. *The rise of China and India: What's in it for Africa?* Paris: OECD Development Centre.

Gomory, Ralph E., and William Baumol. 2000. *Global trade and conflicting international interests*. Cambridge, Mass.: MIT Press.

Gregory, David, Stanley Nollen, and Stoyan Tenev. 2009. *New industries from new places: The emergence of the hardware and software industries from China and India*. Stanford, Cal.: Stanford University Press.

Grossman, Gene, and Esteban Rossi-Hansberg. 2006. *The rise of offshoring: It's not wine for cloth anymore.* Paper prepared for symposium sponsored by the Federal Reserve Bank of Kansas City on the New Economic Geography: Effects and Policy Implications. Jackson Hole, Wyo. (August 24–26).

Halper, Stephen A. 2010. *The Beijing Consensus: How China's authoritarian model will dominate the 21st century.* New York: Basic Books.

Harvey, Fiona. 2009. China signals climate fund shift. *Financial Times* (December 13). http://www.ft.com/cms/s/0/b261d086-e81c-11de-8a02-00144feab49a.html. Accessed April 25, 2010.

Henig, R., ed. 1973. *The League of Nations.* Edinburgh: Oliver and Boyd.

Heritage Foundation. 2010. *2010 index of economic freedom: The link between economic opportunity and prosperity*. Washington, D.C.: Heritage Foundation.

Houser, Trevor. 2010. *Copenhagen, the accord, and the way forward*. Peterson Institute for International Economics, Policy brief. PB10-5. Washington, D.C.: Peterson Institute for International Economics.

Houser, Trevor, Shaskank Mohan, and Ian Hoffman. 2010. *Assessing the American Power Act: The economic, employment, energy security, and environmental impact of Senator Kerry's and Senator Lieberman's discussion draft.* Peterson Institute for International Economics, Policy brief PB10-12. Washington, D.C.: Peterson Institute for International Economics.

Hu, Albert Guanzhou, and Gary H. Jefferson. 2009. A great wall of patents: What is behind China's recent patent explosion? *Journal of Development Economics* 90: 57–68.

Huang, Yasheng, and Tarun Khanna. 2005. Indigenous versus foreign business models. In *Asia's giants: Comparing China and India,* Edward Friedman and Bruce Gilley, eds. New York: Palgrave Macmillan.

Hufbauer, Gary Clyde, Steve Charnovitz, and Jisun Kim. 2009. *Global warming and the world trading system*. Washington, D.C.: Peterson Institute for International Economics.

Ikenberry, John. 2008. The rise of China and the future of the West. *Foreign Affairs* 87 (1): 23–37.

International Energy Agency. 2009. *World energy outlook.* Paris: International Energy Agency.

———. 2010a. *CO_2 emissions from fuel combustion.* Paris: International Energy Agency.

———. 2010b. *Global gaps in clean energy R&D: Update and recommendations for international collaboration.* Paris: International Energy Agency.

———. 2010c. *World energy outlook.* Paris: International Energy Agency.

International Finance Corporation. 2010. *Doing Business 2011: Making a difference for entrepreneurs.* Washington, D.C.: World Bank. http://www.doingbusiness.org/~/media/fpdkm/doingpercent20business/documents/annual-reports/english/db11-fullreport.pdf. Accessed December 11, 2010.

International Labor Office. 2010. *Global wage report 2010/11: Wage policies in times of crisis.* Geneva: International Labor Office.

International Monetary Fund. 2007. *World economic outlook.* Washington, D.C.: International Monetary Fund.

———. Various years. *Currency composition of official foreign exchange reserves.* Washington, D.C.: International Monetary Fund.

———. 2009. *World economic outlook* (April). Washington, D.C.: International Monetary Fund.

———. 2009. *World economic outlook* (September). Washington, D.C.: International Monetary Fund.

———. 2010. *World economic outlook* (April). Washington, D.C.: International Monetary Fund.

———. 2010. *World economic outlook* (October). Washington, D.C.: International Monetary Fund.

Jacques, Martin. 2009. *When China rules the world: The end of the Western world and the birth of a new global order.* London: Penguin.

Jalan, Bimal. 2005. *The future of India: Politics, economics, and governance.* New Delhi: Penguin Books.

Jaruzelski, Barry, and Kevin Dehoff. 2008. Beyond borders: The global innovation 1000. *Strategy and Business* 53 (Winter): 52–67.

Kanbur, Ravi. 2009. Poverty disconnected. *Finance and Development* (December): 32–34.

Kearney, A. T. 2007. *Offshoring for long-term advantage: The 2007 A. T. Kearney global services locations index.* http://www.atkearney.com/res/shared/pdf/GSLI_2007.pdf. Accessed December 8, 2010.

Kempener, Ruud, Laura D. Anadon, and Jose Condor. 2010. *Government energy innovation investments, policies, and institutions in the major emerging economies: Brazil, Russia, India, Mexico, China, and South Africa.* Energy Technology Innovation Policy Discussion paper 2010-16. Cambridge, Mass.: Belfer Center for Science and International Affairs, Harvard Kennedy School.

Kennedy, Paul. 1987. *The rise and fall of great powers: Economic change and military conflict from 1500 to 2000*. New York: Random House.

Keohane, Robert O. 1972. *Transnational relations and world politics*. Cambridge, Mass.: Harvard University Press.

———. 1980. The theory of hegemonic stability and changes in international economic regimes 1967–1977. In *Change in the international economic system*, Oli R. Holsti, Randolph M. Silverson, and Alexander L. George, eds., pp. 131–162. Boulder, Col.: Westview Press.

———. 1984. *After hegemony: Cooperation and discord in the world political economy*. Princeton, N.J.: Princeton University Press.

Keohane, Robert O., and Joseph S. Nye. 2000. *Power and interdependence* (3rd ed.). New York: Longman.

Kindleberger, Charles. 1973. *The world in depression*. Berkeley: University of California Press.

Klare, Michael T. 2002. *Resource wars: The new landscape of global conflict*. New York: Macmillan Holt Paperbacks.

Kohli, Harinder S., and Anil Sood. 2010. *India 2039: An affluent society in one generation*. New Delhi: Sage Publications and Asian Development Bank.

Krugman, Paul. 1986. *Strategic trade policy and the new international economics*. Cambridge, Mass.: MIT Press.

Kupchan, Charles. 2010. *How enemies become friends: The sources of stable peace*. Princeton, N.J.: Princeton University Press.

Kurlantzick, Joshua. 2007. *China's charm offensive: How China's soft power is transforming the world*. New Haven, Conn.: Yale University Press.

Kurup, Saira. 2010. Water wars: India, China and the great thirst. *The Times of India* (July 25). http://articles.timesofindia.indiatimes.com/2010-07-25/special-report/28308457_1_water-wars-water-resources-water-deficit. Accessed December 2, 2010.

Kuznetsov, Yevgeny. 2009. *Diaspora networks and international migration of skills: How countries can draw on their talent abroad*. Washington, D.C.: World Bank.

Kynge, James. 2007. *China shakes the world: A giant's rise and troubled future—and the challenge for America*. New York: Mariner Books, Houghton Mifflin.

Lall, Sanjaya, and John Weiss. 2003. *China's competitive threat to Latin America: An analysis for 1990–2002*. Working paper 120. Oxford: Queen Elizabeth House.

Lederman, Daniel, Marco Olarreaga, and Guillermo Perry. 2007. *China's and India's challenge to Latin America: Opportunity or threat?* Washington, D.C.: World Bank.

Lenton, T. M., and N. E. Vaughan. 2009. The radiative forcing potential of different climate geoengineering options. *Atmospheric Chemistry and Physics*. Discussions (January 28).

Leonard, Mark. 2008. *What does China think?* Philadelphia: Public Affairs/Perseus Book Group.

Lerner, George. 2010. Activist: Farmer suicides in India linked to debt, globalization. *CNN News* (January 5). http://articles.cnn.com/2010-01-05/world/india.farmer.suicides_1_farmer-suicides-andhra-pradesh-vandana-shiva?_s=PM:WORLD. Accessed September 15, 2010.

Lewis, Joanna. 2010. *The state of U.S.–China relations on climate change: Examining the bilateral and multilateral relationship.* Woodrow Wilson International Center for Scholars, China Environment Series. Issue 11, pp. 7–48. Washington, D.C.: Woodrow Wilson International Center for Scholars.

Lieber, Kier. 2007. The new history of World War I and what it means for international relations theory. *International Security* 32 (2): 155–191.

Lieber, Robert J. 2010. Persistent primacy and the future of the American era. *International Politics* 46 (2/3): 119–139.

Luce, Edward. 2007. *In spite of the gods: The strange rise of modern India.* New York: Doubleday.

Maddison, Angus. 2001. *The world economy: A millennial perspective.* Paris: Organisation for Economic Co-operation and Development.

———. 2003. *The world economy: Historical statistics.* Paris: Organisation for Economic Co-operation and Development.

Madsen, Jacob A. 2001. Trade barriers and the collapse of world trade during the Great Depression. *Southern Economic Journal* 67 (4): 848–868.

Malthus, Thomas. 1798. *An essay on the principle of population.* London: Printed for J. Johnson in St Paul's Church-yard.

Martin, Michael F. 2008. *China's sovereign wealth funds.* Report to Congress RL34337. Washington, D.C.: Congressional Research Service.

McDonald, Joe. 2010. China supercomputer named world's second fastest. *Washington Post* (June 1).

McGregor, James. 2010. *China's drive for "indigenous innovation": A web of industrial policies.* Washington, D.C.: U.S. Chamber of Commerce. http://uschamber.com/reports/chinas-drive-indigenous-innovation-web-industrial-policies. Accessed December 24, 2010.

McKinsey Global Institute. 2008. *The carbon productivity challenge: Curbing climate change and sustaining economic growth.* McKinsey Global Institute.

McNeill, John R. 2000. *Something new under the sun: An environmental history of the twentieth-century world.* New York: W. W. Norton.

Meadows, Donella, Dennis Meadows, and Jorgen Randers. 2004. *Limits to growth: The 30 year update.* White River Junction, Vt.: Chelsea Green.

Meadows, Donella H., Dennis L. Meadows, Jorgen Randers, and William Behrens III. 1972. *Limits to growth.* New York: Universe Books.

Mearsheimer, John J. 2001. *The tragedy of great power politics.* New York: W. W. Norton.

Mehta, Pratap Bhanu. 2003. *Burden of democracy.* New Delhi: Penguin Books.

Meredith, Robyn. 2007. *The elephant and the dragon: The rise of India and China and what it means for all of us.* New York: W. W. Norton.

Milhaupt, Curtis J. 2008. Is the U.S. ready for FDI from China? Lessons from Japan's experience in the 1980s. *Investing in the United States: A reference for Chinese investors 1*. New York: Vale Columbia Center and Chinese Services Group of Deloitte LLP.

Milligan-Whyte, John, and Dai Min. 2009. *China & America's emerging partnership: A realistic new perspective*. New York: Specialist Press International.

Money Week. 2010. China prepares for a hard landing—and a trade war (May 28). http://www.moneyweek.com/news-and-charts/economics/china-heads-for-a-hard-landing-and-a-trade-war-48807.aspx#.

Moran, Theodore. 2009. *Three threats: An analytical framework for the CFIUS*. Policy Analyses in International Economics 89. Washington, D.C.: Peterson Institute for International Economics.

———. 2010. *China's strategy to secure natural resources: Risks, dangers, and opportunities*. Washington, D.C.: Peterson Institute for International Economics.

Morgan, Jennifer. 2010. *Cop 15 Copenhagen outcomes*. World Resources Institute. PowerPoint presentation. Washington, D.C. (May 20).

Morrison, Wayne. 2009. *China and the global financial crisis: Implications for the United States*. Report for Congress RS22984. Washington, D.C.: Congressional Research Service.

———. 2009. *China's holdings of U.S. securities: Implications for the U.S. economy*. Report for Congress RL34314. Washington, D.C.: Congressional Research Service.

Mowery, David, and Nathan Rosenberg. 1989. *Technology and the pursuit of economic growth*. Cambridge: Cambridge University Press.

NASSCOM Deloitte. 2008. *Indian IT/ITES industry: Impacting economy and society 2007–08*. http://www.slideshare.net/nasscom/indian-itites-industry-impacting-economy-and-society-200708. Accessed December 12, 2009.

NASSCOM. 2009. *Strategic review: The IT-BPO industry in India*. New Delhi: NASSCOM.

National Academy of Sciences. 2010. *Rising above the gathering storm revisited: Rapidly approaching category 5*. Washington, D.C.: National Academies Press. http://www.nap.edu/catalog.php?record_id=12999. Accessed November 17, 2010.

National Science Board. 2010. *Science and engineering indicators 2010*. Arlington, Va.: National Science Foundation (NSB 10-01).

Naughton, Barry. 2007. *The Chinese economy: Transitions and growth*. Cambridge, Mass.: MIT Press.

Needham, Joseph. 1954. *Science and civilization in China*. Cambridge: Cambridge University Press. (Series started in 1954 by Needham; 27 volumes to date.)

Nilekani. Nandan. 2009. *Imagining India: The idea of a renewed nation*. London: Penguin Press.

Nye, Joseph. 2010. The future of American power. *Foreign Affairs* 89 (6): 2–11.

Nye, Robert. 2007. *Understanding international conflicts* (6th ed.). Upper Saddle River, N.J.: Longman.

Odagiri, H., and A. Goto. 1996. *Technology and industrial development in Japan*. Oxford: Oxford University Press.

Office of the United States Trade Representative. 2009. Special 301 Report. Washington, D.C. http://www.keionline.org/sites/default/files/ustr_special301_2009.pdf. Accessed November 10, 2010.

———. 2010. Special 301 Report. Washington, D.C. http://www.ustr.gov/webfm_send/1906. Accessed November 4, 2010.

O'Neill, Jim, and Tushar Poddar. 2008. *Ten things for India to achieve its 2050 potential*. Goldman Sachs Global Economics Paper 69 (June). http://www2.goldmansachs.com/ideas/brics/ten-things-doc.pdf.

Organisation for Economic Co-operation and Development. 2007. *Science, technology and industry scoreboard*. Paris: Organisation for Economic Co-operation and Development.

———. 2008. *Science, technology, and industry outlook*. Paris: Organisation for Economic Co-operation and Development.

———. 2009. *Science, technology and industry scoreboard*. Paris: Organisation for Economic Co-operation and Development.

———. 2010. *Pisa 2009 results: What students know and can do. Students' results in mathematics, reading and science* (Vol. 1). Paris: Organisation for Economic Co-operation and Development.

Panagariya, Arvind. 2005. India in the 1980s and 1990s: A triumph of reforms. In *India's and China's recent experience with reform and growth*. Wanda Tseng and David Cowen, eds. New York: Palgrave Macmillan.

———. 2008. *India: The emerging giant*. Oxford: Oxford University Press.

Paskal, Cleo. 2010. *Global warring: How environmental, economic, and political crises will redraw the world map*. London: Palgrave Macmillan.

Patrick, Stewart. 2010. Irresponsible stakeholders. *Foreign Affairs* 89 (6): 44–53.

Pearce, Fred. 2010. *The coming population crash: And our planet's surprising future*. Boston: Beacon Press.

Pei, Minxin. 2006. *China's trapped transition: The limits of developmental autocracy*. Cambridge, Mass.: Harvard University Press.

Perez, Carlota. 2002. *Technological revolutions and financial capital*. Northampton, Mass.: Edward Elgar.

Pew Research Center. 2010. *Pew Global Attitudes Survey*. http://pewglobal.org/database/?indicator=3&mode=map. Accessed December 3, 2010.

Pollowitz, Greg. 2009. Chinese geo-engineering. *National Review Online* (February 19).

Prahalad, C. K. 2005. *The fortune at the bottom of the pyramid*. Upper Saddle River, N.J.: Pearson.

Prahalad, C. K., and Ramesh Mashelkar. 2010. Innovation's holy grail. *Harvard Business Review* (July/August): 132–141.

Preeg, Ernest H. 2005. *The emerging advanced Chinese technology superstate*. Washington, D.C.: Manufacturers Alliance (MAPI).

———. 2008. *India and China: An advanced technology race and how the United States should respond*. Washington, D.C.: Center for Strategic and International Studies (CSIS) and Manufacturers Alliance (MAPI).

Public Broadcasting System. 2006. *The tank man*. Documentary. http://www.pbs.org/wgbh/pages/frontline/tankman/view/.

Qiqing, Chen. 2009. *Balanced economic growth: Responsibility and policy of U.S. and China*. Paper presented at the Chinese Central Party School (October). Beijing, China.

Ramos, Joshua Cooper. 2004. *The Beijing Consensus*. London: Foreign Policy Centre.

Ravallion, Martin, and Sudham Chaudhuri. 2007. Partially awakened giants: Uneven growth in China and India. In *Dancing with giants: China, India, and the global economy*, Alan Winters and Shahid Yusuf, eds., pp. 175–210. Washington, D.C.: World Bank and Institute for Policy Studies.

Reinhart, Carmen, and Kenneth Rogoff. 2009. *This time it's different: Eight centuries of financial folly*. Princeton, N.J.: Princeton University Press.

Rhee, Yung Whee, Bruce Ross-Larson, and Garry Purcell. 1984. *Korea's competitive edge: Managing the entry into world markets*. Baltimore: Johns Hopkins University Press.

Roach, Stephen. 2010. *Consumer-led China*. Paper prepared for the 11th annual China Development Forum held in Beijing (March 20–22), Morgan Stanley Asia.

Rodrik, Dani. 2007. How to save globalization from its cheerleaders. *Journal of International Trade and Diplomacy* 1 (2): 1–33.

Ruttan, Vernon. 2006. *Is war necessary for economic growth? Military procurement and technological development*. New York: Oxford University Press.

Samuelson, Paul. 2004. Why Ricardo and Mills rebut and confirm articles of mainstream economists supporting globalization. *Journal of Economic Perspectives* 18 (3): 135–146.

Sanger, David E., and Landler, Mark. 2010. China pledges to work with U.S. on Iran sanctions. *New York Times* (April 12).

Satyanand, Premila Nazareth, and Pramila Raghavendran. 2010. *Outward FDI from India and its policy context* (September). New York: Vale Columbia Center on Sustainable International Investment. Country Profiles.

Science Daily. 2009. Climate change: Halving carbon dioxide emissions by 2050 could stabilize global warming (May 4).

Shambaugh, David. 2008. *China's Communist Party: Atrophy and adaptation*. Berkeley: University of California Press.

Sharma, Shalendra D. 2009. *China and India in the age of globalization*. Cambridge: Cambridge University Press.

Shi, Tianjian. 2008. China: Democratic values supporting an authoritarian regime. In *How East Asians view democracy*, Yun-han Chu, Larry

Diamond, Andrew J. Nathan, and Doh Chull Shin, eds. New York: Columbia University Press.

Simon, Dennis Fred, and Cong Cao. 2009. *China's emerging technological edge: Assessing the role of high end talent*. Cambridge: Cambridge University Press.

Smil, Vaclav. 2003. *Energy at the crossroads*. Cambridge, Mass.: MIT Press.

———. 2004. *China's past, China's future: Energy, food, environment*. New York: Routledge Curzon.

Society for Research and Initiatives for Sustainable Technologies and Institutions (SRISTI). 2010. http://www.sristi.org/cms/.

Steinfeld, Edward. 2010. *Playing our game: Why China's rise doesn't threaten the West*. Oxford: Oxford University Press.

Sturgeon, T. 2002. Modular production networks: A new American model of industrial organization. *Industrial and Corporate Change* 11 (3): 451–496.

Suttmeier, Peter. 2005. China's standards strategy, in short, must accommodate a considerable heterogeneity of interests. *Communications of the ACM* 4 (4): 36–39.

Suttmeier, Peter, Xiangkui Yao, and Alex Zixiang Tan. 2006. *Standards of power? Technology, institutions, and politics in the development of China's national standards strategy*. Seattle, Wash.: National Bureau of Asian Research.

Tang, Rachel. 2009. *The rise of China's auto industry and its impact on the U.S. motor vehicle industry*. Report to Congress R40924. Washington, D.C.: Congressional Research Service.

Tang, Wenfang. 2005. *Public opinion and political change in China*. Stanford, Cal.: Stanford University Press.

Toynbee, Arnold. 1946. *A study of history*. Oxford: Oxford University Press.

Tsai, Kellee. 2007. *Capitalism without democracy: The private sector in contemporary China*. Ithaca, N.Y.: Cornell University Press.

United Nations Conference on Trade and Development (UNCTAD). Various Years. *World investment report*. Geneva: United Nations Conference on Trade and Development.

———. 2008. *World investment report*. Geneva: United Nations Conference on Trade and Development.

———. 2009a. *Handbook of trade*. Geneva: United Nations Conference on Trade and Development. http://stats.unctad.org/Handbook/TableViewer/chartView.aspx. Accessed December 20, 2009.

———. 2009b. *World investment report 2009*. Geneva: United Nations Conference on Trade and Development.

———. 2010. *World investment report 2010*. Geneva: United Nations Conference on Trade and Development.

United Nations Educational, Scientific and Cultural Organization. 2009. *Global education digest*. Montreal: United Nations Educational, Scientific and Cultural Organization.

———. 2010. *Global education digest 2010*. Montreal: United Nations Educational, Scientific and Cultural Organization Institute of Statistics.

United Nations Intergovernmental Panel on Climate Change (IPCC). 2007. *Climate change 2007 synthesis report: Contribution of working groups I, II, and III to the fourth assessment of the Intergovernmental Panel on Climate Change* (core writing team R. K. Pachuari and A. Reisinger, eds.) Geneva: Intergovernmental Panel on Climate Change.

United States–China Economic and Security Review Commission. 2010. *2010 report to Congress*. Washington, D.C. http://www.uscc.gov/annual_report/2010/annual_report_full_10.pdf.

———. 2010b. *Hearings on U.S. debt to China: Implications and 57 repercussions*. Testimony of Eswar Prasad and Daniel Drezner (February 25).

United States Department of Energy, Office of Integrated Analysis and Forecasting. 2009. *International energy outlook*. Washington, D.C.: U.S. Department of Energy.

United States Joint Forces Command (USJFCOM). 2010. *Joint forces operating environment*. Norfolk, Va. http://www.jfcom.mil/newslink/storyarchive/2010/JOE_2010_o.pdf. Accessed May 2, 2010.

United States National Science Foundation. 2010. *Science and engineering indicators*. Washington, D.C.: Government Printing Office.

U.S.–China Business Council. 2009. *U.S. companies China outlook: Recession stings but does not end market optimism*. Washington, D.C.: U.S.–China Business Council.

———. 2010. *U.S. companies' China outlook: China operations profitable and growing: Protectionism concerns real and rising*. Washington, D.C.: U.S.–China Business Council. http://www.uschina.org/public/documents/2010/membership_survey.pdf. Accessed December 15, 2010.

Vernon, Raymond. 1971. *Sovereignty at bay*. New York: Basic Books.

Viner, Jacob. 1948. Power and plenty as objectives of foreign policy in the seventeenth and eighteenth centuries. *World Politics* 1 (1): 1–29.

Vogel, Ezra. 1979. *Japan as number one: Lessons for America*. Cambridge, Mass.: Harvard University Press.

Wadwha, Vivek. 2009. A reverse brain drain. *Issues in Science and Technology* 25 (3). http://www.issues.org/25.3/wadhwa.html.

Wadwha, Vivek, Gary Gereffi, Ben Rising, and Ryan Ong. 2007. Where the engineers are. *Issues in Science and Technology* 23 (3). http://www.issues.org/23.3/wadhwa.html.

Waltz, Kenneth. 1959. *Theory on international politics*. New York: McGraw-Hill.

Washington Post. 2009. Pakistan rejects Indian accusations, plays down tension (January 8).

———. 2010. Faces of the fallen: U.S. service members who died in Operation Iraqi Freedom and Operation Enduring Freedom. http://projects.washingtonpost.com/fallen/. Accessed December 3, 2010.

Webb, Michael C., and Stephen D. Krasner. 1989. Hegemonic stability theory: An empirical assessment. *Review of International Studies* 15: 183–198.

Weiss, Charles, and William H. Bonvillian. 2009. *Structuring an energy technology revolution*. Cambridge, Mass.: MIT University Press.

Winters, Alan, and Shahid Yusuf. 2007. *Dancing with giants: China, India and the global economy*. Washington, D.C.: World Bank and Institute of Policy Studies.

Wolf, Aaron. 2007. Shared waters: Conflict and cooperation. *Annual Review of Environment and Resources* 32: 241–269.

World Bank. 1982. *World development report*. Washington, D.C.: World Bank.

———. 1998. *World development indicators*. Washington, D.C.: World Bank.

———. 1999. *World development indicators*. Washington, D.C.: World Bank.

———. 2004. *Global competitiveness report 2004–2005*. Geneva: World Economic Forum.

———. 2009. *World development indicators*. Washington, D.C.: World Bank.

———. 2010. *World development indicators*. Washington, D.C.: World Bank.

———. 2010a. *Global commodity markets: Review and price forecast*. Washington, D.C.: World Bank.

———. 2010b. *Governance indicators*. http://info.worldbank.org/governance/wgi/index.asp. Accessed September 13, 2010.

———. 2010c. *World development report: Development and climate change*. Washington, D.C.: World Bank.

World Economic Forum. 2004. *Global competitiveness report 2004/2005*. Geneva: World Economic Forum.

———. 2010. *Global competitiveness report 2010–2011*. Geneva: World Economic Forum.

World Intellectual Property Organization. 2009. *World intellectual property indicators 2009*. Geneva: World Intellectual Property Organization.

———. 2010. *World intellectual property indicators 2010*. Geneva: World Intellectual Property Organization.

World Trade Organization. 1998. *Fiftieth anniversary of the multilateral trading system—Press brief*. http://www.wto.org/english/thewto_e/minist_e/min96_e/chrono.htm. Accessed July 3, 2009.

Yang, Dali L. 2007. *Discontented miracle: Growth, conflict, and institutional adaptations in China*. Series on contemporary China. Singapore: World Scientific Publishing Company.

Yao, Yang. 2010. The end of the Beijing Consensus: Can China's model of authoritarian growth survive? *Foreign Affairs* (February).

Yardley, Jonathan. 2010. Maoist rebels suspected as Indian train derails. *New York Times* (May 29). http://www.nytimes.com/2010/05/29/world/asia/29india.html?scp=1&sq=indian%20naxalite%20sabotage&st=cse.

Yergin, Daniel. 1991. *The prize: The epic quest for oil, money, and power*. New York: Free Press.

Yusuf, Shahid, and Kauro Nabeshima. 2009. *Tiger economies under threat: A comparative analysis of Malaysia's industrial prospects and policy options.* Washington, D.C.: World Bank.

———. 2010a. *Changing the industrial geography in Asia: The rise of China and India.* Washington, D.C.: World Bank.

———. 2010b. *Two dragon heads: Contrasting development paths for Beijing and Shanghai.* Washington, D.C.: World Bank.

Zakaria, Fareed. 2003. *The future of freedom: Illiberal democracy at home and abroad.* New York: W. W. Norton.

Index

Italic page numbers indicate material in tables or figures.